CHOOSE MEXICO

LIVE WELL ON
$600 A MONTH

CHOOSE MEXICO

John Howells & Don Merwin

Illustrated by Noni Mendoza

GATEWAY BOOKS

Printed in the United States of America

Gateway Books

Distributed by Publishers Group West

Library of Congress Cataloging-in-Publication Data

Howells, John M., 1928-
      Choose Mexico : live well on $600 a month / John Howells & Don Merwin ; illustrated by Noni Mendoza. — [5th ed.]
          p.   cm.
      Includes bibliographical references and index.
      ISBN 0-933469-30-6
      1. Mexico—Guidebooks. 2. Retirement, Places of—Mexico-
-Guidebooks.   I. Merwin, Don, 1928-   II. Title.
F1209.H77   1997
917.204'836—dc21   97-22083
                                                                  CIP

12 11 10 9 8 7 6 5 4 3 2 1

Contents

This book is dedicated to the people of Mexico. They, above all, are the reason for our choice.

Tijuana
Ensenada
San Felipe

Hermosillo
Alamos
San Carlos Bay
San Ignacio
Mulegé
Loreto

Monte

La Paz
Bahía de Palmas
Todos Santos
Mazatlán
San José del Cabo
Cabo San Lucas

MEX

San Blas
Guadalajara
Puerto Vallarta
Chapala
Ajijic
Moreli
Manzanillo
Me

Ixtapa-Zihutaneo

Acapulco

Introduction

What kind of retirement do you want? Many people are content to spend the years after work glued to the easy chair in front of the TV. Perhaps they'll play an occasional round of golf when the weather permits. If that's what they want, the idea of moving to Mexico will probably seem ridiculous to them.

But there are others who look forward to retirement as an exciting change in lifestyle, not just a break from the workaday world. They want a complete change, perhaps in an exotic setting. (If you are reading this book you probably fall into that category.) Most people dream of a warm, temperate climate, surrounded by natural beauty and friendly people. Life is uncomplicated, easy, yet never boring. Somewhere in the background, music is playing and delicious food is never far away. From the picture window in the living room or from your tree-shaded patio, picturesque mountains form a hazy green backdrop, or is it the gentle swell of the ocean's surf? Maybe you see the wide boulevards and handsome buildings of a cosmopolitan city. We don't all have precisely the same dreams.

Unfortunately, for most people the reality of retirement will bear little resemblance to this ideal. Fantasies are free, but comfortable living normally requires greater means than Social Security or other retirement benefits, given the high cost of living in the United States or Canada today.

Warm, tropical countries abound elsewhere in the world, that's true, but most of them are not places you would want to visit, much less try on for retirement. For a foreign country to be a practical place for most North Americans to live, in addition to a nice climate, it should meet four conditions:

1. *It should be affordable.*

2. *A foreign country should be easily accessible,* so you can return and visit the grandkids occasionally, and they can visit you once in a while. (It goes without saying that it should be a place where they want to visit.)

3. *Your new home should be a safe place to live,* a place where local people like and respect North Americans.

4. *Finally, a foreign retirement location should have large numbers of English-speaking residents*–preferably fellow North Americans–and a well-developed society that welcomes new-comers with warmth and genuine friendliness. This last item is perhaps the most important of all. For many retirees, without an extensive and friendly population of English-speaking compatri-ots, life would be absolute boredom.

Clearly, Mexico fulfills all these requirements. It is affordable. This is a point we will discuss in great detail. It is accessible by air, by bus and by car. Mexico isn't crime free, but retirees there uniformly report that they feel at least as safe as in the United States. And Mexico offers living situations ranging from some where there are great numbers of North American retirees, with a well-developed network of community organizations and ac-tivities, to others where you need see compatriots only when you want to. What is more, unlike most foreign retirement situations, trying Mexico doesn't involve a deep commitment. You needn't bother with complicated visa requirements; a simple tourist card will do. You can drive anywhere in the nation in a matter of days. Should you decide that Mexico is not for you, it's a simple matter to pack up and return home for another look at your retirement menu. This book points out how it can be tried on a no-risk, experimental basis.

Living in Mexico Part of the Year

More and more people are discovering that Mexico is an ideal place for part-time living. Uncounted thousands spend pleasant winters there and return to their homes north of the border every spring. When we first started writing about retiring in Mexico, we tended to underestimate this phenomenon. "Wintering" in Mexico or anywhere else for that matter seemed like something you read about on the society pages, something that only rich people could do. The more we travel in Mexico in winter, the more people we meet who are neither tourists nor full-time residents. Their homes are in Burlington, Vermont, or Duluth, Minnesota. They enjoy a month (or two, or three) in Mexico's sunshine and rejoin their neighbors, children and grandchildren in the spring.

The opposite side of this coin is the great influx of "summer Mexicans" who flee from the heat and humidity of the southern states, especially Texas, to enjoy the moderate climate of Mexico's central plateau. Some are retirees, some are teachers and others whose jobs leave their summers free. They, too, develop strong ties to the country, returning to the same places year after year, but their real homes continue to be up north.

Therefore, although this book was written primarily for people who are planning for retirement, we keep hearing from two other groups: 1) People who are already retired but are unhappy with their current situation and are hoping to find something better. 2) Younger people, particularly those engaged in seasonal work. They find Mexico a great place to live for part of each year. Why not escape winter by relaxing on a tropical beach or enjoying a sunny mountain village? For those planning to retire "at home," a part-time retirement in Mexico is an excellent idea. Reasonable prices in Mexico make early or partial retirement possible on an income far smaller than you might imagine.

Obviously, retirement in Mexico isn't for everyone. (Thank goodness for that, or the country would soon be overrun with North Americans.) Most retirees decide not to move away for retirement or, if they do move, stay in their own country. Others feel that a total change of scenery is called for. For them, the chance to start a totally new life with new friends and experiences can be an adventure in itself. Still others need to move away from the high-cost areas where they presently live, and are looking for someplace more affordable. Fortunately, Mexico is an alternative for both full-time and part-time retirement that doesn't involve a total severing of ties.

When the original *Choose Mexico* was written, the only books available were ten or more years out of date. Many aspects of national character, scenery and customs change slowly, but practical details of living, such as prices, regulations and the availability of foods and medications, tend to change rapidly. Because we offered up-to-date information not available elsewhere, the original book was a success. However, we must repeat the advice we gave in our first edition: when you pick up this book, should you find that the date on the copyright page is more than a few years old, treat many of the specifics in the book with caution, or look for a more recent edition.

What Does It Cost?

In 1983, something happened in Mexico that suddenly created an ideal atmosphere for retirement. Almost overnight, the exchange rate between U.S. dollars and Mexican pesos dropped dramatically. For those who traded dollars for pesos, prices plummeted and the cost of living became so inexpensive it was almost embarrassing. For the first time in two decades, it was possible to retire in Mexico on less than what most people draw in Social Security benefits. With as little as $400 a month, a couple could maintain a gracious lifestyle, with servants, travel and dining in fine restaurants.

The authors of this book were excited about this development, for it came at an opportune time; both of us were approaching retirement age, and we were not optimistic about how we and our wives were going to live on the incomes we could expect. Inflation was a constant threat in the United States, and many thousands of older people weren't doing very well on their Social Security and company pension checks. Therefore, it was quite reassuring to know that it was possible to live well south of the border for a fraction of what one needed to live comfortably in the United States or Canada. Most important, it wasn't just a matter of existing, retirement in Mexico meant living well and enjoying the stimulating atmosphere of an exotic foreign country.

After spending some wonderful months of trying out the lifestyle of retirement in Mexico, we became so enthused that we decided to spread the news, to share this discovery with others. Our retirement guidebook, *Choose Mexico*, quickly became a success, and over the past 13 years has sold almost 200,000 copies. We're proud to know that *Choose Mexico* helped many thousands find their way to an interesting and affordable lifestyle south of the border.

Have prices stood still in Mexico through all this? Of course not. It would be too much to expect such extremely favorable economic conditions to stay just as they were 14 years ago. After a few of those $400-a-month years of bargain paradise, prices started a slow, almost unnoticed rise. After four years, we had to revise our budget for Mexican retirement to $600 a month. This was still an incredible bargain compared to the quality of life the same money would provide up north.

Prices continued their steady upward climb, which wasn't unusual–after all, there was inflation in the United States and Canada, too. In 1992, we had to boost our figure to $800 a month for gracious retirement living, and we had to trim some of the luxuries–items like full-time maids and travel.

A serious complication was that prices increased faster than in the United States, yet the Mexican government clung to an artificial value of the peso, pegging it to about three pesos to the dollar. This had the effect of lowering the value of the dollar as prices rose in Mexico. So prices in Mexico became higher and higher for those with dollars. Economics were returning to the same condition as they were in 1982, just before the peso took its welcome tumble and made prices affordable.

Full Circle

We hinted in our last edition of *Choose Mexico* that prices could possibly fall to a a more realistic level if the government stopped propping up the peso. Well, it happened! Beginning in December of 1994, the value of the peso has fallen from about three to the dollar to almost eight to the dollar. Effectively, most prices have been cut in half.

What does this mean for those thinking about retirement in Mexico? It means that affordable retirement is back in the picture. Unless you are moving from an inexpensive, rural area in the United States to a burgeoning resort area in Mexico–where people on vacation are spending money like people on vacation–your Social Security payments will once again cover all your basic living costs. If you consider what has happened to the purchasing power of the dollar at home in the dozen years since 1985, when this book was first published, the $600 figure in the subtitle of this edition makes living in Mexico an even bigger bargain than it was then!

But, please understand, the thrust of this retirement guide isn't to show you a cheap place to live. Our fervent belief is that Mexico will continue to be a wonderful place to live and would be our choice, even if it were more, rather than less, expensive than the United States or Canada. And many changes during the past decade have been for the good. The transportation system, already good in 1985, is even better today, with luxury buses on many principal routes; faster, more comfortable and more frequent train service; and newer, better-maintained roads throughout the country.

Drivers no longer need to worry about finding unleaded gasoline. It is now available almost anywhere. The frequent and unpredictable shortages of consumer items that were common in the mid-eighties appear to be a thing of the past. Modern shopping malls are springing up in all the large cities. In numerous important respects, Mexico is becoming less quirky. If, as we do, you prize Mexico's differentness, you can only hope with us that it does not become too predictable and modern.

Now, in 1997, having just returned from joint and separate trips to a wide variety of locations throughout Mexico, and having compared our impressions, we are happy to report that Mexico is still that special place where U.S. and Canadian retirees can find and afford the life they've always dreamed of.

That is not to say that prices are uniformly low. Some items are almost as high as in the United States. Airfares, gasoline, highway tolls, imported foods, and long distance calls are no bargains. Yet, these costs aren't quite so critical in a country where good public transportation abounds, domestically processed foods are varied and delicious, and folks have time to cultivate the lost art of letter writing. The room rates for luxury hotels, particularly in resort areas, are pegged to the international, not the Mexican, economy. Yet we found clean, comfortable hotel rooms for as little as $15, and nowhere on our late 1996 trip did we pay more than $45. We ate in good restaurants, paying a maximum of $10 a person for a full-course dinner with beverages. So, Mexico can be a travel bargain, too. But the focus of this book is long-term living in Mexico and what really matters is whether retirees on a limited budget can afford it.

In summary, we find that $600 a month, judiciously spent, will, once again, provide a couple with comfortable and attractive housing, dining out occasionally and, possibly, a part-time maid. This budget allows not merely for subsistence in Mexico, but for enjoyment of what the country has to offer. More money will enable you to live even more comfortably and will widen your choices of retirement sites and provide more travel opportunities. Even if your income is unlimited, this book will be useful to you; most of its sections are invaluable to anyone wishing to live in Mexico.

Singles

Although estimates of living costs are framed in terms of couples, there is no community of retirees in Mexico that does not have a large number of singles, both men and women. In general, women alone seem to feel more comfortable where there are concentrations of their compatriots. Single men, however, can and do go anywhere in Mexico their fancies take them.

New in This Edition

We have been aided immeasurably in the research for this book by a source of information not available when we wrote previous editions. The Worldwide Web and e-mail have put us in instantaneous touch with retired Americans and Canadians all over Mexico. This means that we have been able to obtain up-to-the-moment data on prices and conditions everywhere in the country, particularly those places that we were unable to visit when we traveled around Mexico just before this edition went to press. Also, it provides you, the reader, with the opportunity to ask your own questions of people living there, since we have included in a special appendix a list of e-mail addresses and Web Sites of people who have agreed to do their best to respond to your inquiries.

Another recent innovation is direct-by-satellite television. Now, almost anywhere you go, your favorite anchorperson or sports team is just a twist of the dial away. We're sure that the ability to watch *Wheel of Fortune* reruns will be perceived by some as a dubious blessing. Fortunately, you can turn your TV set off as easily there as here.

There is equally cheerful news for the Price-Costco, Good Sam and K-Mart addicts. Your favorite stores are in all of Mexico's big cities. You will still be able to find those 100-roll packages of bathroom tissue and 50-gallon drums of catsup. And we have included a partial list of locations to tell you where.

To balance out these features designed for those who want the reassurance of similarity to the United States, we've added a section on potential retirement sites in Mexico for the daring minority of retirees who want to experience a more Mexican lifestyle. These sites are places where you won't find an American Legion post or an English-language newspaper. As a matter of fact, in some of them, you'll probably go many days without hearing English spoken at all. What you will find is friendly, welcoming Mexicans who will meet you more than halfway when you try to speak their language and learn about their community.

Why Choose Mexico?

The People

In the course of gathering information for the first edition of this book, we mailed a questionnaire to hundreds of retired Americans living in Mexico. One of the questions we asked was, "What do you like best about Mexico?" To our surprise and delight, the answer most frequently at the top of the list was "the people." What is it about the Mexican people that appeals so strongly to North Americans? What qualities transcend the barriers of language, class, ethnicity and culture to evoke this response so universally? First, it is their friendliness. Mexicans routinely treat strangers with warmth and curiosity. The fact that you are a foreigner as well as a stranger seems to be incidental. Second, it is their happiness. It may be anomalous, but poverty in Mexico is much more common than misery. The people there seem to have the ability to enjoy life, no matter how difficult its circumstances. It is a gift that, as a people, we in the United States do not appear to possess.

Related to their friendliness, but separate from it, is their helpfulness. Mexicans are almost always willing to stop whatever they are doing to be of assistance to a friend, a neighbor or a stranger. They even seem to welcome the opportunity to be helpful (or perhaps to stop what they are doing). Another related quality Mexicans possess is courtesy. Politeness is not enough to make an individual or a people good, and, perhaps as a reaction to our belated recognition of that fact, we in the United States have given up politeness altogether. Mexicans, however, are too deeply steeped in a tradition of courtesy centuries-old to have acquired the knack of rudeness. They still ask to be excused when they must squeeze by you in a crowd, and they still preface every request or order with *por favor* (please).

Then there is the love the Mexicans so obviously feel for their children. Much has been said and written about *machismo* but there is no more common sight in Mexico than a father carrying and caring for his baby or small child. A sensitive observer of the Mexican scene has noted that North Americans are often distressed by the callousness with which the Mexicans treat animals, but that Mexicans are equally scandalized by the verbal brutality North American parents visit on their children. Perhaps if Mexican children were not so extremely well behaved, the sight of a parent screaming at his offspring might be more common, but as it is, we have never seen it.

As you spend more time in Mexico and learn more Spanish, your understanding of Mexicans is likely to undergo many changes. It will become clear, for instance, that easy friendliness will not often evolve into deeper friendship. Despite the contradictions of Mexican character, the appeal of the people remains the uppermost reason for choosing Mexico.

The Beauty

Gorgeous beaches flank both sides of the country, some crowded with sun-drenched tourists happy to escape from northern winters, some beaches silently inviting you to explore miles of untracked sand. From the picturesque desert panorama of Baja California to the tropical jungles of the Yucatán, the country abounds in breathtaking scenery. This draws a multitude of Canadians and Americans who spend billions every year taking in the beauty of Mexico.

Cities with modern buildings and elegant restaurants flowing with excitement thrill many North Americans, while others prefer villages with cobblestone streets and concerts in the town square. Each part of Mexico has its particular character. Each city and village is distinct, its personality differing dramatically from all others. This uniqueness is not found in North America, where so many towns are carbon copies of each other, down to identical restaurants, signs and mass-produced architecture.

We've heard people state that they think Mexico is ugly, because they've visited Tijuana or some other border town and weren't impressed. This judgment is about as fair as one made by a European visitor who, after flying into the middle of Nevada, claimed that the United States was a desert, with almost no one living there! (As you might suspect, we don't particularly recommend border towns as choice places to retire.)

Something that impressed the Spanish Conquistadors was the Indians' love of flowers. There was something almost religious about blossoms, and they were to be found everywhere, in gardens, along roads, painted on walls. Almost five hundred years later the Mexican people's use of flowers continues to impress. No home is complete without some tenderly cared-for potted plants in the windows and perhaps bougainvilleas blooming over the door. In fact, the inhabitants probably don't think of beauty as a luxury. So much of it, provided by nature, is all around them, and what requires a pot, some earth, some seeds, or a brush and some paint is considered as much a necessity as food and shelter.

The Climate

Many people whose experience with Mexico is limited to brief visits to towns on the United States border, or whose picture of the country was formed from cartoons and westerns, think of Mexico as a hot, dry place with endless vistas of treeless desert, spotted with cactus and cattle skeletons bleaching in the sun. Of course, Mexico has its share of places that are unbearably hot, bone-chillingly cold, too humid or too dry. The country is a checkerboard of valleys and plateaus, often with different climates in neighboring sections. In the tropics, for every 300-foot increase in altitude, the temperature drops one degree Fahrenheit. While the Gulf Coast cities like Villahermosa or Veracruz might swelter at 95 degrees, Mexico City enjoys temperatures of 70 or 75 degrees. There is also a difference in climate between the Pacific Coast and the Gulf Coast. The constant sea breeze blowing towards the Pacific Coast keeps summer and winter temperatures pleasant there, while the Gulf Coast can suffocate in the summer and catch chilly northern winds that whip down from Canada in winter. But, not by coincidence, the places where most Americans (and Mexicans) choose to live are either at high enough altitudes to enjoy "eternal spring" or on the Pacific Coast where the temperatures are higher but tempered by continual ocean breezes.

Living in a Foreign Country

On the United States' southern border is Mexico, a truly foreign country. The other two North American nations, Canada and the United States, have too many similarities in language, world views and customs be considered "foreign." Therefore, for millions of North Americans, Mexico is the only foreign country they will ever visit.

Mexico appreciates these visitors, for they pour billions of dollars into the economy. (The Mexican government refers to tourism as its "green pipeline.") Tourists carry away good memories of a vacation well spent–with uncounted tons of curios, weavings, stuffed iguanas, lavender pottery and a host of other bizarre items as presents for their unfortunate friends back home. They enjoy the beaches, mountains and the interesting country-side and cities, yet they often miss the most charming part of Mexico: its uniquely foreign culture. Underlying the tourist traps, American-style restaurants and curio shops is a truly foreign country.

When we talk of foreign travel, we quite naturally think of Europe. Europe is far away, true, but is it really so foreign? After all, most of our ideas, customs and beliefs originally came from Europe. People there think pretty much as we do, behave similarly and see the world in the same terms. Mexico, however, is very different–much more foreign than any European country you're likely to visit.

To be sure, Mexico has European roots, beginning with the Spanish Conquistadors. Yet underlying these roots is a rich tapestry of customs and beliefs that dates back to the Aztecs, the Mayas and even earlier. Folk beliefs, legends, manners and other cultural artifacts are colored by this Indian heritage, just as most Mexicans' skins are colored by their mixed ancestry. This blended culture is neither European nor Indian; it is Mexican. Once you begin to understand the country and its peoples, you discover an exciting new world.

Why the Differences

At first glance, it doesn't stand to reason that Mexico should be so different from the United States or Canada. After all, the only thing that separates us is an artificial line we call a "border." Sometimes a high fence or deep ditch, more often just a shallow river or an imaginary boundary that can only be plotted on a surveyor's map, the border is nevertheless real. Once you step across that line, you enter a profoundly different world. In some respects, you step backward in time half a century or more.

To understand why Mexico is so different from the rest of North America, we need to take a quick glance at history. Beginning in the late 1700s, the United States and Canada experienced heavy waves of immigration which increased in volume for about a century. For the most part, these early immigrants were unemployed workers, displaced farmers and others who longed for the abundant land in America, and sought a new start in life. They brought traditions of individualism and valued hard work. They knew how to till the land, how to build houses, how to work in factories. They brought the technology of the Industrial Revolution, which was sweeping Europe at that time.

The new immigrants discovered that the choice lands were occupied by Indians. The newcomers solved this problem by slaughtering the original owners or moving them ever westward. Small, family-operated farms sprang up in the forests and prairies. In the towns, small mercantile or manufacturing enterprises arose. The United States and Canada thus began as working-class and middle-class societies, and they have more or less retained these traditions through the centuries.

But Mexico was settled much earlier, in the 1500s. This was long before the Industrial Revolution wrought its changes upon the world. The original Spanish settlers in Mexico were *hidalgos,* the minor nobility and warrior class of Spain, which after several centuries of fighting had just defeated the Moors. Eager for adventure, the *hidalgos* leaped at the chance of conquering new vistas, of becoming lords in a new world.

These soldiers brought with them the ideas of feudalistic Spain with its notions of nobility. (Traditionally, European nobles don't work with their hands; they oversee others who do.) The *hidalgos'* ideas of farming weren't small farms, but huge estates operated by serfs, just as was the custom of nobility in Spain.

The conquerors came as an army, without women or wives. But, instead of killing off the Indians, as their northern counterparts were to do two centuries later, the early Spanish married Indian women and merged their European genes with the Native American ones. Cortez himself started the ball rolling by marrying Malinche (or Marina), the Aztec girl who had been a Mayan slave and who guided the Spaniards to the Aztec emperor.

From the Spanish point of view, it would have been pointless to exterminate the Indians; they were needed to operate the huge farms or *haciendas.* Indian tenant farmers simply shifted from serving Aztec overlords to Spanish ones; the Indians went on tilling the same lands their ancestors had for centuries. As Indians intermarried with the Spanish, a new race, called *mestizo,* was created. The *mestizos,* with their darker skins and slightly Indian features, became the racial cornerstone of Mexico. As the races blended, so did the customs, traditions and folklore to create a new culture, uniquely Mexican.

With the conquest, Spain quickly divided Mexico's land among the nobility, and within a few decades the entire country was solidly under the control of the new owners. So, unlike the British colonies of North America, Mexico was colonized rather swiftly. Then immigration slowed to a trickle, so modern European traditions were slow in reaching Mexico. While the United States and Europe were undergoing industrialization and modernization, Mexico remained an agricultural country with world views formed by feudal Spaniards of the 1500s.

To this day, Americans are puzzled at upper-class Mexicans' apparent lack of interest in labor or anything mechanical. Up north, for example, being able to repair a car or perhaps to turn it into a "hot rod" is prestigious for American youngsters, no matter how wealthy their families. In Mexico, only low-income, working-class people would think of with fixing their own cars. Often, upper- or middle-class drivers have no idea of how to change a flat tire and often wait until someone who knows how comes along. Mexican businessmen will buy expensive equipment and, instead of scrupulously maintaining it as one might expect, will run it until it stops and then buy a replacement. All of this is understandable if you have historical perspective.

Many Different Mexicos

As you travel about the United States and Canada, you'll find remarkable similarities between one section and another. To be sure, the scenery in Maine is different from Alabama or Nevada, but many, many things are the same. Meals served in Denny's or Howard Johnson's are indistinguishable, for example. People read the same books, watch the same TV shows, discuss the same current events, and generally speak the same dialects of English, using common slang words and sharing common humor, likes and dislikes.

Mexico is not so homogenous, and its diversity is part of its charm. It is divided into many physical segments, each separated by geography and history. Each section has its own traditions, cuisine, climate and, often, even its own language.

If you take a look at a map of Mexico, you'll begin to see why these differences exist. You'll notice a long, narrow country, with several mountain chains that run north and south, splitting the country and forming barriers against east-west communication. In pre-Colombian times, trails across these sierras were few in number and difficult to travel. Indian tribes living in the valleys developed unique languages and different civilizations. You'll also notice that most highways and railroads run north and south. This is not only because of the mountain barriers, but also because most of the highways and railroads were built years ago by U.S. manufacturing and mining interests who wanted to ship raw materials out of Mexico to feed northern factories and then ship saleable goods back into Mexico.

Furthermore, the country is laterally sliced by rivers and canyons, sometimes thousands of feet deep, that made north-south communication difficult in olden days. It's still not easy today. Each of these sections, over thousands of years of settlement, developed its own variants of culture, food, housing and style. Today, even though TV and radio have bridged many of the gaps, these differences persist and are a source of local pride. Almost any Mexican you meet will inform you that his particular section of the republic is universally recognized as the very best place in the whole world!

Selection of Climates

The resident or retiree can choose from an amazing variety of individual cultures as well as climates, each one distinct and a delight to discover. Each is a microcosm with its own cooking techniques, styles of dress and accents. When you get away from the big towns, you often hear people conversing in *Nahuatl* or *Quechua*, the languages of the ancient Aztecs and Mayas. The Mexicans themselves often look physically different from section to section. Because geographical barriers kept them apart for thousands of years, individuals tended to marry within tribes, keeping bloodlines relatively pure and developing tribal differences in appearance. At least 40 distinct racial and language groups are represented in Mexico.

On the eastern coast around Veracruz, home of the Huastecan tribes, typical clothing is tropical white, with the men wearing shallow straw hats. The women love bright embroided trim on their dresses. On the west coast around Tehuantepec, where the temperature is equally tropical, for some reason women tend to wear ankle-length skirts. A bit farther north around the Costa Chica area, the Indian women wear long woven skirts of cochineal-dyed yarn and occasionally go topless. Yes, you read correctly, topless. The early missionaries weren't able to completely wipe out the custom, although they did convince most women to wear a white, flouncy kind of overblouse. This outfit is worn today; however, a few women still insist on going topless. As time goes on, this custom is becoming rare and only the very old women still observe it–the younger set long ago replaced the purple woven skirts and white tops or bare bosoms with blue jeans and designer blouses.

In the Yucatán, women prefer to wear a loose dress of light cotton (a *huipil*), and the men often work bare chested, wearing lightweight, white muslin trousers. Because temperatures and humidity can be oppressive, this kind of dress is very practical. On the other hand, the northern part of Mexico is influenced by the "western" clothing of Texas and Arizona. There the climate is similar to Texas, Arizona and New Mexico, so it isn't surprising that clothing styles should be influenced by fashion in those states.

In the southern part of Mexico, nearby Guatemalan tribes affect styles with bright, colorfully woven garments. Depending upon the particular tribe, men may wear woolen mini-skirts or knee-length trousers. The patterns of the weavings denote which village the wearer is from, and the color of the ribbons in the hair indicates whether the person is married or single.

While each section of the country has its own clothing styles, styles from New York, London, Paris and Mexico City invade the fashions of young Mexicans, particularly in the larger, more cosmopolitan cities. The smaller the town or village, the more likely you are to find older, more traditional dress.

Different Diets

Mexican food varieties are another joy to the authors of this book. Each section of the country is proud of its own kind of dishes, its own style of cooking. Part of the fun of traveling in Mexico is sampling menus from one section of the country to another.

Most tourists think of Mexican food in terms of tacos, burritos and chili con carne. This is understandable since these dishes are just about all that's served in most Mexican restaurants in the United States. Similarly, most foreigners believe that typical American cuisine consists of hamburgers and hot dogs. Just as you can find hamburgers in the United States, you can find your fill of tacos in Mexico, if that's your dish. Most restaurants that cater to Americans include tacos on the menu, but a really good Mexican restaurant would no more offer tacos and burritos than would a gourmet restaurant offer hamburgers and hot dogs. There is so much more to Mexican cooking!

In the Yucatán, you'll discover such treats as venison cooked with a vinegar-cream sauce, or smoked *jaibali* (wild peccary) or *cochinito pibil* (roast suckling pig, cooked in a pit with a delicious sauce). In the mountains, you'll find succulent quail, delicately flavored with herbs and grilled over a charcoal fire, or eggs cooked with a dry cheese that transforms them into a delightfully textured breakfast. Mexican seafood is fabulous. Some of our favorite dishes are *huachinango al mojo de ajo* (grilled red snapper with garlic-butter sauce), *langostinos* (charbroiled fresh-water lobsters), and a bewildering variety of shellfish dishes. As an example of menu variety, one Mazatlan restaurant offers almost 20 shrimp dishes! One of the authors even tried iguana stew on a recent trip to Mexico. It tasted a little like chicken, but very bony and with not much meat. It's not recommended unless you're truly hungry.

One of the delights of living in Mexico is being able to cook some of these regional dishes at home, to experiment and learn. A trip through a typical market, with its variety of fresh fruits, vegetables and meats, makes shopping and menu planning a pleasant adventure rather than a chore. With their tropical climates, many parts of Mexico have year-round growing seasons for produce that is seasonally unavailable in the north. Just about any time of the year is good for incredibly sweet strawberries or luscious melons. Tropical fruits such as mangoes, pineapples, avocados and bananas are picked for the Mexican market when they are ripe, not days or weeks ahead to allow for ripening en route, as they must be when destined for the United States.

Shopping is also fun because foods are not only fresh but also available in a profusion and quality that most of us barely remember. In time, Mexican agriculture may become sufficiently mechanized and chemical fertilizers may become cheap enough to mass produce the tasteless fruits and vegetables that we have learned to settle for in the United States. But for now, Mexican fruits, vegetables, eggs, chicken and pork burst with flavor and enliven any cuisine in which one chooses to use them.

Retirement Choices

The difficulty of choosing the right retirement or long-term living spot is finding the section of Mexico that is just right for you. This is where this book should be of help. You can choose a tropical climate to escape winter, or you might want a dry, pleasant summer season. Like cool evenings and warm days? Balmy to warm evenings? Many people select the best of all worlds by living by the beaches in the winter, then, when humidity and temperatures begin to rise, they move to their favorite village high in the mountains.

The nice thing about making a search for the right place is that it's fun to do, and you can do it simply by using your tourist-card privileges. You can travel about, live a few weeks here or there and make comparisons. You can see what kind of North American neighbors you will have and get their opinions on living there. One thing you'll find out: there is no one place that can suit everyone. Your needs and desires are unique, so only you can decide.

Two Mexicos

Many people find it hard to believe that living in Mexico can be economical. "Why, we paid $300 a day for our condominium in Cancun," said one indignant couple, "so how could you possibly live there for $600 a month?" Admittedly, this was an extra-luxurious, three-bedroom condo with a balcony overlooking the beach. Yet numerous tourists report paying $100 a day and more for rooms.

For tourists, Mexico is a real mecca. On a two-week vacation, they can escape the snow and ice of New York or Chicago, and do it in real style. In Mexico, the beaches are marvelous, and restaurants offer great service, with white-jacketed waiters and menus that are as good as any at the Sheraton or Hilton in the United States. For only two weeks, what difference does it make if you pay $100, maybe $150, a day for a room? One Acapulco hotel charges $300 a day, but this includes your own private swimming pool and a car. If it's 20 below zero back home, you may decide you've earned a little luxury in your life. Besides, a

$100-a-day room in Mexico is a marvel compared to a $100 room in New York. But with prices like this, how can you possibly expect to live or travel in Mexico on $600 a month?

Two Realities

The answer is that Mexico is divided into two realities, one for tourists and one for residents. Tourists pay different rates, often for the same items. Tourists make their reservations with travel agents, who earn their living from ten percent commissions. They aren't likely to even have the $30 rooms among their listings. But most North Americans who live in Mexico would think it absurd to lay out that kind of money, not when a $30 room is more than adequate. They can't afford to pay $200 a day for a condo, not when $200 a month is considered moderately expensive by a retired couple. People who *live* in Mexico consider it ludicrous to go to a high-priced hotel restaurant and dine on Holiday Inn cuisine, especially when so many marvelous local restaurants offer tasty specialties at a fraction of the cost.

One of the most important changes we've observed in the 15 years since the first edition of *Choose Mexico* was published is the increased difference between the tourist and resident economies. It seems that Mexican entrepreneurs (and the international ones who run the fancy hotels and restaurants) have learned that tourists are willing to pay much higher prices than are common in Mexico.

Is the secret of inexpensive living to stay away from luxury resorts, like Acapulco, Cancun or Puerto Vallarta? Not necessarily. Acapulco, for example, can be one of the cheapest places to live in Mexico! From its initial marketing as a beautiful place for beautiful people, Acapulco has consistently overbuilt hotels and apartments. As soon as one high-rise is completed and half-full, another is started. There are plenty of $30-a-day hotel rooms and $300-a-month apartments. The bargains are to be found away from the beach, sometimes on hillsides with gorgeous views of the Pacific. Twenty years ago, these were top-of-the-line accommodations, but in order to compete, the owners of these properties had to continually lower their rents. When you save $100 a day, so what if you have to walk five blocks to the beach! If you are going to be a resident, this type of bargain is what you look for.

One thing to keep in mind about living expenses in Mexico is that foreign tourists make up but a tiny part of the population. The vast majority of the tourists are Mexican wage-earners who can't possibly afford to spend like the foreigners. A $30 hotel room represents about two days' wages for most Mexican workers. Ninety percent of the people in a resort town work there. They average about $200-$300 a month in wages, so they can't afford to pay much for rent or groceries. Most of the housing market is aimed at them, so rents and prices are scaled accordingly. You are either a rich tourist or a resident.

As a potential resident or retiree, you must make this a do-it-yourself project. Might as well start out traveling like a resident from the beginning! At your bookstore or library, pick up one of the low-cost travel guides to Mexico–the "Mexico on a Budget" type. They tend to be accurate about inexpensive hotels and travel tips. Except for the Christmas holidays and Easter week, you will seldom have any problems booking the hotel of your choice.

Don't bother with a travel agent, because the kind of hotels that budget books recommend usually don't pay travel agents' commissions and therefore aren't on their computers. In 40 years of traveling in Mexico, we've never had problems finding an inexpensive hotel. Cab drivers are helpful, but often they get a tip from the hotels for bringing guests, so naturally they want to take you to their special hotel. Take with a grain of salt anything a cab driver tells you. Don't be persuaded to deviate from your original choice, even if the cabby tells you the hotel is closed or that he knows one that is cheaper. See it for yourself first. The guidebooks are pretty accurate; cab drivers are not.

Once you arrive and are safely entrenched in an economical hotel, you can start searching looking for an apartment or a house to rent. If you are in a place where there are a lot of North Americans, you'll usually find listings and announcements posted on a bulletin board in the favorite "gringo" supermarket. Sometimes you'll see "for rent" signs in windows or advertised in the local English-language newspaper. But the best way to find rentals is to ask other foreign residents. They always seem to know what is vacant or what is about to be vacated.

Often, your hotel will have an apartment or suite for rent. This is a great way to test the town for its potential without getting involved in long-term rental agreements. (Few landlords are willing to rent for less than two or three months.) A hotel rents by the day, week or month, and often charges only a little more for an apartment than for an ordinary room. We've rented some nice apartments for between $15 and $20 a day. Particularly common are hotel "efficiencies" in resort places like Acapulco and Puerto Vallarta.

Like most furnished apartments, hotel kitchens come equipped with dishes, silverware, pots and pans, five-gallon jugs of purified water and even dish towels. The bonus is that every day, a brace of efficient maids scours the tile floors, changes the linen and brings in fresh water, exactly as in a hotel. In addition, they do your breakfast dishes and put them away in the cupboard! We usually leave a small tip every day, and it's greatly appreciated.

In some areas, such as Guadalajara and Lake Chapala, many apartments are owned by North Americans. It seems that every time a gringo couple decides to retire in the mellow climate of Lake Chapala or Ajijic, they think about building a house. Next, it occurs to them to build a few rental units for supplementary income. The result is a predictable oversupply of rental units. Rents are forced to a low level to keep the apartments rented. The only drawback to renting one of these units is that you will probably have to wash your own breakfast dishes and sweep out the place yourself or hire a maid to do it for you. In 1997, the going price was about $15 to have a woman come in two days a week to clean and do the laundry. Can you handle that?

Our recommendation to non-tourists is to take a hotel-apartment that rents by the day or week, even if it costs a little more than an ordinary hotel room, and even if you have no intention of cooking many meals. There is nothing like starting off the day by having breakfast on your patio or balcony. Planning the day's adventures while you relax in pajamas is infinitely more fun than spending half the morning getting dressed and then wait for a slow waiter to bring a second cup of coffee.

For the finicky or those worried about the dreaded "tourist disease," you have the satisfaction of preparing your own meals, using purified water and taking other hygienic precautions. Your food is as safe as if it were cooked in Omaha.

A few tips about apartment-hopping in Mexico:

–Invariably, you won't find a can opener in the kitchen. Don't ask why; just bring or buy one.

–Be sure you have matches for lighting the stove and candles for candlelight dining on the balcony (and for frequent power outages in some areas).

–When freezing ice cubes for drinks, use bottled water, not tap water, which may or may not be drinkable. As an aside, we note that many tourists religiously avoid drinking tap water, then brush their teeth with it. And they wonder why they get the trots! Remember that when taking a shower, if you open your mouth to sing, you are going to get water in your mouth. You can safely hum to your heart's content, however. Bottled water or boiled water in any form is the only kind that should enter your mouth.

–It isn't necessary to avoid fresh fruits and salads. Just wash everything in a solution of bottled water and water purification pills, which can be purchased at any drug store for pennies a box. (Doing this won't spoil the taste.)

The "Tourist Disease"

Why do they call it the "tourist disease?" Many people believe that only tourists are affected, that natives "build up an immunity." In fact, no one, including local residents, builds up an immunity to the most serious of these disorders, amoebic dysentery. By observing some simple rules of hygiene, residents avoid getting sick. When they don't follow these rules, they get sick just as the tourists. We know of many people who have been scared off by an unhappy experience with *turista* or have heard of others who suffered through their whole two-week vacation in Mexico. It doesn't have to be that way. Ask anyone who lives there.

Everyone has bacteria in their digestive systems; they are necessary for good health. But a phenomenon common to anyone who travels from one place to another is encountering a new strain of bacteria. The resident bacteria fight the intruders and the intestines finally get tired of all the fuss and decide to produce a little diarrhea. This is a mild form of the "tourist disease," and nothing to worry about. It's the bad-guy amoebas you must worry about. But common sense can avert problems. Most Americans who live in Mexico report that they seldom if ever have "tourist problems."

As a potential resident, you must relearn a few basic habits. These will distinguish you from the two-week tourist and keep you from a lot of misery. Before long, these rules become automatic, and you won't even have to think about them.

Of course, don't drink the water in any form other than boiled or bottled. By the way, you don't have to boil it for hours and hours. Since no organism can survive at temperatures higher than 150 degrees Fahrenheit, just bringing it to a boil is sufficient. Some water systems are all right, but we recommend boiled or purified water anyway; make it one of your automatic habits. Always soak salad vegetables (lettuce, tomatoes–anything that isn't going to be cooked or peeled) in a solution of water and purification tablets for 20 minutes.

Finally, one of the most valuable pieces of advice this book can give you about avoiding dysentery: when selecting a restaurant, don't be impressed by the nicely dressed waiters, immaculate linen and sparkling silverware; check out the clientele. Notice if local people eat there. If local people don't patronize a place, there's one of three explanations: the food is overpriced; poorly prepared; or not fit to eat.

Too often, a "tourist" restaurant is owned by absentee owners and operated by low-paid employees who really don't care if you get sick or not. They know you won't be back again anyway, and you eat in so many places you won't know where you got the "bug." But a family-operated restaurant, one that caters to local people, can't afford to have anyone get sick. When word gets around, the place is out of business. One of this book's authors as a youth lived in Mexico for many years and has traveled extensively throughout the country for the past 40 years. Only twice has he caught the curse. Both times he ignored his own advice and patronized a spiffy, tourist-only restaurant where no Mexicans ate!

Why all this fuss about boiled or bottled water? Isn't any Mexican water fit to drink? If not, why not? The answer is that some water is probably okay, particularly that coming from desert areas where the water is pumped from deep wells, or that flows from the high mountains, where few people are around to pollute it. The problem is that Mexico has many priorities well ahead of the construction of modern sewage disposal plants. The costs would be astronomical, and the money is simply not there. Even where there are facilities for modern disposal, expanding home and hotel construction assures that sewage production exceeds the capacity of these plants. So, most of the sewage goes into septic tanks and eventually seeps into the ground water. Where there is a high water table, such as you find at the coastal resorts, some sewage, with its amoebas and bacteria, inevitably finds its way into the water system. Wherever water is drawn from shallow wells, you can have problems. A further complication in Mexico City is that the water and sewage pipes are often damaged by earthquake activity, and they leak, not much, but enough to sometimes make you sick.

To become a healthy non-tourist in Mexico, you have to continually follow common-sense rules. Before long you will become so used to the drill that when you return to the United States, you will hesitate before using tap water to brush your teeth.

Two Price Systems in Mexico?

You often hear people claim, "There are two prices in Mexico, one for the Mexicans and one for the gringos." Some believe, for example, that different menus are handed to gringos and Mexicans. This simply isn't true. Most prices are fixed by government decree, and the government is serious about enforcement. When you rent a room, for example, the ceiling price is supposed to be clearly displayed at the desk and in your room.

But, as we have observed earlier, there are two price systems—not for Mexicans and foreigners but for residents and tourists. You won't find different prices being charged to the two groups in the same restaurants and hotels, since menus and room rates are prominently displayed. You will, however, find higher prices at the hotels into which tourists are booked by travel agents, and the restaurants in those hotels. Ironically, the government often turns its head at violations by tourist hotels. Residents, whether Mexican or foreign, know of equally nice places that charge a fraction as much.

Restaurants and stores, particularly the non-tourist places, are anxious to have residents' repeat business, so they can't very well overcharge you, or you'll never return. However, that old game of bargaining does go on in Mexico. Some merchants feel obligated to quote an unrealistic price, and they often feel cheated out of the fun if you go ahead and pay without a little arguing.

How do you know if you're paying the right price or the tourist price? Don't all Mexicans expect you to bargain? Should you offer one-third the asking price? These questions are relative to the product being offered and the price asked. For example, if you are in a market, and the vendor wants the equivalent of a dime for a handful of onions, ask yourself: "What do I gain by arguing him down 20 percent?" A few pennies or a nickel means nothing to you, but plenty to the vendor. Actually, individual entrepreneurs face a lot of competition in the native markets, so they try to keep their prices attractive. They want to see you become a regular customer, and they usually go out of their way to make you happy.

On the other hand, if you're buying something that costs a lot of money, then a 20 percent discount would be significant. If it's big money, sometimes it's worth bargaining hard, just as you would when buying an automobile or house back home.

Bargaining is an art form that you might enjoy, but accept the fact that you will never win. Just as you never really beat an automobile salesman at his game, you'll never quite get the final value in Mexico. Bargaining is fun to do, and no one gets hurt feelings. Yet serious hassling over pennies doesn't mark an American as an astute bargainer; it marks him as a cheapskate.

It's interesting to watch the tourists bargain. As soon as they settle down on the beach, a swarm of eager vendors begins landing like flies on a lollipop. They'll offer jewelry, blankets, sweaters, you name it, and the bargaining begins in Spanish, English and sign language. Everyone has a glorious time, and in the end, the poor merchant reluctantly agrees to drop the price of the $40 necklace to only $10. The tourist is delighted at his prowess in saving $30, and the vendor is discouraged that he allowed such a fine $1 necklace go for only $10. Like the automobile salesman back home, the beach salesmen are experts. But don't get the idea that everyone you meet is trying to scalp you. Most merchants you deal with in everyday living situations are anxious to do business with you and take pride in having a good relationship with *norteamericanos.*

If you visit a store with price tags on all items, it's pretty sure that they mean business, unless you are talking big money. If you are thinking about a $100 purchase or a $1,000 deal, then maybe it's worth your while to bargain against the posted price. You may not be successful, but it's worth the try to shave off ten or 20 percent. But if the price is only $2, you're wasting your time haggling.

One complaint occasionally heard about *Choose Mexico* is that it is drawing more and more North Americans into the country. "They come down here, throw money around, pay big wages, leave big tips and ruin things for the rest of us!" is the way one woman put it.

It's true that when more foreigners move into a town or village, the demand for domestic help creates a boost in wages. It's also true that foreigners tend to pay more than the going rate for lots of things. This means more money circulating in the community, and slightly higher prices all around. The final result is that Americans pay a few cents more for goods and services, and the Mexicans have more money in their pockets, more food on the table and better clothing for their children. Because Americans are known to pay higher wages, the local people are eager to work for them. Working for an American family is prestigious, and workers try very hard to be good employees and keep their jobs.

Our stock answer to complainers: Mexico is not your private discovery. Mexico is not for the sole benefit of a few stingy gringos who want to keep the local economy depressed so they can save a few pennies. We are guests in that country, and as guests we should rejoice in any improvement in the living standard of our hosts. If you have to pay $1 an hour for help instead of 75 cents an hour, just remember how much you would pay back home and think of what that extra money will buy for a Mexican family.

Yes, there are two Mexicos. One is for tourists; the other is for residents. The happiest residents are those who consider themselves part of the community, and by the same token, they are the best liked by their Mexican neighbors. The unhappiest residents are those who try to change things and make Mexico into a bargain-basement copy of the United States.

Successful Retirement in Mexico

Finances in Mexico

As we stated earlier, our most recent research suggests that a retired couple can live in Mexico today on a budget of $600 a month. This amount covers most basic, day-to-day living expenses. What does $600 mean in terms of purchasing power? It amounts to more than *six times* the minimum wage for a Mexican who works six days a week. (Many employers in Mexico believe that "minimum wage" and "maximum wage" mean the same thing: less than $4 a day.) Another way to look at it is that $600 a month is twice as much as skilled technicians earn at IBM's Guadalajara disk drive plant. (And IBM pays much higher wages than most manufacturers in the country.) Or, $600 is significantly more income than a school teacher, an accountant or an electrical engineer enjoys. In other words, a Mexican family considers a $600 monthly income to be generous.

We don't suggest that you can live luxuriously on $600 a month, but the fact is, a retired couple can cover their basic monthly expenses on this amount. They can afford a house-keeper/maid (on a part-time basis), medical insurance and a certain amount of entertainment and travel expense. Some people manage to include routine maintenance and insurance for an automobile on this amount. But clearly, this minimum budget provides a significantly higher standard of living than the vast majority of Mexicans enjoy. Unquestionably $600 a month provides a higher quality of life in Mexico than it does in the United

States or Canada. However, as we've stated many times, we do not encourage anyone with extremely limited funds to move to Mexico. There is no "safety net" in Mexico—no welfare, no food stamps, no one to take care of you. Also, those who move to Mexico just because they think living there is cheap could be making a serious mistake. Nothing is a bargain if it is not what you want, and life in Mexico is not for everyone. That is why we so strongly and so repeatedly suggest that you "try it before you buy it."

Why is Living in Mexico Affordable?

Economic conditions in Mexico tend to move in regular, predictable patterns. Over the years, we've seen cycles of rising costs—which cause prices to rise to almost the same levels as in the United States—followed by abrupt slumps which bring the cost of living to very low levels. That's where we are today, near the bottom of the trough. For those of us with dollars in our pocketbooks, most prices are at a 15-year low. Once again, we find the opportunity to enjoy at exceedingly affordable prices all that Mexico offers. Food, labor and goods manufactured in Mexico are especially inexpensive, although anything imported will be expensive.

Now, what does this favorable exchange rate mean in terms of your retirement lifestyle? The following paragraph is a quote from Nadine and Henry Laxen, who live in Mazatlán:

"We go to the movies here every week, and a ticket costs $2, while popcorn is 80 cents. Our full-time maid [who comes in six days a week] is paid approximately 350 pesos or $50 per week, and she is very well paid by Mexican standards. On the other hand, if you want to buy imported electronics or appliances, be prepared to pay double for it. A 32-inch Sony TV costs over $2000, as does a large Whirlpool side-by-side refrigerator. All in all, I would say that you can live *quite* well on $1000 per month, and live like a king, or at least a high level prince, on $2000 per month." Henry Laxen maintains a very interesting Web Site: (http://www.maztravel.com)

Inflation and Currency Exchange

The devaluation of the peso in late 1994 and early 1995 is an almost exact repeat of the peso's last big slump back in 1982, when its value slipped from 20 to the dollar to 38 to the dollar in one afternoon. A year later, it fell to 150 to the dollar and kept on falling. This was a major bonanza for retirees and others living in Mexico who exchange dollars for pesos to pay bills. However, it wasn't quite as good as it sounds. Even though they received 20 times as many pesos for their dollars, they couldn't buy 20 times as many goods and services. That old demon, inflation, marched side by side with exchange rates, climbing upward as the peso's value went downward. The same thing could very well happen again.

But, shouldn't retirees living in Mexico worry about inflation, devaluation and falling peso values? Not really. When your income is in American or Canadian dollars, the phenomenon of inflation-devaluation is purely academic. When you pay more pesos for rent, groceries or taxi fares, it really doesn't matter because you receive more pesos for your dollars. You break even. For example: at one point in time, the price of a bottle of beer was 100 pesos (75 cents). Gradually the price rose to 2,250 pesos. That sounds like a whopping increase, but since 2,250 pesos were worth 75 cents, what did it matter?

This wild devaluationary ride was finally contained through drastic action, when the Mexican government imposed strict controls over exchange rates. Quickly, devaluation leveled out to almost nothing. The government then clipped three zeros off the end of the currency (magically changing 3,000 pesos into three pesos) and declared the peso to be worth about three pesos to the dollar. Of course, that didn't make things less expensive or more expensive; this change just made it easier to count your money.

Please, don't confuse a stable exchange rate with a stable rate of inflation. Most people do. Just because the dollar-to-peso exchange rate remained constant, it didn't mean prices in pesos couldn't rise. And rise they did.

From outside Mexico, things appeared to be going along quite well; after all, the peso-to-dollar ratio remained comfortably constant. But prices in pesos didn't. Prices in stores increased, yet number of pesos to the dollar remained constant. For foreigners, the problem was no longer academic. Their money was worth less every day, and prices were higher every day; that's inflation, no matter *what* the exchange rate is!

John Howells predicted that this condition could not continue. The government was using its dollar reserves to protect the peso, just as they did before the 1982 slide. The peso clearly needed to realign itself with world currency. He warned anyone who would listen that the peso would crash as soon as the new president assumed office. Sure enough, overnight the peso lost more than 40 percent of its value! The surprising thing was the number of financial "experts" who professed to be surprised.

Mexican devaluation is hardly unique; it's happened over and over and over in the course of the past half century. Devaluation inevitably happens when the peso is artificially supported at an impossibly high value, forcing the dollar to be undervalued. When these conditions exist, something has to give. The first devaluation John personally remembers was in 1948, when the peso dropped from five per dollar to seven–the day after his father switched several thousand dollars into his peso checking account. Then it slipped to eight, where it stayed for several years, then to 12 and then to 20, to 40, to 80, and so on. In February, 1982, John happened to be sitting in a Mexican bar, just about to change dollars into pesos, when Presidente de la Madrid came on television to announce a 50 percent devaluation. Suddenly, John's dollars were worth twice as much! The price of the next beer dropped from two dollars to one dollar and a half by the time the newscast ended.

That famous 1982 devaluation was a disastrous lesson for those who kept large investments in peso bank accounts. Those with dollar accounts were hurt even worse because, when the government took over control of banks, dollar accounts were converted into pesos at the official rate of exchange–representing a fraction of the dollar's true value. The horror of this gambit is legendary. Before 1982, someone with two million pesos in the bank ($100,000) could live quite luxuriously on the interest. Today, those same two million (old) pesos would be worth less than $500.

Most retirees and other foreigners in Mexico weren't hurt as badly in the 1994–1995 devaluation–for two reasons. For one thing, the United States government pumped billions into the Mexican economy to prevent a total melt-down. (Let's be honest; this wasn't done to help the Mexican people, but rather to protect massive American investment in Mexican manufacturing facilities.) The second reason is that most foreign residents did as we so strongly recommended in our first edition. We urged that North Americans keep the bulk of their funds at home and arrange for a monthly transfer of only as much money as needed for living expenses. While acknowledging the lure of Mexico's attractive interest rates, we advised that the temptation to make a killing on interest rates should be avoided. Our caution has been vindicated. This time, aware North Americans heeded the obvious warning signs and converted their peso investments to U.S. money-market funds in the nick of time. Those who didn't, lost 40 percent of the value.

What are the warning signs? When the peso becomes dramatically over-valued against the dollar, watch out. When Mexicans start shopping across the border in the United States because goods are cheaper there, you know the peso is in for trouble. When wealthy people begin changing pesos for dollars to invest in U. S. real estate or when Mexicans start going to the United States for vacations because Mexico is too expensive, then it's time to convert your pesos to dollar accounts in U.S. or Canadian banks!

How Safe Are Mexican Banks?

Don't confuse the instability of the exchange rate system with the stability of Mexican banks. By and large, they are quite safe. Bank accounts are guaranteed by the Mexican government, and it can be confidently stated that no one has lost a peso over the years. The *value* of those pesos is another story. Our advice is, once again, keep the bulk of your money in your hometown bank and transfer money to your Mexican bank only when you need it. And transfer only as much as you need, not more.

Of course, you will open an account with a Mexican bank from which you will pay your bills and into which you will have your Social Security checks or other pension or investment income deposited. In an emergency, you can get "cash advances" at most banks using a MasterCard or Visa, but just as you do back home, you pay a premium for this service.

Long-distance banking can be a headache as well as expensive for several reasons. You usually have to pay up to a one-and-a-half percent service charge to your Mexican bank to accept your foreign check, and you must pay an equal percentage to convert your pesos into dollars. We're talking three percent per transaction just to use your own money! However, retirees here have discovered a couple of ways to get around these fees.

One way is to open a peso account with a reputable Mexican investment firm such as Allen W. Lloyd's. An account can be opened for less than $1,000, and current interest is paid on the investment. The interest rate varies from month to month, and the rates are always high. (That interest looks good, but you must keep your eye on the exchange rate and be prepared to switch over to a dollar account if you become leery.) Once you have an account, you can cash without charge personal checks from your U.S. or Canadian bank. Local residents typically drop into Lloyd's once a week for pesos to pay operating expenses.

We mention the Lloyd's company because it has branches in the major retirement areas and because the company specializes in dealing with English-speaking investors. There may be other equally reliable investment companies, but most people seem to use this one. One retiree we interviewed said, "I keep $5,000 in my account, and I'm very pleased with the interest. I was even more pleased when it was drawing 42 percent. However, I'd advise against keeping more in the account than you can afford to lose, just in case another deflation happens." Other residents are less cautious, keeping much more money in the accounts. One single man said, "I could damn near live on the interest until it dropped to 24 percent!"

(For more information: Allen W. Lloyd, Apdo. 1-1470, Guadalajara, Jalisco, Mexico; tel. 121-9050.)
e-mail, lloyd@infosel.net.mx

A second strategy is to open a "Friendship Senior Checking Account" with Los Angeles's California Commerce Bank (a subsidiary of Mexico's BANAMEX which has 700 branch offices throughout the republic). As a chartered U.S. bank, California Bank of Commerce is insured up to $100,000. These "Friendship" accounts are designed specifically for American senior citizens (55 years or older) who live in Mexico.

Then, you open a peso account with BANAMEX, where you can deposit or cash checks from its United States subsidiary without incurring a service charge. With a checking account at BANAMEX, you also receive a free credit card and an ATM card, so you can draw cash from an automatic teller instead of having to stand in line to cash a check.

Dollars on deposit in California Commerce's unique Friendship Senior Checking Program earn an extra one percent over current U.S. interest rates for regular depositors, and there is no monthly service charge. To get the high current rate of Mexican interest, you need to invest about $1,500 worth of pesos (the amount varies), although it isn't necessary to do this in order to open a convenience account. You can draw up to $200 at a time from BANAMEX without any service charge.

(For more information: California Commerce Bank, P.O. Box 30886 Terminal Annex, Los Angeles, CA 90030; 21624-5700. Or BANAMEX, Banco Nacional de Mexico, International Dept., Isabel La Catolica 43 44, 06089 Mexico.)

Current Investment Strategy

What's the potential for investing in Mexico? (If we could predict the future, do you think we'd be writing books instead of counting our money full time?) Okay, if you insist on our unqualified opinion, we'll hazard a guess that the financial picture in Mexico will follow the familiar scenario of 1982 to 1994. That is, there'll be a period of stagnation—with prices in dollars exceptionally favorable for *norteamericanos*. Then, the peso will begin to rise in value. It will slowly gain against the dollar through two Mexican presidential terms, possibly three. Then, at the end of the second or third term, the world's economists will once again express astonishment when devaluation hits! You needn't have a PH.D. to figure this out. Just look at history. It happens over and over, yet economists always seem bewildered by it.

Now, many retirees are fascinated with an interesting side effect of devaluation: bizarre interest rates. As the peso falls, interest rates soar. For example, in 1995–after the initial devaluation–interest on money-market accounts (in pesos) swung from a low of 30 percent to a high of 86 percent! These rates varied monthly, depending on the paranoia of the market. Unfortunately, dollar accounts aren't permitted at this time, so all your investments are automatically converted to pesos. Of course, there's no reason you can't convert your profits to dollars and put them into your hometown bank.

If you take a look at the chart below, which shows interest rates, and if you consider that the peso has spells of holding steady for several months at a time, investing in pesos would seem to be a good deal. Many people do invest, some enough to live off the interest. On paper, it appears that US$20,000 invested in a peso money-market fund would bring in enough income for a couple to cover all living expenses each month. One fund we've looked at paid over 40 percent interest over a one year period, which would bring in almost $700 a month.

However, bear in mind that one swift, overnight devaluation could wipe out your profits, and then some. When the economy is riding the trough, the peso is almost sure to lose value. Whether devaluation will be a slow, gradual slide or a roller coaster ride is anybody's guess. High interest rates often compensate for this loss as well as turn a nice profit, but you must realize that keeping large sums of money in peso accounts is a gamble. Like all good gamblers, you need to know the chances you're taking, calculate your odds of making money, and most important, not gamble any more than you can afford to lose!

Here are some interest figures for 1996:

1996	AWLASA FUND	LOYPLUS FUND
JANUARY	31.936 percent	32.755 percent
FEBRUARY	40.408	43.840
MARCH	57.980	66.302
APRIL	76.044	86.117
MAY	65.372	69.121
JUNE	47.794	50.372
JULY	40.271	42.516
AUGUST	33.729	36.746
SEPTEMBER	30.296	35.279
OCTOBER	33.076	35.248
NOVEMBER	45.662	46.381
DECEMBER	48.993	52.990

Mexican Stock Investments

Mexico's stock market is known as the Bolsa. It is similar in many ways to securities markets in America and Europe, but there are important differences. For one thing, the Bolsa is on a smaller scale. Not only are far fewer issues traded, but the daily volume is a tiny fraction of that on the New York Stock Exchange. The market is so thin–there is so little activity–for most issues that liquidity can be a very serious problem. And, of course, a sudden devaluation can wipe out a large part of your investment over-night. However, people who bought Mexican stocks early in 1995 and have held onto them through the Bolsa's impressive recovery are sitting pretty. If Mexico's economy continues to expand, there is probably still much money to be made on the Bolsa. Some retirees, those who read the Mexican financial pages daily or who find a trusted financial adviser, may raise their standard of living to celestial heights and leave princely inheritances. But for the average person of moderate means, we strongly counsel prudence and patience. In Mexico, there are many ways to enjoy oneself without being a millionaire or making financial gain the focus of one's life.

Real Estate as an Investment

At the time our first edition was published, Mexican real estate was selling at prices unthinkable in the United States or Canada. This was soon after the devaluation of 1982, when property values dropped dramatically. Early readers of *Choose Mexico* rushed down to snap up these bargains. As you can imagine, when a flood of buyers waving fistfuls of dollars hit the retirement areas, housing prices shot up. They doubled, then doubled again. However, since the prices were so low in the first place, even at these quadrupled prices, the homes were bargains compared to similar homes in California or Florida. Those who bought property as the cost of living was rising did quite well on their investments.

What happened to the real-estate market after the devaluation of 1994–1995? Did it suddenly crash as it did in 1982? Not this time, at least not in the same way. Those who paid their rents in pesos found their rents had dropped by 40 percent, but those who rented from other *norteamericanos* were paying in dollars, so nothing changed. Mexicans who were selling their property were forced to drop the asking price, especially when selling to other Mexicans, because they were trading in pesos, not dollars. Retirees who owned property, on the other hand, thought in terms of dollars, and saw no reason to drop asking prices because the peso was worth less.

Prices on choice retirement property could possibly drop as time goes on, but our guess is that the market won't change significantly. The bottom line is that the real-estate market works on the age-old principle of supply-and-demand. With today's conditions so favorable for retirement in Mexico, even more *gringos* will be going there, looking for property. And, as long as there are buyers, prices probably won't fall very low. (This is just a guess, so please don't make any real-estate investments based on it.)

To sum up, real estate can be an excellent investment, provided you make rational decisions and bargain for a good price. Buying on the open market from Mexican sellers will undoubtedly give you an edge. Some things you ought to know before buying a home are discussed in elsewhere in this section, but our principal caveat bears repeating here: know or be advised by someone who knows a lot about the area, the laws, the real-estate market and construction.

Finding a Place to Live

For some reason or other, we North Americans think we have to own a house. Maybe it's something left over from the depression, a security blanket of sorts. It's more than that, of course; during the past decades in the United States, home ownership has been a way of keeping ahead of inflation and, in many parts of the country, achieving great appreciation of value. We write loan interest off our income before taxes, and overall we come out pretty well financially.

But things aren't necessarily the same in Mexico. For one thing, few homes are sold with bank loans (although the owners of new developments will sometimes finance through U.S. or Canadian banks). Buyers customarily pay cash for property, so you'll have no interest payments to deduct from your income. Therefore you'll have a large investment in a home–money that otherwise would have been bringing in dividend or interest income. Also, since you're retired, or perhaps living on savings, you probably won't have much income tax to pay, or much income to deduct from in the first place.

But doesn't property ownership protect you from inflation? Not necessarily. Get rid of the notion that during times of inflation, property is *always* a hedge against falling purchasing power. When you are in a country undergoing hyper-inflation, property doesn't usually rise in value with the economy, instead it can *drop* in value! This was clearly the case during Mexico's period of hyper-inflation in 1982. Why? Because in order to keep ahead of the inflation game, people need hard currency (meaning dollars) in their hands to manipulate and invest in things that go up in value. It wasn't until inflation in terms of dollars set in that values went up; then folks did okay.

Figure it this way: real-estate value is partially determined by how much rental income a property might bring in if rented to a tenant. However, when inflation eats into tenants' incomes, their ability to pay good rents is lessened. Property becomes a lousy investment when owners reason, "Better sell and get some dollars!" Then, when everybody wants to sell and nobody wants to buy, prices tumble even faster.

This is what happened during the inflationary jump in the early 1980s. As the value of the peso plummeted, so did dollar values of real estate. In the last part of the 1980s, however, prices stabilized and began creeping upward. In fact, within a short time, real-estate prices regained the losses incurred after the initial devaluation and more. This was due to the increased demand by North Americans and the liberalized Mexican laws concerning property ownership.

Where we once might have cautioned against buying, the recent devaluation makes some properties once again bargains, making us less cautious. As we pointed out earlier in the book, the prime real estate in the hands of foreigners didn't lose value as it did in 1982, but then there has been no hyper-devaluation this time. It could be that property will hold its value and even continue to appreciate.

Having pointed out that property ownership is different in Mexico, we need to add that, despite the drawbacks, many North Americans find great joy in buying old colonial homes and restoring them. Others want to build their own places, doing their own designing and testing their artistic abilities as architects. Fortunately, with the low cost of labor and the availability of unusual building materials such as custom-made tiles and hand-formed bricks, the cost of redoing a home is certainly reasonable.

Can Foreigners Own Property ?

A common misconception is that Americans can't own property in Mexico. For years, the government tried to foreign ownership of land with diminishing success. The fear was that Mexican citizens would have little chance to compete with affluent foreigners; property ownership for Mexicans could be a thing of the past. In fact, this is one of the fears most often expressed by Mexicans when discussing the NAFTA treaty.

Despite the Mexican government's efforts, the foreigners seem to have won. For the first time in several generations, all restrictions are off in most parts of Mexico. In most of the country, you can buy and sell property just as you might in Omaha or Ottawa. Because of this change in federal law, foreigners can hold an *escritura,* or fee-simple title deed, for the property in their own names.

Foreigners are still restricted within specified distances of the seacoast or international borders, in that you can't own the property outright; even if you have FM-2 status (see p. 73 for definition) you must go through the lease process described below.

The way it works is that you purchase the property through a bank. You establish trust of which you are the beneficiary, and order the bank to buy the land in the name of the trust. Then, the bank leases the property back to you for a period of up to *50 years,* renewable in perpetuity. This is a government-approved maneuver which, as one man put it, "... is a way for the Mexican government to save face. They can sell beach property to foreigners while claiming that they aren't." Formerly, the leases were for 30 years; what isn't clear at this point is whether the 30-year leases already in effect will be extended to 50 years.

This bank trust is known as a *fidecomiso* and since it's renewable, the time limit doesn't really mean much except that you have to set up a new trust when it expires. In the meantime, you can do anything you want with your property–live there, rent it out, whatever. The bank charges an administration fee which varies between $250 to $1,000 a year. When you're ready to sell, the buyer pays you the money and you assign the lease to the new owner. Of course, a legal immigrant with FM-2 papers can buy the property in their own name, without bothering with trusts.

A welcome change in the Fidecomiso rules is the elimination of an onerous part of bank trusts. Previously, a lease was valid for just 30 years and not renewable; the property had to be sold to a Mexican citizen. That is, if you bought a house with a 30-year lease and decided to sell after 10 years, a new buyer would only have the remaining 20 years of the lease. This meant that the longer you owned property, the less valuable it was for a new owner. But today leases are indefinite and can be renewed without restrictions. Also, leased property can be changed over to private ownership upon payment of fees if and when you decide to go to FM-2 status.

Exactly how these laws are going to work out for foreigners remains to be seen. The laws are too recent to be sure of their application. For example: we understand that if you buy a house as a tourist–with an *escritura*–you are not permitted to rent the house during your absence. If indeed this is the rule, we don't know that it's being enforced, or for that matter how it could be enforced. NAFTA can, and probably will, influence these and other restrictions; only time will tell.

When considering property in the late 1990s, our continuing best advice is to consult with local expatriates, real-estate experts and a recommended lawyer to make sure of what you are getting into. Under no circumstances let any money change hands before you have assurances that everything is in order; people have been hurt by real-estate salesmen who say, "We'll take of the details *mañana*.

A major caution still is that many desirable properties, often choice ocean-front parcels, once belonged to *ejidos* (community-owned farms) that could not be sold without government permission. When those rules were in effect, many North Americans lost money by buying from someone who really didn't own the property. It wasn't always that the seller was cheating intentionally. He may have sincerely believed land that his family had farmed for generations was his to sell. The laws changed drastically during the Salinas administration, and precisely how they work today is a question you need to go over with your lawyer. If nobody knew who owned the property before, how do they know today?

Looking at Property

One thing we need to make clear: real-estate agencies do *not* operate under the same rules as where you came from. The United States and Canada have very strict regulations, and every broker and salesperson is held to certain ethical standards. They must undergo training and pass tests to obtain their licenses. Not so in Mexico. This is not to say that real-estate people in Mexico are all crooked. Most are very ethical, but many of them are amateurs. It turns out that selling real estate to other gringos is the easiest way to get work that pays anything. And just about all that's required to deal in properties is the desire to sell something and make money. It's worth your while to make inquiries among residents as to who they recommend for agents. The better ones gain their reputations just as the bums gain theirs.

The first thing you'll discover is that the term "multiple listing" doesn't necessarily mean the same as back home. Many real-estate agencies will show you only the properties they have under contract, while giving you the impression that this is all there is available through all other companies. The result is that you are going to waste your time looking at a small range of properties, probably in the upper range of your price level.

The solution is to visit several real-estate offices, and ask to see a complete list of what they have. This is the only way you can be sure you have access to all the available properties. In some of the larger areas, you'll find flyers with pictures of homes for sale and sometimes a multiple-listing catalogue.

Finally, when you've found your dream home, be sure you have a reputable attorney, one who is comes highly recommended by your fellow expatriates. Of utmost importance, be sure that he is *not* the same attorney who represents the buyer. (That can't happen back home.) You want someone to represent your interests who is on your side exclusively.

Mexican Real Estate Today

As detailed in earlier sections of this book, real estate has had its ups and downs in Mexico. And, at the moment it seems to be a mixed bag. Gringo-owned properties are holding their price levels pretty well, but asking prices for homes in all-Mexican neighborhoods can be described as bargains. Around the Lake Chapala/Ajijic area, where most buyers and sellers are gringos, the market seems to be relatively steady–although this could change. A pleasant two-bedroom, two-bath furnished home in Ajijic costs between $70,000 and $100,000 for 1,000 to 2,000 square feet on a nice-sized lot. Closing costs are about $1,200 dollars, which includes drawing up a trust deed (*fidecomiso*) or a direct, fee-simple title (*escritura*). By the way, many choose to go the *fidecomiso* route, rather than buying outright, because it is slightly easier.

There are some great bargains to be found in Mexico today. This is particularly true if you want something away from the usual gringo circuit. When buying away from foreign enclaves, the kind of homes Americans typically buy are often priced a higher, simply because sellers know we *norteamericanos* can and will pay more. For this reason, it helps to have a Mexican friend do the looking and bargaining for you. (Make sure he or she is a *friend* and not a commission-seeker!) And, look carefully before you force your money on a seller of a truly cheap house in a Mexican neighborhood. It can be, and probably is, very rustic, inside and out according to our standards. The plumbing could be sluggish, inadequate, maybe even non-existent, and the electrical wires strung around the walls and ceilings like spider webs, as if the electrician weren't serious. The inside walls will probably need plaster, and the doors and window frames, new wood. The whole place will be begging to be rebuilt. That wonderful bargain could be a nightmare.

For others, remodeling a home is a project of love. Shopping for just the right tile, looking for tropical woods for the doors, and working with a contractor to rebuild a house is fun for certain people. You must know yourself before undertaking something like this. The payoff, if you decide to go ahead, is that you can build your dream home through the investment of a little money and a lot of effort.

Do You Really Need to Buy?

Before you plunk down your savings on a home in Mexico, you ought to question some of your basic beliefs about real estate–beliefs that may be valid at home, but not necessarily in Mexico. Property ownership in the United States has many advantages. One is the tax break on interest payments. Often it's cheaper to own a house than to rent when everything is considered, including the almost certain annual appreciation in a home's value.

In Mexico, however, if you have to pay cash, you won't have interest to deduct from your income. And, you can't count on your home's increasing in value; sometimes they do, sometimes they don't. But most important, you probably can rent much cheaper than you can buy. For example, a house that sells for $80,000 (a really nice one) can usually be rented for $400 to $550 a month–sometimes much less. Is it wise to tie up $80,000 of your savings for a place you could have rented for only $550 a month? It may be worth it if you are thinking of the fun you are going to have fixing it up or if you have a need to *own* your own place. If you are selling a house in the United States and will have a capital gain larger than the $125,000 (on which those over 55 can get a one-time tax forgiveness), you may want to check with your tax adviser on the renting vs. buying question.

If cost is your primary consideration, you can't beat renting. But in any event, *please* do yourself a favor and rent for a period of time to make sure you want to live in Mexico. As we stress repeatedly, Mexico isn't for everyone, and you might be unhappy to have your life savings stuck in a house that isn't selling because of a slow market condition.

Fortunately for the renter, rentals are abundant in most areas. Prices for a small apartment or house can start at less than $250 a month, depending on the neighborhood. Many people we interviewed seem to think $350 is an ordinary rent, and $500 a month and over can rent a very acceptable place. You can pay much more, and if you want to rent a Mexican-style house you can pay far less. In Lake Chapala we met one man who indignantly denied that a person could live in Mexico on less than $1,500 a month. It turned out that he had read *Choose Mexico* and immediately, without ever having visited the country, phoned a real-estate agent and rented a large, four-bedroom home in a luxury retirement area, sight unseen. It was a nice place, and he could afford it. But he was correct in saying he needed $1,500 a month to cover his basic expenses. (By the way, this book never suggests that you can live *anywhere* in Mexico on a short budget!)

Recent Examples

To illustrate the rental market, here is our experience on a recent trip to San Miguel de Allende. For $500 a month (on a one-month basis), we rented a nice place–two large bedrooms and a bath upstairs, another bath downstairs, a large living room, a small dining room and a kitchen. Had we taken a lease, the rent would have been lower. Everything was furnished, including extra bed linens and tasteful wall hangings and folk statuary. The furniture was typical colonial-style: made of massive, dark wood and bright fabrics. We had a lady come in two mornings a week to clean the house, and she did the laundry, including the bedding, twice, a week. The going rate for maids is 50 pesos a day, or 25 pesos for a half day (early 1997). Renting an apartment for a month at a time is a great way to study a town and see if you want to stay permanently or not.

Of course, if you wanted to, you could look into even cheaper housing. After all, to the local people (who earn between $100 and $300 a month), rents like we were paying would be out of the question. We've heard of houses renting for $35 a month or less. But be prepared for something quite rustic. Whereas an American landlord is expected to fix things when they break or wear out, Mexican custom makes maintenance the responsibility of the renter. Therefore, when the plumbing fails or the roof leaks, you are on your own. Nothing is done by the owner, and the condition keeps deteriorating until everything collapses. Then he sells it, buys another, and starts all over.

Finding Rentals or Homes for Sale

Looking for rentals or homes to buy can be a pleasant adventure. Simply walking around town may give you some leads; a *se renta* or *se aquila* sign might be showing in a window here and there. Don't be put off by the outside appearance of a building. A rough adobe facade with cracked plaster could conceal a beautiful patio with delightful apartments clustered about a flower-perfumed garden. Colonial buildings tend to look inward, rather than show themselves to the passerby.

You can usually find a bulletin board in the local *supermercado* (supermarket), where ads for apartment and house rentals are placed, along with ads by domestic servants looking for work. If there's an English-language newspaper or newsletter, it will also contain such information. English paperback exchanges and English-language libraries usually have bulletin boards. However, most news of rentals or homes for sale is spread by word of mouth. This is particularly true of Mexican landlords; they seldom advertise in newspapers and depend on friends and neighbors to let the word out that their house is for rent. It's okay to stop fellow *norteamericanos* on the street or in a restaurant and ask them for leads. Eventually you'll find something.

We know of at least one retiree who returned from Mexico quite disgruntled because he couldn't find suitable housing the first week he was in Guadalajara. Just as in the United States or Canada, you can't expect a "dream house" to suddenly appear the moment you step off the airplane. You have to look, search and bargain to find your ideal place. Temporarily rent a hotel apartment, and you won't feel pressured to take the first thing that comes along. You'll have time to explore, compare housing, and you might even have fun making decisions! Our advice is to take your time, and don't expect miracles.

Some of the best housing bargains can be in house-sitting arrangements. Many foreigners who own or lease property in Mexico like to return to the United States for three or so months every year and want other Americans to watch their homes while they are gone. They are also happy to derive a small income to help with the upkeep of the house. Keep your eyes and ears open. You might try placing your own ad in the local English-language paper or posting your availability on a bulletin board. These homes are furnished, of course, and usually come with a maid and/or gardener. (The homeowners don't want to risk losing good help while they are gone, so they pay the wages while they are away.) To be a house-sitter, be prepared to furnish good references.

Cultural Differences

Mexican kitchens are remarkably different from your kitchen back home. In the United States or Canada, the kitchen–roomy, with colorful curtains in the windows and a large kitchen table with comfortable chairs–is an important part of the household. Back home, we spend a lot of time in our kitchens; we eat most of our meals there, at least breakfast and lunch, and when company comes to call, we naturally invite them to have a cup of coffee at our kitchen table.

But middle-class Mexican families wouldn't any more dine in the kitchen than we would take our meals in the garage. In middle-class Mexican homes, the kitchen is the domain of the maid, the cook and the gardener; the lady of the house seldom enters. Therefore, Mexican kitchens are often stark and utilitarian, with a minimum of conveniences and ugly plumbing fixtures; they look as if they belong to another house. If the kitchen has a table and chairs, they're only used by the servants to take their meals.

In some of the more luxurious homes, the kitchen is actually separated from the main part of the house by a locked door. The kitchen, along with the maid's quarters, bath and garage are the domain of the servants, who have their own keys that unlock their section of the house but not the owner's living quarters.

However, neither the authors nor most of the readers of this book are members of that tiny upper-class society in which the presence of domestic servants is taken for granted. In fact, many of us are uncomfortable with the very idea of having people around the house who are paid to do things we could do for ourselves. While we love to have a housekeeper clean our place on a regular basis, we also value our privacy and hate the idea of a person living with us 24 hours a day, continually scurrying around the house trying to look busy. Therefore, some North Americans never think about hiring servants. They enjoy yard work and think washing dishes and making beds is a normal part of living.

We initially resisted the idea of employing a maid, but then compromised by hiring a woman to come in just in the mornings.

She arrived just after breakfast, cleaned the kitchen, scrubbed the tile floors, did the laundry, and sometimes prepared the noon meal. Gradually, we became used to her, because she was so unobtrusive and careful to keep busy in some part of the house where we were *not*. Her not living with us left the maid's room available as a guest room or a place for a house-sitter while we visited Acapulco or Mexico City.

Another reason you may not wish to hire a full-time maid or gardener is the legal obligations you have toward them as employees. They have certain rights under the law: annual vacations, severance pay, notice of dismissal and things of that nature. People who do employ full-time servants recommend that you have your lawyer draw up a one-year contract. As one expatriate from Acapulco says, "You can't argue with the intent of the laws. These people have been taken advantage of for years, so maybe it's a good thing the law is slanted in their favor."

Leases and Rental Agreements

If you enter into a rental or lease agreement, you may find yourself signing an official-looking document complete with colorful government stamps. If it's a long-term lease, there will probably be an escalation clause that pegs the rent to the value of the dollar vs. peso. More than likely, if the property owner is a gringo, the rental terms will be in dollars rather than pesos. An item to insist upon is a clause on subleasing rights. Many landlords, particularly Mexicans, don't like the idea. Nevertheless, in case you decide to take a long vacation to visit friends and family in the United States, or you feel you've had enough of Mexico and need to get out from under the lease, you should protect yourself against liability. Furthermore, should you obtain a very long-term lease and you plan on putting money into the house to fix it up to your specifications, you'll need a way to recoup this money if you decide to move on. Be sure you have a complete understanding of the rental terms and insist on a receipt each month as proof that you are living up to your end of the rental agreement or lease.

An important consideration in renting or buying a house or apartment is the presence or absence of a telephone. Depending on the location, it sometimes takes an inordinate amount of time to have a telephone installed in Mexico. With a phone in place, you are assured of communications, and when you decide to sell, rent or sublease, you'll have an easier time finding clients.

A final caution about rental agreements. Should you decide to rent your Mexican home while you are back in the United States or Canada, you need to be aware of your lease agreement. As in many Latin American countries, the laws are definitely stacked on the side of the renter and against the landlord.

You must be very sure of the person to whom you rent, and you must have an iron-clad rental agreement. Once a person is living on your property and decides he or she doesn't want to leave, it can be difficult to get them out as long as they pay rent. We've heard horror stories about tenants refusing to pay rent and staying for long periods of time before they could be evicted. This rarely happens with gringo tenants; it's the shrewd Mexican who works these kinds of scams.

You could have a similar problem when you sell your property and allow someone to move in before you receive your cash. One reader reported that he believed a buyer when he said he wanted to move in and make improvements on the house so he could receive a higher mortgage. The unfortunate seller said he had already spent $8,500 in legal fees to get the swindler out of the home, and the problem still hadn't been resolved.

Market and Kitchen

Long before the Spanish arrived, the *tianguis* (open-air market) was a prominent feature of Mexican life. A few tables shaded by awnings, farmers with something to sell and towns-people with money or items to trade were all that were needed. From Mexico City to the smallest villages, that tradition is still alive today and continues to be much more than just a commercial institution.

Outdoor markets are common throughout the world. Even in the United States, where they seemed to be disappearing, they are staging a comeback in the form of farmers' markets (in big cities) and garage sales and flea markets (just about everywhere).

In few places, however, are open-air markets as prominent or as important to the life of the community as they are in Mexico, where on one or more days of the week, a whole neighborhood will be transformed into a sprawling marketplace with most of the residents drawn into its transactions.

Fun and Savings

For the North American resident or visitor, these markets are an opportunity not only to buy everything from produce to machine parts at substantial savings but also to observe closely the inner workings of Mexico. One thing that fascinates us is the juxtaposition of items as traditional as tethered chickens and trussed-up (live) pigs with other articles as contemporary as transistor radios and cassette tapes.

In addition to these informal, weekly outdoor markets, every city and town has one or more permanent *mercados*, usually under public auspices. Usually these markets are housed in great tin-roofed sheds but spill out into the surrounding streets. They, too, are operated by a collection of entrepreneurs, each offering his or her own specialty–be it fruits or vegetables, meat, or even clothing and hardware. At first you might feel intimidated by this seemingly disorderly hive of vendors vigorously hawking their wares, but remember they cluster according to the products being offered. Thus, for vegetables, you wander about the section where stand after stand of produce–tomatoes, onions, avocados and potatoes–is displayed in attractive arrangements. Wander a few steps away, and you might find yourself in a profusion of clothes, or birds in cages, or perhaps stands where cassettes and records are sold, with boom boxes blaring at top volume. If you live near the ocean, look for the area where fish is wholesaled. Fishermen bring their catch to sell to the wholesalers, who in turn sell it to the stores. By going directly to the fishermen, you not only save money, but you buy the freshest possible catch.

Many Other Shops

Not everything in the *mercado* will appeal to you, at least not until you are used to the system. Those stalls where sides of beef, dotted with flies, hang in the open can be passed by in favor of meat markets with sanitation and refrigeration. Modern meat markets can be usually be found inside the *mercados* or at least nearby.

Melons and other displayed fruits are often cut and sliced. These are best enjoyed for their aesthetics. Make sure the melon you buy is whole; when you get home, you can slice it with the assurance that it hasn't been a parade ground for flies. Any fruit that can be peeled is perfectly safe to eat on the spot. With fruits and vegetables that need washing, better wait until you can purify them in your kitchen.

Before you begin to worry that you are going to have to do all your buying from street vendors, rest assured you that the *supermercado* has arrived in Mexico. Even smaller towns have miniature versions of the United States supermarket. Although you could do all your shopping there, you would not only miss one of the delights of Mexican living, but also severely limit your choices. Like its counterpart in the United States, the *supermercado* is a convenient, usually economical place to buy packaged foods, domestic paper goods, laundry soap, beer and liquor. For fresh fruit and vegetables, meats and poultry, and baked goods, go to the *mercado*, or community market.

Fruit and Vegetables

Because most fruits and vegetables sold locally are grown in small family plots, without the aid of United States mass-production techniques and not force-fed with chemical fertilizers, they taste great. The variety of oranges (which have seeds) is amazing. Their juice is sweet and refreshing. Avocados are an adventure. There are at least a hundred different kinds, each with a slightly different flavor and texture. The bland U.S. varieties pale in comparison. Carrots are often small, but they are so sweet and tasty that you could make a meal on them alone. Asparagus, broccoli and swiss chard are so flavorful that you wonder if they're the same varieties as we get up north. Indeed, they may not be. This is not the produce that Mexican agribusiness ships to the north. Like its U.S. counterpart, it concentrates on a few varieties of produce–generally those that will survive the long journey. In the *mercado*, however, you are buying from small farmers who raise the same crops their fathers planted. The emphasis is on flavor, not convenience or uniformity.

Meat

Cattle are seldom grain-fed in Mexico, which means it takes longer–six months to a year longer–to raise them for market. This extra maturity accounts for the rich flavor of Mexican beef. Of course, range-fed beef is tough and stringy, which for some folks, counterbalances the tasty flavor. Beef can be aged in your refrigerator, and it can be cooked in ways to compensate for toughness. At better meat markets, you can purchase grain-fed beef if you prefer an extra-tender steak. Most good restaurants serve tender beef–well, tender for Mexico.

Pork is another story. Most pork sold in the markets does not come from pig farms where animals are penned so tightly they can't move and fed garbage until they pack on enough weight to go to market. In Mexico, pigs wander loose around farm houses and in small villages, almost as if they were family pets. They exercise and run free until they are ready for market. The result is a lean, red-meat pork, sometimes with the consistency of steak. The flavor can be incredible. If you cook this pork until it is well-done, it is perfectly safe.

Outside of the *mercado* you'll find many other food shops, bakeries and small markets. Those that cater to foreign residents have higher prices. Yet food prices are so low in Mexico that it is difficult to be concerned that the dozen eggs that cost the equivalent of one dollar in the *mercado* are selling for 25 cents more in the shop where the proprietor speaks English.

Food Prices

For a time, before the peso's 40 percent devaluation, food prices in Mexico were approaching those in the United States and Canada. Then prices on most food items fell to a level far below what you would pay north of the border. Thus, one of the more expensive cost-of-living categories became cheaper for those with dollar incomes. Our impression, after many hours of comparing prices during our latest visit, was that, overall, food is at least 30 percent less expensive in Mexico than in the United States.

Here are some recent (early 1997) examples:

Meat and Dairy

Whole Chicken	$0.93 per pound
Bacon	$2.28 per pound
Hamburger	$1.00 per pound
Pork Chops	$1.95 per pound
T-Bone Steak	$2.56 per pound
Eggs	$1.10 per dozen
Milk	$0.86 per 2 liters

Fruit and Vegetables

Tomatoes	$0.39 per pound
Cucumbers	$0.11 per pound
Potatoes	$0.36 per pound
Cabbage	$0.05 per pound
Broccoli	$0.17 per pound
Strawberries	$0.70 per pound
Oranges	$0.08 per pound
Bananas	$0.22 per pound

Miscellaneous

Parkay Margarine	$1.26 per 400g
Flour	$0.70 per pound
Regular Grind Coffee	$3.46 per 1-pound can

Bottled Drinks

Corona Beer	$1.27 per 6 pack
Coca-Cola	$0.78 per 2-liter bottle
Fruit Juice	$1.15 per liter
Assorted soft drinks	$0.25 per can

Liquor

Kahlua	$8.85 per 946 ml
Passport Scotch	$12.38 per 700 ml
Don Pedro Brandy	$5.50 per 940 ml
Bacardi Carta Blanca Rum	$4.41 per 946 ml
Smirnoff's Vodka	$4.81 per 915 ml

One difference between food shopping in the United States and in Mexico is the frequency with which one needs to shop. You can buy food so fresh in Mexico that it seems a shame to let it sit for several days in the refrigerator. In addition, going to the *mercado* is fun. People who normally shop once a week at the U.S. supermarkets quickly fall into the Mexican habit of shopping daily. They discover the fun of planning a menu around what looks enticing in the market, rather than what's available in the freezer or fridge. Shopping is an engaging form of social interaction and a fine way to practice Spanish. The standkeepers quickly recognize you and often, as a token of good will, put something extra in your bag after you've paid. Once, when we bought a cut-up chicken at our favorite poultry stand, the owner placed an extra neck and two gizzards into our basket. When we indicated that we really had no use for the extras, he nodded his head in understanding and replaced the neck and gizzards with three large, yellow chicken feet.

You can bargain in most markets, but it is hardly worthwhile because of the low prices. You will quickly learn to identify those who take advantage of your relative wealth by jacking up their prices. In this case, rather than waste time bargaining, simply avoid those stands and deal with friendly merchants who give you the right price and who show you they appreciate your patronage.

Outside of a few convenience foods, most items that Americans are used to are available in Mexico. Food packaging of local products, however, tends to be several years behind. Maybe this is because people prefer fresh foods to prepackaged mixes or frozen TV-dinners. Bacon, for instance, is usually sliced to order rather than prepackaged in transparent material. Sometimes, seemingly arbitrary little shortages can be annoying if you allow them to be. Once, for several weeks, we searched for oatmeal that was not pre-sweetened, although it had been available a month earlier and was available again later. Some things are sold in different base quantities. For example, eggs can be bought by the dozen, but are cheaper by the kilo. Oranges, though available by the kilo, are cheaper when bought by number. Go figure.

When you shop every day, getting your purchases home is not a serious problem, even if you don't have a car. All over Mexico, Americans and Mexicans can be seen carrying groceries in locally produced straw bags. In some parts of the country, the bags have straps that go over your shoulders, in others, straps that you hold in your hand. (If you get tired of walking, taxis are affordable.)

Wherever you are, the straw bag filled with groceries proclaims that you are not a tourist, but someone really living in Mexico. Lately, however, plastic shopping bags have been pushing aside the straw woven ones. Although they're cheaper and can be thrown away without regret, they will never be quite the same as the straw bags.

Mexican Cooking

Once you get those delicious meats, fruits and vegetables home, what you make them into will be up to you. There are Americans in Mexico whose menus seldom stray from those of their former neighbors still living in Dubuque or Toronto. (We think they're missing something.) On the other hand, if you want to experiment with the varied cuisines of Mexico, your kitchen is an excellent place to do so. You are in control and can adapt seasoning to suit your taste.

Diana Kennedy's *The Cuisines of Mexico* is the standard English language cookbook for Americans who want to share what Mexico's many peoples have to offer. You can use this book as a source of recipes, as a guide to ordering in restaurants where menus aren't in English, or as a source of answers to your maid's questions about what you'd like for dinner. Don't expect your maid to be able to prepare all the dishes in the book; however, if you speak Spanish well enough, or are skillful at teaching by example, you may have your maid cooking Mexican food of which the neighbors have never heard.

A pleasant, though not essential, part of your preparation for retirement in Mexico might be studying Mexican cookbooks and trying some dishes. Even if the ingredients are not all readily available, you will find some recipes you can make with what is at hand.

As we've asserted several times in this book, Mexican cuisine is rich and varied and by no means limited to chiles, beans and tortillas. Nevertheless, were it not for the creative use of maize (corn) tortillas, beans, chiles, and cheese, there would be many more people suffering from hunger and malnutrition in Mexico. These inexpensive ingredients formed the foundation of the pre-Cortes diet and are staples of Mexican cooking today. Meat, poultry and fish are used sparingly, almost as a seasoning is. The result is comparable to much Asian cooking: delicious, inexpensive food that is actually more healthful than the standard American diet, which emphasizes red meat.

Years ago, nutritionists wondered why Mexicans seem to thrive on a combination of foods that violate many of the basic nutritional values held by most Americans. They discovered that the nutrients, particularly the proteins, in the daily Mexican fare fit together in an almost perfect balance. The U.S. scientific community now believes that fats, not carbohydrates, are the cause of America's endemic obesity and the resulting heart and circulatory problems. Also, the Mexican custom is to eat the principal meal, *la comida*, in the middle of the day. Traditionally, this is a leisurely meal that is eaten during the long siesta hours and that might include a nap afterwards. Mexicans tend to limit *la cena*, or evening meal, to a light snack. Elaborate evening meals, if eaten at all, are eaten very late. In Mexico City, for example, many restaurants don't even open their doors until nine o'clock, and are still serving meals at midnight. Enjoying the main meal during the siesta is ideal for the retiree. The maid will be there to prepare it, and you can make your own supper from the leftovers or enjoy *la cena* in a restaurant with your friends. In addition, it is healthier and more comfortable, particularly as you grow older, to avoid heavy meals late in the day.

Most Americans of moderate means have had no experience with servants, or perhaps they have had a cleaning woman come in once or twice a week. During the past 40 years, even in homes affluent enough to afford hired help, the trend has been to substitute "labor-saving" devices for human assistance. The middle-class homemaker spends more time in the kitchen and laundry or behind a vacuum cleaner than his or her counterpart of a generation ago. Not only has help become expensive, but in the United States it is a rare employer or employee who is fully comfortable with the employer-servant relationship.

When Americans hear that domestic help is readily affordable in Mexico, they often wonder whether they would like to hire someone to cook, clean and do laundry. They visualize someone who is a servant because he or she is unable to find other employment, someone who deeply resents his or her situation and feels demeaned by having to take orders and work in someone else's home.

In Mexico, as we've said, domestic service is considered an entirely acceptable occupation. Despite low wages, there are enough benefits to make domestic service desirable and satisfying for many. Some benefits are tangible, like the guarantee of one or more nutritious meals each day and the higher wages usually paid by foreign residents. Americans often treat their help better than local employers and are more egalitarian and generous in ways that sometimes aren't apparent. Other benefits include the status a domestic servant gains from close connection with relatively affluent foreigners. In short, domestic service is not considered a last resort as it often is up north. When American residents speak of the loyalty and good nature of their servants, they are neither being naive nor condescending. Servants can truly help increase your involvement with the country, as well as making life easier and more comfortable.

Often a person will work for more than one employer and will be happy to work for you two or three hours a day, doing the breakfast dishes, scrubbing the tile floors, as well as doing laundry. For these chores, the maid will need no English and you, no Spanish. The workers' energy and efficiency will amaze you. They evidently feel that since they are being paid by the hour, they must fill up each hour and thus will look for things to do. With one maid, we had to be careful not to lay clean clothes on the bed so we could wear them after showering, for when we were ready to put them on, they would be hanging on the line, already washed. Anything that wasn't hanging up or in a dresser was fair game for the wash tub. If you wish your employees to do anything complicated, they must be taught procedures that will be strange to them unless they have had experience working for Americans. If you want a roast chicken for lunch, you must make clear how long you want it cooked, what kinds of seasoning you want and what, if anything, to put inside. Even something as simple as making picnic sandwiches can be a mystery to someone for whom bread is a luxury, seldom if ever used in her house. If, on the other hand, you want to try *chile con queso* or *chiles rellenos* the maid will need no instruction. Unless you're willing to take time teaching and explaining, you're better off doing the complicated American cooking yourself and letting the maid help you with shopping and cleaning up the kitchen afterward.

Gardeners

The gardener, sometimes called a *mozo*, is usually more than simply a gardener. He not only cares for the flowers, but also is a repairman, a bartender and a watchman. He helps the maid, runs errands, and negotiates with local business people for you. If you're going away to Acapulco for a week, often the gardener will stay in your house to watch things. Many gardeners have several clients, so it's easy to find someone who only wants to come in for an hour or two a day to water plants and make sure everything is working properly. Above all, do treat your servants with respect, and don't talk down to them. Being a domestic servant in Mexico isn't a low-status job, and you want your employees to be proud of working for you.

Do You Need to Know Spanish?

If you're going to fully enjoy Mexico, of course, you will need to learn to speak Spanish. However, you won't starve if you don't know Spanish, and you won't lack for social connections just because you are too lazy to learn more than a few phrases of the language. You'll survive. Many North Americans have lived in Mexico for years and learned just enough Spanish to ask where the bathroom is or order another round of drinks. Occasionally, they enter the wrong bathroom, that's true, but rarely does a waiter misunderstand an order for more drinks. If you plan on hanging around with Americans for your entire stay in Mexico, or if you insist on living in expensive hotels and condos, then it really doesn't matter whether you learn Spanish or not.

But, once you learn to communicate in Spanish, you suddenly find new doors open to you. Mexico becomes a totally different place. Instead of being limited to a small circle of English-speaking friends, you can venture out into the exciting world of Mexico. You can participate in everything that is going on around you instead of being puzzled and mystified by it. You will find yourself being invited to visit homes and join in festivities that before were inaccessible. You will have fun dealing with merchants, servants and neighbors, entering into much closer relationships with them. You will no longer fear hassling with bureaucrats or arguing with policemen and taxi drivers. When traveling like a resident in posh resort towns, you will be in a much better position to locate those $20 hotel rooms. In short, when you learn Spanish, you truly become a resident of Mexico who is ready to enjoy the country to the fullest.

But isn't it difficult to learn a foreign language? Yes, it is; language learning is not easy. You often hear someone say: "Oh, I won't bother studying the language now. I'll pick it up when I get there." Unless you are under ten years old, the chances that simply by being around Spanish speakers you will be able to "pick up" the language are less than zero.

The only way adults learn a foreign language is the old fashioned way: through study, practice, and more practice. Studying Spanish can not only be enjoyable, it can be a rewarding activity, part of getting settled in your new home.

Even if you already speak some Spanish, we highly recommend that one of the first things you do upon arriving in Mexico is to enroll in a language class. Besides polishing your command of the language, you'll find classrooms excellent places to meet people and enlarge your circle of friends. Your fellow students will form their own social groups, which hold parties and get-togethers–any excuse they can find to practice Spanish. Spanish classrooms are among the very best places to meet fellow retirees in the community and to start making friends.

Living with Mexican Laws

Your Legal Status

We are often asked, "Do I have to give up my citizenship if I retire permanently in Mexico?" Of course not. Very few North Americans would consider Mexican retirement if this were the case. Fortunately, there are a number of ways to become a legal resident of Mexico, and none of them affects your citizenship in any way. The options open to you range all the way from using the tourist cards (readily available to anyone wishing to visit Mexico) to *Inmigrado* status, which gives you all the rights of a Mexican citizen–except the right to vote.

The following is a brief description of the documents and statuses available to those who want to visit or live in Mexico.

The rules have been undergoing changes since the original publication of this book, and even more changes are possible. For example, it used to be that the income requirement for long-term residency was very low–with a minimum of $550 a month for a couple. That figure climbed at one time to as much as $2,200 monthly. Now, pegged to a multiple of the minimum wage, it is about half of that.

We list below the four kinds of residence permit and a brief summary of the advantages and disadvantages of each.

Tourist Visa (FM-T)
Advantages: No income requirement. No need for legal help to obtain. No cost to obtain.
Disadvantages: Must be renewed every six months by making a trip to the border. Does not allow you to legally bring in household goods, appliances, etc.

***Visitante Rentista* (FM-3) Available to those over 55.**
Advantages: Applications processed rapidly and routinely. Cheapest (when you figure in cost of trips to the border to renew tourist cards) and easiest way to reside in Mexico, according to the government. May bring in household goods tax-free within three months of securing status.
Disadvantages: Income requirement currently about $700 a month for the head of a family plus $350 per dependent. (These requirements are tied to the minimum wage. They fluctuate

both with changes in the exchange rate and in the minimum wage, and are likely to go up. They are halved for those who own homes in Mexico.) Must be renewed yearly with current proof of income.

Inmigrante Rentista (FM-2)

Advantages: Leads, after renewal for five years, to *Inmigrado* status.

Disadvantages: Need to show much higher monthly income. Longer, more difficult process to obtain.

Inmigrado

Advantages: Possessor has all the rights of a Mexican citizen, except the right to vote. Can work or operate a business.

Disadvantages: Granted only after five years as *Inmigrante Rentista*. Same income requirement as for FM-3.

The process of obtaining the longer-term residential statuses is, like any dealings with the Mexican bureaucracy, complicated and exasperating. If you are blessed with the patience of a saint, you can probably do it all yourself. If not, it may be worth the additional expense to retain a Mexican lawyer. Whereas this status is not difficult to obtain, if you are going to Mexico for relaxation, you may not want to spend your time in lines in government offices. Besides, in Mexico, even lawyer's fees are moderate.

Which status is right for you? You will probably have gone through one or more 180-day tourist cards before making any binding decisions, so you will undoubtedly have received the advice of many long-time residents (and will have heard more arguments than we could possibly make for or against each possibility). Above all, we emphasize once again that the current, unrealistically high income requirement for the permanent resident statuses need not be an insurmountable barrier to happy, affordable retirement in Mexico. This requirement, like all the regulations we have listed above, is subject to change.

Differences between U. S. and Mexican Laws

Many Americans are concerned about the differences between the legal systems of Mexico and the United States. Some dread the possibility that they might, because of some misunderstanding, end up in a dreary Mexican jail. This fear evaporates in the Mexican sun, however. We have found no American resident there who expressed concern about the law. Of course, if your retirement plans include dealing illegal drugs, this reassurance does not apply. On the other hand, we've encountered a few gringos who, for one reason or other, spent some time in a Mexican jail. From their experiences, we can safely say that you don't want to do time there! Mexican law, like most European systems, is one of codified statutes. This is often referred to as Roman Law or the Napoleonic Code. North American law, on the other hand, is based on English common law, in which each case may be considered unique and each decision may be based on prior decisions in other courts. Under Mexican law, almost every possible violation or transgression is thoroughly codified or listed in law books, and extenuating circumstances play little role. Instead of long jury trials to determine punishment or damages, the magistrate simply looks up the law code that applies–and that's it. Awards in damage suits are usually limited to the actual proven losses.

Sentences for criminal acts are longer, and parole is not as easily available as in the United States. On the second conviction (even for relatively minor offenses), a criminal is judged to be a "habitual" criminal, and upon a third conviction, is sentenced to 20 years away from society. That doesn't mean nine months in the slammer and then parole. It means 20 years. Perhaps as a result, serious crime– particularly in smaller towns and cities–is much less frequent than in most places in the United States.

Bringing Your Car into Mexico

In January, 1992, Mexican border officials started enforcing some new regulations designed to prevent tax dodging by Mexican nationals who were illegally importing American cars. These rules apply to anyone who drives more than 25 kilometers into the Mexican mainland (but not to any of Baja California or other *zona libre* area).

The most recent rules now require that you must present at the border:

1. The original certificate of title, in the name of the driver. No borrowed vehicles are permitted to enter.

2. If you don't own the car outright, an affidavit from the lienholder authorizing the temporary importation of the car.

3. A valid state registration.

4. Proof of nationality with picture identification (driver's license or passport will do).

5. A Mexican Tourist Card, which you can get at the border when applying for an importation permit.

6. A valid driver's license issued outside of Mexico, bearing the same name as the title.

7. MasterCard, VISA, Diners Club or American Express, in the car owner's name. The credit card will be used to pay a $12 vehicle permit and to post a bond based on the vehicle's value. If you don't have a credit card, you'll be required to post a cash bond. The car permit is good for multiple crossings during its six-month life.

When you apply for the car permit, you'll be required to sign a promise that, when you leave Mexico, you'll take the car with you. You are not permitted to sell the car while you're in Mexico. If the car is stolen or completely wrecked, then you'll be required to obtain from the Mexican government additional documentation and verification to that effect.

You should also carry a copy of a U.S. or Canadian insurance policy, effective for at least two months from the date of entry, and Mexican automobile insurance.

Don't think you can just hand out a few dollars and cross into Mexico without all of the foregoing documents. The Mexican government is serious about enforcing these laws.

Of utmost importance is a Mexican insurance policy. Technically, Mexican insurance isn't required, but if you don't have it, you are taking terrible chances. Your U.S. or Canadian policy won't help you, because Mexico does not recognize any insurance unless issued by a legitimate Mexican company.

The reason we stress adequate car insurance is that, in the event of an accident, Mexican law requires that your vehicle be held until damages are paid or until you guarantee proper payment via an insurance policy. If bodily injury is involved, police can detain you until the problem is resolved. Since courts usually grant compensation for the actual damages to the car and, in case of an injury, for a stipulated amount of damages for time off from work, an insured driver never has to worry about lawsuits. But if you don't have insurance, you could have a lot to worry about.

Mexican cops are not empowered to assign fault for the accident, so whether or not it was your fault, you'd better have the appropriate proof of insurance with you; always keep the policy with you when you drive. The good news is that Mexican insurance companies are very good about helping you and making sure your auto is fixed. We've heard of them finding hotel accommodations for clients whose autos are being repaired. So, drive as carefully as you do in the United States and stop worrying.

Mexican Labor Laws

In many aspects, Mexican labor laws are similar to those in the United States as they apply to the maximum work day and week and the employment of minors. There are, however, some special rules regarding vacations, bonuses and termination of employment that have particular relevance to those of you who plan on hiring a maid or a gardener to work around your home.

Workers with more than one year's service are entitled to an annual vacation of at least six workdays. This increases at the rate of two workdays a year for the next three years (to a total of 12 days vacation a year). In subsequent years, two workdays vacation are added for each five years of employment. Thus, if someone worked for you for 19 years, he or she would be entitled to a vacation of 18 workdays, or three six-day weeks.

After one year of employment, workers are also entitled to an annual bonus equal to 15 days wages (paid before December 20). Those who have not been employed for a full year get a bonus prorated for the time they have worked. This is not a gift, you understand, it's required by law.

To avoid having a terminated employee bring a case to the State Labor Board, an employer should insist that the employee sign a form in front of witnesses and then file it with the authorities. There are a number of grounds for which an employee can be dismissed for cause (including more than three unauthorized absences from work within a 28-day period). The rules, and their enforcement, vary from one locality to another. So check with your neighbors as to the guidelines in effect for hiring help. In general, the labor laws do a good job of protecting workers without unduly burdening employers.

Police in Mexico

Police officers in the United States and Canada are generally thought of as highly trained and professional. Taking bribes is considered sleazy in the extreme; we are horrified when a cop is "on the take." Although not exactly highly-paid, most United States police officers earn $30,000 to $50,000 a year, sometimes more with overtime and bonuses. American taxpayers consider this a good investment; they feel they get what they pay for.

But Mexico is reluctant to pay public employees decent wages, sometimes even living wages. Therefore, many government employees, including police, feel they should be compensated by the public for any services they perform. North Americans have difficulty accepting this practice; they harshly refer to it as bribery and corruption. However, Mexicans choose a softer term, *la mordida* (the bite), and take a more tolerant attitude. They consider these payments tips, just as one might tip a waiter for his services.

In contrast with the adequately paid and professional U. S. cop, police in Mexico come from the lower socio-economic classes, have little or no training and are pitifully underpaid. Many Mexican police earn the minimum wage. From this meager amount, they must pay a *mordida* to their superiors for the "privilege" of holding this low-paying job.

Now, nobody could possibly expect a policeman to feed and clothe a family on minimum wage, not even in Mexico. Therefore, he is expected to supplement his salary by "collecting fines" or taking *mordidas*. Officially, this is frowned on, but the officials who frown disapprovingly over the practice fully expect the collection of *mordidas* to continue, and they encourage it when refusing to pay a living wage. Furthermore, some officials hold their hands out for their share of the *mordidas* collected by the cops. Again, a policeman feels that he's doing nothing wrong by collecting the fine from you. He considers it a favor to you by not issuing a traffic ticket and making you go to police headquarters to stand in line to pay your fine (while, outside, another cop is removing your license plates because you've parked in a no-parking zone).

If you ask Mexican taxpayers why they don't pay police a living wage, you'll hear: "What? Spend my taxes to pay a cop to chase speeders? Let the foolish speeder pay the cop's wages, not me. If and when I get caught speeding, I'll pay. Not before!"

This author, who over the years has driven nearly 100,000 miles in Mexico, affirms that he has never been stopped for an offense for which he was not guilty. He's paid more than his share of *mordidas,* but then he admits to doing more than his share of speeding and selecting bizarre parking places. The other author says that, perhaps because he has not driven nearly so much or perhaps because he speeds less, he has never been stopped, never paid a *mordida* and does not personally know anyone who has been hassled unfairly for a traffic offense.

North Americans universally detest the idea of bribing cops, but detest it or not, that's the system, and there's not a thing we can do as individuals to change this system. Raising hell with the cop or accusing him of being a crook will do nothing but aggravate the situation–seriously aggravate it. The policeman feels he is just doing his job, and doesn't appreciate being yelled at or called names.

What to do if you're stopped? Remain cool, determine what the problem is and then decide whether to pay or not to pay a *mordida.* If you feel you are innocent, insist on a ticket. This will mean a trip to the police station to pay a moderate fine, but it will deprive the cop of his earnings for that incident and helps discourage harassment of other foreigners. (As a matter of common practice, a cop won't bother stopping you unless he thinks he can convince you that you've done something wrong– and that he can earn his *mordida.*) If the cop refuses to give a ticket and still wants money, insist on a receipt (a *recibo)* for your fine. Also, do bargain. Offer half of what he asks–but only if you are guilty.

This is not to say that all Mexican cops lack professionalism and pride or that they cannot be honest, competent and conscientious. (Again, they don't consider taking *mordidas* to be dishonest.) They can be very tough on real criminals. As a matter of government policy, when it comes to minor indiscretions, police are far more tolerant with foreigners than with Mexican citizens. We've seen North Americans get away with offenses (such as public drunkenness) that would land an ordinary citizen in jail for three days. Treating tourists or foreign residents roughly or unfairly is a serious matter, which can cause repercussions throughout a department. Should you have an unpleasant experience, you are morally obligated to report it by calling the Ministry of Tourism's 24-hour hotline (in Mexico City) at 5-250-0123.

In Mexico City, you'll encounter "tourist police" who speak English and whose job is to see that the tourists are assisted. They have a tendency for overkill, however, and will attack you with friendliness, practically insisting that you visit the places they think you should. They'll flag down a cab, push you inside and send you off to the tourist market before you know what's happening. (While this may seem very friendly, you must realize that the cab driver is probably the cop's brother-in-law, and they split the commission for delivering you to the tourist market.)

Not every Mexican cop will be patient with every faceless tourist, and if, like a few Americans, you think you can get away with treating policemen like flunkies, you may be in for some unpleasant moments. They have as much pride as any Mexican and will usually treat you with the respect you show them.

Mexicans Are Serious about Their Laws

Many laws in Mexico seem to be honored in their violation, which sometimes gives an American the wrong impression. For example, the largest piles of trash and garbage are invariably found stacked around signs that proclaim, "Do not throw garbage here!" Speed limit signs have no relation to the speed of the traffic. Stop signs seem to be invisible to most drivers, and stern prohibitions are simply a challenge. The foreigner residing in Mexico, however, would be wise to consider himself or herself a guest. Obeying laws should be no more an imposition than it would be in the United States. If you park in a no-parking zone, you might find your license plates impounded. To get them back, you must first go to a bank where you get a receipt for the fine you must pay, and then to the central office where confiscated plates are held.

Some legal matters are taken more seriously in Mexico than back home, especially business relationships. If you break a lease, for example, you may discover that the landlord has impounded your belongings and the judge agrees with him. The law might come down very heavily on you if you cheat someone out of money or refuse to pay a legitimate bill. As we've noted above, there are special rules for hiring employees, such as your maid or a gardener. Trying to get away with something on a real-estate deal can be expensive, as many an American who tried to circumvent the laws against buying *ejido* property (reserved in perpetuity for indiginous residents) and lost all his investment can attest.

A North American who normally obeys the laws in his own country can expect no more trouble in Mexico than he would at home–probably less, since he usually behaves as a guest in a foreign country. But those who think that the law applies only to others, those with contempt for the customs of their host country or those who feel that the law shouldn't apply to Americans as it does to Mexicans, are likely to be quickly disabused of these attitudes.

Staying Healthy

Far too much of the discussion of whether Mexico is good for your health boils down to the question, "Can you drink the water?" The short answer to that question is, "Yes, but not water from the tap." We'll cover that in detail a little further on, and we hope that we can persuade you that it is a relatively trivial concern. Far more important is the fact that the vigor and happiness of the typical U.S. retiree in Mexico points to the ways in which the country is indeed a very healthy place for older people.

There are both physical and emotional reasons for their well-being. The climate in most places where retirees have chosen to live is healthier in several ways than in the communities they have come from. For one thing, it is dryer. For generations, the attractions of a low-humidity climate have been bringing people who suffer from respiratory and rheumatic diseases to the American Southwest. With the exception of its coastal areas, Mexico is blessed with a climate that is at least as dry. In addition, Mexico possesses something the United States' southwestern states do not. It has (again, in the communities favored by retirees) temperatures that are moderate year-round.

Too many people avoid Mexico because they fear for their health. They have heard that no one escapes *turista* or "Montezuma's Revenge" and imagine a stay made miserable, if not dangerous, by gastrointestinal woes. Some Mexican water supplies are indeed contaminated, but clean, safe water is available everywhere. Furthermore, the contaminated water can be purified easily, as can vegetables and fruits that have come into contact with that water. As we've noted, every prudent Mexican and foreigner recognizes the importance of guarding against the hazards of impure water and untreated raw fruit and vegetables. The necessary steps are incorporated into his or her life, so that these precautions become as natural as washing one's hands before meals. (This practice is a very good idea in Mexico as elsewhere. Recent studies report that one's hands are likely to be the source of the bacteria that gets into one's mouth.)

Water is safe after being boiled for a few minutes. Treating it with chlorine tablets or a reliable filtration device also takes care of bacteria or amoebic problems. If you have a maid, she will make sure you always have an ample supply of purified water both in the kitchen and in the bathroom so that you will not be tempted to brush your teeth or swallow a pill with tap water. Fruit and vegetables fresh from the market are stored separately from those that have been made safe by a brief soaking in purified water to which some chlorine tablets have been added (available inexpensively at any drug store).

Ice must be made with purified water and, like fruit and vegetables, should be consumed only in places where you can be confident that the necessary precautions have been taken. The law in Mexico is that ice cubes must be made from purified water. That requirement, however, does not extend to bulk ice. Almost always, restaurants and stores will use purified water for ice cubes, since it is so inexpensive there is no reason not to. If a restaurant doesn't follow the law, cheating by using tainted water, its customers will soon know about it and will no longer patronize the place. Bad restaurants don't remain in business long. In the beginning, you'll have to rely on the knowledge of the local Americans about which restaurants to avoid. In time you'll develop your own sound instincts.

Some travelers, worried about gastrointestinal illness, dose themselves with antibiotics which are readily available in Mexican pharmacies. However, this is a dangerous practice; these medications have dangerous side effects. Recently, the fad has been to take hefty dosages of Pepto Bismol as a preventative. Carl Franz (in *The People's Guide to Mexico*) swears by the efficacy of Pepto Bismol and confirms that it works. This is fine for travelers, but if you are going to be living in Mexico, you don't want to spend the rest of your days pouring that pink stuff into your stomach! Once you've settled into your new life, you'll find these kinds of self-medication unnecessary.

Good health, however, is more than avoiding unfriendly bugs. It involves your total physical and mental well-being and your whole outlook. If Mexico is the right place for you, you can be healthier there than you could be anywhere else. Almost everything that can make you happy–the climate, the good food, the constant activity–will also make you healthy. These elements, in addition to the common-sense principles of sanitation discussed above, are the essential prescriptions for good health. If you have a chronic illness, your doctor will have some additional rules and perhaps some medications for you, but you should find them no more onerous in Mexico than in your home town.

Health Care

Americans living in most parts of Mexico report the availability of competent English-speaking doctors and dentists. The questionnaires we mailed to retired Americans devoted special attention to the quality of medical and dental care, access to hospitals, and the availability of medications. We emphasized these areas because books written a couple of decades ago treated health care, at least outside of the biggest cities, as a problem. We are gratified to report however, that today (according to responses received from retirees in every part of Mexico) there are good doctors and dentists in most cities of any size. Quality hospitals are within easy traveling distance, and most of the commonly prescribed medications are stocked by Mexican pharmacies.

A few of our respondents stated that they might go to Mexico City or to the United States for an unusual or extremely serious illness, but most indicated that they thought that in the nearest big city, they could find sophisticated facilities and personnel. Since we know of people who, if they became ill in Miami or Los Angeles, would go to hospitals and doctors in New York, we are inclined to conclude that the needs catered to by air evacuation services are more emotional than medical.

Doctors

Many doctors in the United States are Mexican trained. As the number of qualified students seeking entrance to U.S. medical schools exceeded their capacity, many young Americans went abroad for their medical educations. Mexico was one of the countries in which they found training facilities of top quality. In short, there is no more reason to be concerned about the qualification of a reputable Mexican doctor than there is to be about an American one. Two nice things about Mexican doctors: they still make house calls and office visits are usually not much more than $20. Specialists, of course, are more expensive.

Although not every town is blessed with a first-rate hospital, few are far from one. Few drugs require prescriptions in Mexico, and those that do can be filled at any pharmacy. If, however, you need some special or unusual medication, it would be wise to bring a supply with you on your initial visit to Mexico and, if you find it is unavailable there, to confer with your physician when you return to the United States. He can tell you what may be substituted. If there is no substitute available in Mexico, receiving a regular supply from the United States, though a nuisance, should pose no problem. Incidentally, in Mexico, many prescription and over-the-counter drugs cost less than 40 percent of their United States price.

Dentists

Because in Mexico, quality dentistry is available at exceptionally low prices, many Europeans as well as North Americans travel here to have work done. Often, patients save enough to pay for most of their vacation expenses. For those who live in Mexico, the low cost of dentistry is part of the low cost of living. Prices will vary between locations and the type of practice a dentist maintains. That is, one who specializes in wealthy, Mexico City patients will, of course, be more expensive than a dentist in a small village. Very likely, the quality of care will vary as well; ask for recommendations from friends and neighbors before choosing a dentist. Below is a chart of typical fees charged by English-speaking Mexican dentists. (Prices are in U.S. dollars.)

Cleaning	$ 25
Root Canal	$ 65
Filling, amalgam	$ 20
Filling, porcelain	$ 45
Filling, gold	$ 65
Cap, porcelain	$ 70
Cap, gold-porcelain	$110
Gold Crown	$ 75
Dentures, porcelain	$675

Medicare

As we've said, routine and emergency medical care of high quality is available many places in Mexico. Nevertheless, those retirees who are eligible for Medicare (which does not pay for care or treatment received in Mexico) or who have a trusted physician in the United States will wish to return there if they become seriously ill. If they're not well enough to travel by routine means, there is a commercial "air evacuation" service that provides emergency air transport to destinations north of the border. For a monthly fee, one can arrange to have this service available when needed. Air transport of casualties, which was first employed in Korea and came into its own in Vietnam, has been adopted in civilian medicine and without question has saved many lives. How appropriate this air service is (except to enjoy the financial benefits of Medicare) may be a moot point. If nothing else, it gives Americans in Mexico the emotional security of knowing that in the event of serious illness, within a few hours they can be under the care of American doctors in an American hospital.

On the other hand, we've interviewed retirees living in Mexico who are convinced that medical care there is as good as back home. One man claimed that hospitals here don't have a "factory" mentality, where doctors worry more about about malpractice lawyers than they do about patients. Also, physicians here are willing to prescribe medication for pain, which the doctors in the United States will only do "if you are screaming and threatening bodily harm." To this, add the practice of doctors making house calls instead of requiring you to travel back to the hospital for post-operation followups.

Of course, you must recognize that not everywhere in Mexico will offer top-quality care; some clinics–especially rural ones–are quite rustic, at best. You'll need to check out facilities and make your own decisions.

Health Insurance

Of course, many Americans retiring in Mexico are too young to qualify for Medicare and have to rely on other health insurance to pay major medical expenses. Some U.S. insurance companies cover you wherever you travel or live. Certain carriers pay a slightly smaller percentage of the total when you are out of your home area, but since health care in Mexico is so inexpensive relative to U.S. costs, that won't be a problem. Most Blue Cross plans will pay for your hospital stays while in Mexico, but usually require that you lay out the money and wait for reimbursement. We advise that you check with your insurance broker to determine the extent of your coverage while in Mexico and to discuss any adjustments necessary to maximize your protection at minimum expense. In Guadalajara, the American Society offers low-cost health insurance to its members.

Another option available to North Americans in Mexico is very low-cost medical coverage by the national health system. Twice a year there are open enrollment periods when you can join. The cost, in 1997, was less than $200 a year–for full coverage! This plan covers medical, hospital, prescription drugs, even dental care and eye examinations. We believe this is something to investigate after you have been here awhile and have had the opportunity to check out the quality of the hospitals and physicians in the community in which you decide to live. Our understanding is that there is no age limit; we know of a lady who joined the plan when she turned 86 years old.

Several folks we interviewed stated that, although they had insurance coverage back home, they rarely used it. One man said, "I have a major medical plan that covers everything over $15,000. But when I went to the local hospital here for emergency treatment, the bill came to less than $2,500! This covered several doctors for separate opinions, surgeons, anesthesiologist, hospital stay, laboratory work, X-rays, electrocardiograms, sonograms, prescription drugs and follow-up care for three months following surgery." He added, "A friend of mine paid more than $2,500 for just one night in a Las Vegas hospital!"

People with Disabilities

Many of our readers have inquired about the provisions Mexico makes for people with disabilities. From what we have observed and been told by people who face the problem, Mexico is still far behind the United States in dealing with air pollution, accessibility and the myriad other issues that we also neglected until fairly recently. On the positive side, the gentle climate does make getting around somewhat easier, and the low pay scale enables people who need help to afford it more readily. Also, on recent visits we noted more curb cuts, particularly in the larger cities.

Most airports and many railroad stations and bus terminals have wheelchair access. Sources of detailed information:

1. Mexican National Railways Estación Central de Buenavista 06358, Mexico, D.F. Mexico

2. Greyhound Lines, Director of Customer Relations, Greyhound Tower, 111 West Clarendon, Phoenix, AZ 85013

Each airline, domestic or foreign, can give you information on the arrangements it can make for wheelchairs or other assistance.

Climate and Health

Mexico's varied climates offer a choice of temperatures and humidities, but almost all–particularly those where North Americans have established their homes–have earned the label "eternal spring" because of the lack of extremes.

With one's energies freed from combating the winter winds and the humid summer swelter, flourishing health immediately feels attainable. Life in Mexico is outdoors year-round. Most houses have little or no provision for heating or air conditioning. If the weather becomes brisk, you simply put on a sweater. When warm, you stay indoors for a siesta during the hot part of the day. One doesn't breathe air stale with artificial heat or chill but rather air crisped by mountain altitudes, softened by warm oceans and dried to crystalline clarity by empty deserts.

Diet and Stress

For the tourist traveling in Mexico and eating in restaurants, adhering to a special diet–perhaps one low in sodium, sugar or fats–could be difficult, though clearly not impossible. For someone who lives there and prepares his own food (or has it prepared by a servant) there is no special problem. One of the delights of living in Mexico is the abundance of fresh fruits, vegetables and poultry. In many places fresh fish is always available. Most diet convenience foods are now available in

Mexico, and with reasonable inventiveness, almost any dietary prescription can be followed.

Mexican cuisine is discussed in greater detail elsewhere in this book. But we add a brief reassurance here for those potential retirees who may feel intimidated by the food's notorious spiciness: you could live in Mexico for years without ever being forced to eat anything the least bit *picante*, even if all your dining were in restaurants. Any town is likely to have several restaurants where the food is "continental" rather than Mexican, and not all dishes in thoroughly Mexican restaurants are highly spiced. In the more elegant restaurants, the dishes are not spicy at all, but with an emphasis on French sauces, they are not guaranteed to be low calorie.

Volumes have been written about the role of stress in causing illness. Stress has been implicated as an aggravating factor in chronic conditions that are common in people past middle age. Visitors to Mexico, almost without exception, comment on the lack of stress and the relaxed atmosphere there. Perhaps it is the absence of many negative and unnecessary forms of stress that makes so many Americans consider Mexico a healthful place to live.

Mexico offers freedom from the nagging annoyances of unpleasant weather, unpleasant people, economic insecurity, relentless status seeking and the nagging, confining fear of crime. Relaxing doesn't mean doing nothing; it means taking part in exercise and outdoor activities that are fun, not chores.

Lethargy comes from inactivity, from boredom and fatigue. Perhaps because of the stimulation of the unfamiliar or because of the vibrancy of Mexican culture–its sights, sounds and smells–one encounters few bored and unhappy retirees there. Visitors to Mexico, almost without exception, comment on the relaxed and healthful atmosphere. It can be healthful for you, too, if you learn to live in it.

Getting Around Mexico

One big advantage to living in Mexico is the opportunity for travel. You have the entire country to choose from, with many interesting locations just a few miles from anywhere you decide to live. At your leisure, you can afford to visit little-known or out-of-the-way places that ordinary tourists seldom see. You can lope on down to Acapulco for a weekend as casually as you might visit the local lake or seashore back home. All of those exotic beach towns you've read about are just a bus ride away: dream places like Mazatlán, Puerto Vallarta, Cancun, plus dozens of hidden beaches and fascinating villages no one outside of Mexico has ever heard of. You'll probably discover your own personal hideaway.

Mountain gems such as Zacatecas, San Cristóbal de las Casas or Taxco beckon to you, while, for a welcome change of pace, the cosmopolitan atmosphere of Mexico City invites shopping and elegant dining. Fortunately, travel in Mexico costs far less than it does in the United States. Most people find they can take regular excursions and still stay within the boundaries of their basic $600 a month budget. With abundant hotel rooms under $30 a night, how can you miss?

Because Mexican culture–cuisine, handicrafts, music and architecture–is, like the climate and scenery, intensely regional, travel within the country offers the stimulation that people living in the United States and Canada have to go abroad to find. Another advantage of traveling *and* living in Mexico is that when, in your travels, you come across the unusual piece of pottery or furniture you just can't resist, getting it home is easy–there are no shipping and customs problems caused by crossing an international border. Many North American retirees' homes in Mexico look like miniature museums, because their owners are so carried away are by the beauty, variety and inexpensiveness of the handicrafts they encounter on their trips around the country.

Bus Travel

The mainstay of the Mexican travel system is the nation's vast network of buses. Bus travel in the United States, where one company has a virtual monopoly of interstate service, is neither particularly inexpensive nor enjoyable. In Mexico it's a different story. Many companies, each one eager to take you anywhere you can possibly wish to go, compete for your business. You get the feeling that your business is important to them. The government is building new terminals–central depots where all bus lines meet–as quickly as possible in each town. There's little waiting time because buses for most destinations depart every few minutes. Yet, the cost of a ticket is a fraction of the price charged by intercity, monopoly bus lines in the United States. The latest thing in Mexican bus travel is the "Executive" bus, which is equipped with an amazing bump-free suspension, a restroom, latest-release films shown on closed-circuit TVs and a friendly stewardess who serves coffee, tea and soft drinks, hands out pillows and generally assists the passengers on the trip. By the way, all seats are reserved on first-class service in Mexico.

The best part about the Mexican bus system is that rural areas are not devoid of bus lines as they are in the United States. We've traveled in some of the most remote areas in Mexico–to high mountain villages, through jungle country and desert terrain–but no matter how isolated the area might seem, before long a bus comes rumbling and bouncing along, carrying passengers from one village to another.

Mexico offers several levels of bus service, and not all operate with the newest equipment. Sometimes the vehicles are ancient, dented and in need of paint, and sometimes, the equipment is the latest in air-conditioned luxury. Officially, there are two types of service, first and second class, but these names don't necessarily describe the equipment. The main difference between first and second class is that first-class buses take reservations, and they can only sell as many tickets as they have seats. Second-class buses are permitted to crowd on as many passengers as possible, allowing people to stand in the aisle. Additionally, second-class buses are slower because they make many more stops, sometimes stopping to pick up passengers whenever anyone waves a hand at the driver. Also, some second-class buses traveling through isolated rural areas permit passengers to carry produce, chickens and piglets to market. This adds immensely to the adventure of bus riding in Mexico! Your living adventure in Mexico isn't complete without at least one ride on a second-class bus with a squealing pig in the aisle!

Most North Americans choose first-class service. However, if you'd like to see Mexico on a different level than other tourists and you speak some Spanish, second-class travel may be an adventure you'd enjoy. Second-class buses are usually older and always slower. They turn off the pavement at every opportunity and bump their way over unpaved roads to visit any number of picturesque villages. While the bus takes on passengers and disposes of cargo, you often have 15 or 20 minutes to wander about the square, inspect the inevitable church or order a bowl of steaming chicken *caldo*. If you were driving, it would never occur to you to detour off the busy highway. The other passengers take pride in pointing out landmarks as you go along; they seldom have the chance to talk with a real *norteamericano*.

Mexican Railroads

For the adventurous, particularly those with a sense of humor, rail travel in Mexico is a must. Much of the equipment is old hand-me-downs from the U.S. rail system. The coaches are right out of the 1920s, with the luxurious decor of those days still more or less in place. Other equipment is more modern and made in Mexico. You can reserve *camarines* (one-room Pullmans with individual toilet facilities) or luxurious drawing rooms with full bathrooms (including showers) and lounging sofas. The first-class section has ordinary recliner chairs, and the dining cars (when available) serve surprisingly tasty meals.

At least on some key routes, service is currently being upgraded and the travel time cut. Fares on the special trains making these runs are somewhat higher but are still extremely affordable. There is now an excellent first-class train from Monterrey to Mexico City which you can reach via luxury bus from Brownsville, Texas, where many travelers leave their automobiles. Reservations can be made through a travel agent in the United States.

Train fare is usually less expensive than bus transportation for the same route, but trains can also be much slower, particularly when rolling over the mountains. Many travelers prefer trains because they can schedule their long, grueling trips at night; they can climb into a Pullman bed and wake up in the morning at their destination, refreshed, and not very damaged in the pocketbook.

Second Class Trains

On Mexican trains, second class is exactly what the name suggests. Sometimes the coaches are equipped with wooden benches for seats, and the restrooms are always dirty. Despite this, some North Americans prefer to ride second class for the atmosphere. Fellow passengers are Indians, soldiers, farmers and anyone else too poor to afford the luxury of reserved first-class seats. These trains are guaranteed to contain a vendor's stand offering sandwiches, cold beer and soft drinks. You'll often find an American or two leaning against the improvised bar and practicing Spanish with the second-class passengers.

Automobile Travel

Chances are, wherever you live in the United States or Canada, existing without an automobile is next to impossible. Our society has forsaken public transportation to the point where it's almost nonexistent. We depend on our cars just as cowboys depended on their horses back in the Wild West days. Without an auto, even the simplest shopping errands are all but out of the question. Fortunately, Mexico hasn't "modernized" itself to the point of phasing out public transportation. Taxis are cheap and plentiful, and buses are everywhere. Just stand still, and before long, one will come along to take you where you want to go. Because public transportation is so convenient there, many retirees elect not to have an auto in Mexico, particularly if they're trying to live on a budget. Nevertheless, there are times when an auto comes in handy. You might want to show visitors the sights or drive to the next town to do some heavy shopping. Car rentals are readily available and relatively inexpensive for these special occasions. We recently rented an auto for $35 a day, which included insurance and unlimited mileage. By renting a car whenever you need to make a jaunt to Acapulco or Guadalajara, you can enjoy motoring without the expense of maintaining an automobile.

But many North Americans are so automobile-dependent they can't visualize life without a car. They either bring one with them or buy one in Mexico.

The requirements for bringing cars into Mexico are constantly being revised. The sites listed in our section on the Internet are likely to have the most up-to-date informaton. At one time, you couldn't keep a U.S. car there for more than six months. This rule has been changed several times, and we suggest you get the most recent regulations just before you move. If you enter the country on a tourist card good for a six-month stay, make sure you get an auto permit of the same duration. Otherwise, you will have to drive to the border after three months to get a new auto permit.

Any current driver's license from the United States or Canada is valid in Mexico. You need no other. However, you *must* have Mexican automobile insurance, which can be bought at the border and renewed most places in Mexico. This is just about the most important advice you'll find in this book! The law doesn't *mandate* that you have insurance, but common sense does. Also, bring proof of your U.S. or Canadian insurance. (We've never been asked for it, but everybody seems to think it's necessary.)

We've heard several horror stories about Americans who drove without insurance in Mexico. Even in the case of a non-injury accident, the police must, by law, arrest anyone who doesn't have insurance–at least until they can prove financial responsibility. You can't blame them for this; a gringo would be sorely tempted to abandon his wrecked auto and return home if the damages might be more than his car is worth.

To make another point: it's important not only to have insurance, but also to carry the name and phone number of an insurance agent with you at all times. Lately there's been a disturbing trend in the way the police handle accidents. When a traffic accident occurs, the police have the right to impound your vehicle. They don't always do this, but they can. When this happens, you need to have an insurance adjuster or an attorney come to your defense.

An injury accident, however, is considered more serious; police may hold a driver for up to three days to make sure there is no criminal fault. Usually, when it's pretty clear what happened and criminal intent doesn't enter into the picture, they won't. But they can. So, make sure your insurance policy provides for the services of a lawyer in the event of an accident. For example, if someone is injured and it's your fault, you could be held financially responsible not only for damages to the car of and medical expenses for the injured party, but also for supporting the victim's dependents until he or she recovers. The insurance company should be liable for these expenses, but it takes an attorney to keep you out of the fray.

We've heard many heartwarming stories of insured motorists who were given excellent treatment by their Mexican insurance companies. Typically, the insurance agent found them a place to stay and had someone watch over the vehicle to supervise repairs and make sure the work was done satisfactorily.

Another tip on insurance: report any accidents *as soon as possible!* If you wait until you return to the United States to make your report, there's a good chance you've lost your claim. You must report the accident where it happens. And, if you are driving a rental car, you must report an accident within six hours of its occurrence, or the insurance company won't pay! Too often, the driver of a rental car simply leaves the car where it was damaged, thinking it is the rental agency's problem and that the insurance will cover it. Days later, by the time the rental agency appears on the scene, the auto may have been vandalized or stripped to the frame. Again, it's your liability if not reported within six hours, and the insurance company will refuse to pay.

Buying Insurance

Insurance rates for daily insurance coverage in Mexico are set by the government, so there is very little difference between companies. However, when buying policies for six months or more, you can save a bundle by shopping. Some companies only sell by the day, so a one year policy would be astronomical, as much as $2,500. But insuring by the year might cost $600 with another company. It used to be, the only way to save money on insurance was to go through an RV travel club or special brokers. However at least one U.S. company, Sanborn's, also offers

Mexican long-term insurance at discounts. One insurance strategy is to purchase enough daily insurance coverage to get you to the region where you want to settle, and ask local residents which insurance agents they recommend. They'll have the up-to-date information on rates and coverages.

A typical policy on a recent model car should cover: collision, upset and glass breakage, with $100 deductible; fire and "total theft," wind, hail, flood and earthquake with no deductible. People often decline full coverage on older cars; auto repair in Mexico is cheap, they're willing to gamble. It would have to be a serious accident to cost more to repair an old car than the cost of an extended, full-coverage policy. While you might gamble on collision, property and bodily injury insurance are essential–no matter what you are driving. Only a fool would drive in Mexico without liability insurance. On the other hand, it's unnecessary to over-insure; since insurance awards in Mexico are usually limited to actual damages, it isn't necessary to insure more than $25,000 for property damage and $30,000 per person bodily injury.

Although these amounts are adequate under Mexican law, there's always the possibility of having an accident involving a U.S. citizen, with subsequent litigation in U.S. courts. Therefore, some people feel better with higher liability insurance.

Buying an Auto in Mexico

Many residents avoid the problem of importing an auto simply by buying one in Mexico. For our money, the most practical and economical car in Mexico is the good old VW "Bug." This reliable machine is still being manufactured in Mexico by the Volkswagen people. As of early 1997, you could buy a brand new one for about $4,000–half of what the cheapest import costs up north! Used cars in Mexico are proportionally priced. With VW's so popular, you'll find mechanics all over who are expert in VW repair. One bit of advice: don't think about buying a new VW and bringing it back to the United States. It won't pass the rigid U.S. specifications for items like smog, safety glass, etc. Mexico also manufactures Datsuns, Toyotas, Fords and Chevys.

Gas Station Smarts

Gasoline comes in two flavors. There's the old-fashioned leaded gas, which is used in older cars and some economy cars like the VW. This gasoline is called *regular* or *Nova*; it's about 30 percent cheaper than the higher-octane, no-lead Magna-sin. Important: regular gas comes from the blue pumps, no-lead from the silver pumps and diesel from the red pumps. Watch which kind goes into your car! Filling your gas tank with diesel will cause no end of trouble. Occasionally those working around *gasolineras* know very little about autos, other than how to pump gas into your tank. Don't let anyone tell you that the red pump is gasoline!

Beware of cute little tykes who come running to start pumping gas into your car before you have a chance to think. Some of these kids have a scam where they clown around and get your eyes off the pump so you don't know how much gasoline has been put in. They then quickly set the meter back to zero, quote you an outrageous amount and pocket the difference. In addition, if a pump isn't brought back to zero before starting, you'll pay for fuel you haven't received.

Here is a little advice, which if followed, will prevent you from ever being taken at a gas station. Before you pull into the station, make a close estimate of how many liters you will need. (There are 3.64 liters to a gallon.) Then multiply the number of liters by the price, which is standard at all stations. Round this figure off to the nearest even amount, and try to have the exact change ready. Next, get out of your car and carefully watch the whole proceedings. Check that the pump has been turned back to zero; don't let anyone distract you from this mission. Always have a calculator in your hand. This makes the person pumping gas think you know what you are doing (even if you don't). Then ask for the exact amount of pesos you want to spend, rather than the number of liters. *"Setenta pesos, por favor."* (Or write it on paper: "70 pesos.") This way, you only have to watch the pesos meter on the pump. If you have exact change or ask for an even amount, you cannot be shortchanged. If you hand the attendant bills larger than the amount on the pump, carefully count it out to him; a favorite trick is for him to innocently say, "But señor, you handed me a 50 peso bill, not a 100!" (The bills look enough alike that you can feel you've made a mistake.)

When a boy wants to clean your windshield (this service is never provided by gas stations), remember that he is doing it for tips. We usually say yes, even if the windshield doesn't need cleaning, because it's probably the boy's only way to earn a peso. The spare change isn't going to make a difference to us; it will to the boy. If a herd of kids comes around, choose one youngster and wave the rest away, or you'll have a forest of hands seeking tips. Once, a little entrepreneur (about five years old) pounded all four of our tires with a chunk of wood, then seriously announced that he had checked the air in the tires and that they seemed to be full. We gave him the customary coin plus an old tennis ball for his services. His look of delight told us that he will be pounding on tourist's tires for some time to come.

Rules of the Road

As in all countries, there are special customs and rules for driving in Mexico. When you are on the road, you need to know these rules in order to understand what's going on around you. These customs vary from region to region. For example, in the northern desert, where you might expect lots of high-speed driving, you'll find that some Mexican drivers refuse to drive faster than 30 miles an hour–in the belief that slow driving prolongs the life of the car. They're probably right–you'll find a plethora of 1970-vintage cars still creeping along the highways. They aren't driven fast enough to wear out.

Slow driving may be interesting, but it is also dangerous for the American who whips along at 60 miles per hour while others cruise at 30. A good rule is to drive as if there were a 25-mile-an-hour car around every curve, and be prepared to slow down. On the other hand, in Mexico City, where congestion can be appalling, drivers go as fast as they can. Sixty miles an hour seems perfectly reasonable to a cab driver in the capital, after all, he is getting paid by the mile, not by the time.

We try to avoid driving in Mexico City. If possible, we enter early Sunday morning, when traffic is lightest, park the car and take buses or taxis for the rest of our stay. Anywhere else in Mexico is a piece of cake, but Mexico City turns many a macho driver into a trembling wimp.

Turn Signals and Right-of-Way

In the United States, our system of turn signals seems self-evident. When the left signal is blinking, it means, "Be careful, I'm going to turn left!" However, in Mexico, a blinking signal could mean any number of things, depending on what the driver wishes it to mean. Often a left signal doesn't mean a left turn at all! It means, "It's okay to pass if you want; I don't see anyone coming in the opposite direction, but if I do, I'll pull over to let you get by safely." On the other hand, it could mean the driver is actually planning on turning left! If there's any possible left turn ahead, better wait. A flashing right blinker usually signals a right turn–but not always. Sometimes the driver is saying, "Don't pass," or he may just be blinking for the hell of it. You never know. A flashing of both lights at once seems to say, "Look out, I'm going to do something silly, so stay clear!"

All of this makes sense of some sort when you consider that, under Mexican law, the vehicle in front has the right-of-way. If the guy in front of you decides to make a left turn, make a right turn, swerve into the next lane, or suddenly stop and ask directions, you have to be prepared to avoid him, while the people in back of you give you the same courtesy. Well, usually they do.

At first, this system of right-of-way can be puzzling for the tourist, especially in heavy city traffic, with cars swerving from lane to lane in front of you. What you must realize is that you have the right-of-way over all those behind you. Therefore, instead of worrying, as you must in the United States, about *all* the cars in the road, you can concentrate on trying to outguess the idiot in front of you. Whatever lane changes you make are cool because those behind you are watching you very carefully. You'll find that when you cut in front of people, they will obligingly drop back and give you room, instead of honking their horns and waving their fists as *gringo* drivers might. Actually, we consider it a fairly good system, and most drivers, once used to it, find it rather easy to get around in Mexico (except in Mexico City). The smaller the town, the lighter the traffic and the slower people drive. Again, remember that the guy in front is always right. If you're in front, that guy is you. Having said all of this, we urge you not to totally give up worrying about the driver behind you who could be a *gringo* who doesn't understand the system!

One exception to this rule is when someone is passing you; then you *must* concede the right of way. Always be prepared to help him get safely around you. Even if the other driver is breaking the law by passing on a hill or curve, you are equally guilty if you don't drop back and let him pass.

Highways and Byways

During the oil bonanza of a few years ago, Mexico embarked upon an ambitious road-building project. The emphasis was on constructing new highways to reach areas that were previously accessible only by dirt or gravel roads. So you'll find miles of fine highways that lead you to some great places, areas where you can drive all day on new roads and seldom see another vehicle. But because of a lack of funds, many other highways, the busy ones, haven't been maintained so well, and they tend to disintegrate rapidly.

North American drivers aren't used to watching out for road hazards. We take it for granted that manhole covers will be in place and that a sign will give adequate warning when a bridge is out ahead. We assume that shoulders are safe to park on in an emergency and that farmers will keep their livestock off a busy highway. But in Mexico, the motto is "Driver Beware!"

What does this mean for the novice driver in Mexico? Simply that you must slow down and drive cautiously, just like most of the Mexican drivers. So, you take an extra 20 minutes for your trip because you drive 50 miles an hour instead of 70. You'll find that you'll see more of the country and arrive a lot more relaxed.

The most important motoring advice we can give is *never attempt to drive the highways at night!* There are several good reasons for this. One is that livestock roam freely throughout the country. It can be somewhat distracting to be driving along at 70 miles an hour on black asphalt and suddenly come across an almost invisible black bull sleeping on the road. Animals love to bed down on the pavement at night, because it holds the daytime heat and makes a cozy place to sleep. A 1,000-pound animal can neatly remove the wheels from your car if you collide with it at high speed. Even worse is clipping a burro. This cute little animal also finds the warm asphalt a great place to stand and snooze. When a driver zooms around a curve and cuffs a burro with his bumper, he finds that the animal is just the right height to flip up in the air and glide across the hood at 50 miles an hour. Burros stop looking cute when 200 pounds of bone, hide and muscle come crashing through your windshield.

Another hazard of night driving is suddenly finding the lane blocked by a line of large rocks. "What the devil are rocks doing across the road?" you may well ask. I once heard a nervous American speculate that maybe "bandidos" had placed the rocks as a roadblock. No, no. No "bandidos"! The rocks are actually placed there by truck drivers. Here's what happens: truckers prefer traveling at night because the traffic is much lighter and they make better time. When a truck breaks down (a frequent occurrence), the driver has no choice but to stop in the right-hand lane of the pavement (there's rarely a roadside shoulder). But he doesn't want to crawl under the truck to make repairs if it means taking a chance that another driver will not see him and will crash into the back of his truck. So, he first goes back fifty yards and places rocks–the biggest rocks he can carry–across that lane of the pavement to warn other truckers and motorists. Oncoming drivers are thus alerted that something is wrong up ahead and will have time to stop or swerve. If the oncoming driver doesn't see the rocks, his vehicle will tangle with a barrier of 50-pound boulders, and the trucker will be safe. Usually, when the repair job is finished, the trucker rolls the rocks off the pavement. But not always; the driver is anxious to get on his way.

A related problem occurs when a truck has to stop on a hill for any reason. Once he's ready to get started again, the driver finds it a hassle trying to work clutch, brake and accelerator at the same time. So he puts a heavy rock behind each rear wheel to prevent the truck from rolling backward. With the truck wheels braced against the rocks, it's much easier to get going. The rocks remain on the pavement, waiting for you as you round a curve. You can imagine the damage they cause. Rocks are easy to avoid in the daylight, but not so at night.

Another hazard about night driving is that some Mexican drivers routinely turn their lights off, to see if anyone is coming, when passing on a curve. Guess what happens when the car coming the other way also has its lights out. Also, some older cars don't have working tail lights. Occasionally, a car won't even have headlights; its driver is content to drive along simply using the moonlight for illumination.

Do you now understand why you don't want to drive at night? We have to admit that we violate these warnings from time to time, when we have a schedule to maintain and driving after dark is the only way to do it. We've never had an accident, but the tension level involved tells us it just isn't worth it.

The speed limit on good highways is usually 100 kilometers (60 miles) per hour; the posted limit is much lower in towns. Sometimes that limit is ridiculously low, and you'll notice that few people observe the signs unless a cop is in sight (which is rare). Without many cops around to enforce the rules, your chances are excellent for getting away with driving 50 kilometers an hour in a 30-kilometer zone. Yet why take the chance? Drive slowly and safely in Mexico, and you'll never get into trouble.

Traffic Tickets

If you are stopped for a violation such as speeding or failing to observe a stop sign, the cop will probably hint that you can save a lot of time if you pay the fine directly to him. That way, he won't have to take your driver's license and license plates to ensure that you'll show up at the police station tomorrow to pay the fine.

Now, don't get upset and accuse the cop of being a crook. In the unofficial system of Mexican traffic rules, a traffic cop can accept a cash donation in lieu of a ticket and keep the money as part of his salary. Most cops are paid minimum wage or less, so they're expected to catch speeders to earn enough money to live on. Technically, they aren't supposed to do this, but in practice, almost all of them do take payoffs, or *mordidas*. For the policeman, it's sort of like working on commission. Even with low prices in Mexico, a person can't feed his family very well on minimum wages, so most Mexicans expect the cops to take the money.

If you've actually violated the law, you have no cause to complain; just negotiate the fine and pay it. The policeman is actually doing you a favor by not taking your license plates. You either pay the cop, or you waste a day by going to the police station (tomorrow) to pay. Haggling over the amount of the "fine" is usual, and the money is traditionally folded and passed surreptitiously. We keep a couple of dollars worth of pesos folded behind our drivers' licenses and simply hand it over when we're caught doing something wrong. You can expect the cop to lecture you as to how dangerous it is to be going the wrong way on a one-way street, or whatever, then apologize for stopping you, and that's that.

What's the safeguard against a cop's stopping you for some thing you *didn't* do? Simple: insist on taking the ticket. That way he's wasted his time by stopping you, because he gets nothing if you pay at the police station. For that reason, a cop seldom hassles motorists unless he can convince them they've broken a law. So, if you're innocent, say so and don't even discuss paying a fine. It will be an inconvenience for you, but it will make it easier on the next driver. If you're guilty, just pay up; that's the system in Mexico. Until Mexican taxpayers agree to pay police decent salaries, as we do in the United States, the system of *mordidas* will continue. You don't have to like the system, but don't try to change it single-handedly, or you may make an enemy of the cop. We've often been criticized by people who point out that the practice is morally wrong for suggesting that drivers pay *mordidas* to cops. But we have to tell it like it is, and not how we'd like it to be.

Help on the Road

Don't be discouraged about driving in Mexico. If you take normal precautions and understand what is happening around you, it is perfectly safe. (John Howells has driven many thousands of miles in Mexico, with only two minor accidents. Don

Merwin has never had an accident in Mexico, but admits to having driven far fewer miles.) What if your car breaks down on the road? Chances are one of the first cars along will stop to help if you are stranded on the highway. You'll quickly find that mechanics are everywhere: men who've spent their lives keeping their old machines running with innovative, creative repairs.

If you sit long enough, you ought to see a Green Angel coming to the rescue! What's a Green Angel? To promote tourism and to help motorists in general, the Mexican government has a fleet of repair trucks that cruise the highways, looking for cars in trouble. These "Green Angel" trucks (painted green, of course) patrol the major routes and try to cover each highway at least once a day and often twice a day or more. The trucks are loaded with gasoline, oil, spare parts of all descriptions, plus two trained mechanics. Usually, one of them speaks English. If you are in trouble, it is their duty to stop and make the necessary repairs. You pay the cost of parts, gasoline, and oil, but the labor is courtesy of the government.

You might want to take note of this phone number; it's the 24-hour "hotline" for the Green Angels: 520-0123. You can call from anywhere in the country (assuming you have access to a telephone), and the dispatcher will get in touch with a Green Angel by radio. If you park by the side of the road and raise the hood, someone will surely stop to help. At the next town, this good Samaritan will phone the Green Angels for you or notify the police, who can call the hotline.

Also, during peak tourist times, the Mexican army is utilized for tourist assistance. As you drive, you'll see olive-drab jeeps and trucks with soldiers sitting alongside the road or patrolling the countryside. The jeeps sometimes carry signs that read: "*Asistencia Turistica.*" While it's doubtful that the soldiers could repair a car, they have radios in their jeeps and can call a mechanic or the Green Angels quite quickly. These troops are generally used on the least traveled routes, where the Green Angels don't patrol, but they can sometimes be seen on major highways.

If you drive very much in Mexico, you will from time to time come across random customs inspections on the highway. Officials, sometimes military, sometimes civilian, stop traffic and check for contraband. The main items they are looking for are drugs, guns and ammunition. Please, don't carry any guns or ammo unless you have the proper permits, or you can really get into trouble!

Often, a tourist misunderstands and feels threatened by these inspections. This misunderstanding, we fear, has given rise to stories of "bandidos" or shakedowns. We've heard of people nervously thrusting money into the inspectors' hands, thinking that's what they want. These stories would be funny if they weren't so damaging to tourism. The inspectors aren't interested in tourists other than to make sure they are really tourists and not loaded down with illegal contraband or.30-caliber ammunition. They neither want nor expect anything other than your cooperation in letting them look in your trunk or under the hood. But if you are going to force money upon them, most will gratefully accept it.

One-Way Streets

Perhaps a word or two about a few other traffic customs are in order here. The system of one-way streets puzzles some American drivers. Since the streets in most older towns were designed for horse traffic, they are often quite narrow and, by necessity, one-way. The direction is indicated, *not* (as you find back in Omaha) by a large sign on the street corner, but by small arrows high up on the corners of the buildings. These signs also control traffic in a unique and common-sense manner. The arrows come in three colors: red, green and black. If the arrow you can see on the building is green, that means you are on a major street and have the right-of-way over any car coming along the cross street. A red arrow means you must yield. Black means it's first come first served. But remember that the first one there always has the right-of-way. Actually, this system works rather well and keeps traffic flowing along the narrow streets with a minimum of congestion or accidents. Of course, just because you have a green arrow doesn't necessarily mean you can charge ahead with confidence. Always slow down and look both ways; you might run into a tourist who doesn't know the system.

Please don't let any of these cautions frighten you. Driving is an excellent way of seeing the country. You can amble along at your own pace and stop where you like to explore villages or have a picnic on a country lane. The pace of driving is slow in Mexico, but it matches the pace of living. Above all, don't worry about getting off the road and into remote areas. Just as in the United States and Canada, the more rural the countryside, the more simple and friendly the people. Farmers and other Mexican villagers are every bit as hospitable as farmers in Tennessee or Iowa, maybe more so.

New Toll Roads

A fairly recent innovation is the extensive construction of toll roads. For those accustomed to driving on the parkways of the northeastern United States, these pay-by-the-mile super high-ways should feel familiar. However, California drivers are often shocked by the frequency (and voracity) of the toll booths. But, if they are far from inexpensive, they are certainly convenient, often getting you to your destination in less than half the time the journey over the free roads would take.

RV Travel in Mexico

The first thing many people do when they retire is buy a motorhome or a travel trailer. They envision themselves living the carefree life of bohemian vagabonds, following the pleasant weather and enjoying the good life. A few actually do this; they become full-timers, as RV people call folks who live the year round in their rigs. But most end up using their RVs for temporary escapes. A much larger number of people "become part-time retirees," driving or dragging their portable homes to winter quarters in Florida or Arizona. In the summer, another sizable group heads for Oregon or Montana to escape the scorching heat in their home states.

Given Mexico's variety of climates and interesting places to stay, it's only natural that many RV retirees are interested in Mexico as a place for full- or part-time retirement. As it turns out, RV travel in Mexico is quite popular with RV enthusiasts; untold thousands return year after year. From our perspective, there are several drawbacks to using RVs for retirement in Mexico, although we admit there are some positive aspects of seasonal RV living there.

First, let's dispense with the idea of *mobile homes* in Mexico. With few exceptions, dragging one of those monsters into Mexico for retirement living is highly impractical. By the time you purchase a mobile home, struggle to move it to your location, set it up and make the connections, you could have built a quality home and saved money in the bargain. The exceptions we've found are mainly in Baja California, just a short distance from the United States border. Because mobile homes contain wiring and plumbing, all set up and ready to use, they have the advantage of being able to be installed on a lot–ready for immediate occupancy. Getting them to some sites in northern Baja is relatively easy because of an excellent four-lane highway that extends as far south as Ensenada. However, according to Mexican law, anything over 40 feet long or eight feet wide requires special permits, which could mean yards of red tape! There's good reason for this law: Mexican highways are simply not designed for 12-foot-wide packages. When you try to haul that clumsy box through towns where the narrow 400-year-old streets were laid out for horses and carriages, you could learn the full meaning of the word "impossible."

Vacation RV travel in Mexico is fun; it's a convenient way of visiting Mexico. John Howells and his wife traveled many thousands of miles through the republic via camper, trailer and motorhome. John liked RV travel in Mexico so well that he wrote a book–cleverly titled: *RV Travel In Mexico*–on the subject. Unfortunately, it's now out of print, but you probably can scrounge a copy at your public library.

However, living full time in a tin box in Mexico leaves a lot to be desired. First of all, in many desirable places to which you might wish to retire, RV facilities aren't all that great–in some places, they are non-existent. As a rule, trailer parks are located on the outskirts of town, so you end up living somewhere because that's where the trailer park is rather than because it's where you might *like* to stay. This leads to our second objection to long-term RV living in Mexico: it separates you from the everyday life of the community. You'll be staying in an enclave of North American RV travelers and will have few Mexican neighbors to interact with. You'll be insulated from the traditional Mexican neighborhoods and the everyday events that make life in Mexico so fascinating. Instead of living near the *zócalo*–where you can stroll around in the evening, socializing with friends, or you can lounge on a bench while reading the morning papers--you'll be parked out in the boondocks. You'll have to make a special effort to get into town. You might as well be camped in an RV park in Kansas, for all the special ambiance you'll be experiencing.

Having said these negative things about RV living in Mexico, let us examine the positive side for a minute. Many RV people regularly travel to Mexico for seasonal retirement and wouldn't consider any other style of travel. They counter my objections by pointing out that they *enjoy* living in a closed, United States-style community. "We don't *want* to learn a foreign language," one woman emphasized, "and we didn't come here to absorb another culture. We simply want to spend a pleasant winter with our friends and return home when the weather thaws out back home." One couple we know drives to Guaymas every winter, parks their rig in the enclave and, for the entire season, hardly ever sets foot outside the protected walls of the trailer park. That behavior is a little extreme, but makes them happy.

For those who are somewhat paranoid about Mexican food, having their own kitchen continually at their disposal is very comforting. Not having to depend on Mexican restaurants means a lot to them; they can prepare their own meals and feel safe. "Most RV people eat out occasionally," said one woman, "but the rest of the time, we want to eat the same kind of meals as we do back home." (Frankly, one of our favorite pastimes is trying different Mexican restaurants!)

Others disagree that you necessarily have to be isolated from the Mexican community. One woman told of a Halloween party held in San Carlos Bay. "We informed a few taxi drivers that we were having a 'trick or treat' party for kids, and could they find some kids to attend. Come Halloween night, and the taxi drivers brought over 250 children to the party! Most were dressed in costumes, and we gave out 150 pounds of candies and treats! What a wonderful night!" Halloween has become an annual event, looked forward to eagerly by *gringo* and Mexican adults and, of course, the kids of San Carlos Bay.

One huge advantage to RV retirement in Mexico is that you can find lovely places to stay that are only accessible by motor-home or travel trailer. You can camp on the beach, with the surf rolling in just yards from your home, in locations where there are no habitations of any kind, other than RVs.

One couple we interviewed regularly bivouacs next to the Seri Indian camp, on the mainland side of the Sea of Cortez. "The Indians came to expect us for a visit every winter," they said, "and we always bring them old clothes and toys for the children. They treat us with love and respect that's truly heartwarming."

RV people tend to return to the same Mexican RV parks every year for their "winter retirement," just as they do to parks in the United States. They eagerly look forward to meeting their friends of last season. Many parks hold holiday celebrations, with parties and dinners for the incoming RVers. Many long-term friendships have been forged in Mexican RV parks. Residents organize and plan activities, from potlucks to dances. RV owners probably aren't any more friendly than other travelers in Mexico, but perhaps because they are quartered so close together, they have more opportunities to be friendly.

Where do RVers Go in Mexico?

Although RV retirement in Mexico isn't nearly as popular as living in traditional Mexican homes, there is one place where RV inhabitants probably outnumber conventional retirees: Baja California. Both the Pacific peninsula and the mainland side of the Sea of Cortez see an ever-increasing number of regular winter retirees. At last count, more than 100 RV parks in Baja cater exclusively to North Americans. Also growing in popularity, the mainland side of the Sea of Cortez–particularly places such as Puerto Peñasco, Bahía Kino and San Carlos Bay–is drawing winter visitors.

For a desert sojourn in the warm sun, hundreds of thousands of motorhome, trailer and truckbed-campers head for the southern parts of Arizona, Nevada and California. It's not surprising that many of them have discovered Baja. Those snowbirds who usually nest in the Yuma, Lake Havasu or Phoenix areas are learning about San Felipe, on Baja's Sea of Cortez coast.

About a two-hour drive south of the border–over a lightly traveled, well-paved highway–San Felipe is the winter destination of thousands of RVers. Well-equipped parks–some right on the beach–offer complete facilities, even visiting mechanics who will perform maintenance and repairs on your vehicle while you lounge in the sun or catch fish for dinner.

Although a few basic necessities may be less expensive here than in Yuma or Phoenix, most people don't travel here to cut expenses. A trailer space costs about $240 to $300 a month in most parks–about what you would pay in the United States–and other prices are on par. "We don't expect to save money by spending our winters here," said one couple, "but we don't spend any more than we used to spend in Yuma–and we have a lot more fun!"

On the mainland side of the Sea of Cortez, RVers head for three favorite locales. The first is Puerto Peñasco, about a hundred miles south of the border. It's a sprawling town situated on a long stretch of pristine beach. The town of Puerto Peñasco has little to praise as far as scenic values go; people come here mainly for the beach, warm winters and companionship with other snowbirds. Several conventional neighborhoods contain homes, ranging from scruffy to elegant, as well as many RV parks. The park we stayed in one winter was enormous; it had a large restaurant, a nightclub and a well-stocked grocery store. Most people were settled in for the season. They reserve the same RV lots every year.

Bahía Kino

The second favorite short-term retirement spot along this coast is Bahía Kino, also known as Kino Bay. Because it's the closest beach place to Hermosillo, Kino is a favorite place for well-heeled Hermosillo farmers to build beautiful, bougainvillea-covered mansions. Some North Americans are building; report-edly, an increasing number of retired United States military personnel are spending winters here.

But the vast majority of winter residents here are *norteameri-cano* winter retirees who, hauling trailers or dragging or driving motorhomes, rendezvous here in October or November. The RV population increases by at least a thousand vehicles, filling a huge trailer park and spilling over into several smaller ones. Most visitors come here every year. They routinely organize into temporary clubs, elect officers for the season, and celebrate their yearly reunion.

Kino is divided into two sections: Old Kino and New Kino. The old part is basically a fishing village, holding little attraction for tourists or retirees. New Kino is where the retirees live. The town spreads out for nine miles along the beach, and several impressive condominium developments are underway. The streets have been laid out and the utilities are in place, waiting for someone to build houses on the lots.

Here's where you'll meet the Seri Indians, a semi-nomadic tribe who formerly lived on Tiburón Island, in the Gulf. A few years ago, when existence on the island had become too precarious, the Mexican government moved them to the main-land. The Indians brought with them their skills at carving driftwood and the super-hard ironwood. When living in Kino, you can see them in their workshops, where they'll offer beautiful sculptures at irresistible prices.

A third major destination for winter retirees along this coast is San Carlos Bay. San Carlos had its start as an RV destination about 30 years ago. At that time, there were only two small hotels–and beaucoup trailers and campers (motorhomes weren't too plentiful back then). As the trailer parks grew in number and size, so did the number of hotels, condos and private homes. San Carlos has become a year-round retirement town, with an emphasis on traditional housing.

Pacific Side of Baja

From the border down to Ensenada, throughout the *zona libre* (free zone), where some entry laws are less restrictive than elsewhere in Mexico, many thousand "winter Mexicans" (temporary retirees) settle in each year. All along the coast, you'll find parks near the surf or on hills overlooking the Pacific ocean. Because summer temperatures here are pleasant–about what they would be in San Diego–some residents do use RVs for longer periods of living. We suppose that, after a while, though, folks might feel compelled to switch to larger, more conventional living arrangements.

The accepted way of life here in the *zona libre* is to reside in commercial trailer parks; sometimes retirees purchase lots and set up their trailers on a permanent basis. But farther south, where the population is almost nil, there's a different way of RVing. It's called "boondocking"–parking for free or almost free for months on end. In fact, boondocking is the *only* way you'll have the opportunity to enjoy some of these beaches. Because of the absence of fresh water, there are no hotels or tourist accommodations of any sort. Unless you camp, no matter how rich you might be, you can only glimpse these beautiful sights as you drive past. But park your rolling home on the sand, and you can enjoy beaches and scenery that money cannot buy. A weekly trip to the nearest town to replenish the drinking water and stock up on groceries is all that's needed for a winter's stay.

Like birds flocking together, winter retirees cluster along the shores and congregate wherever fishing and scenic attractions beckon. Our favorite string of beaches is located just south of Mulegé about halfway down the peninsula. Santispac, El Coyote, Requesón and several other well-known boondocking places dot the sandy shores of the Sea of Cortez.

Hundreds of RVs arrive here every October and stay until the weather begins heating up in April. With their rigs lined up along the beach, campfire pits in front and sometimes a palm thatch-*palapa* built for shade, the campers enjoy a bountiful season of companionship, fishing, swimming, boating, hiking and just plain loafing.

Not unexpectedly, as more and more winter Mexicans crowd the beaches, natives are beginning to see commercial possibilities, and they naturally want their share. Beaches usually belong to an *ejido* (Indian communal land) and nominally are under tribal or communal control. And, even though all Mexican beaches are open to the public, the *ejido* is permitted to charge for overnight parking. That's why some beaches today are no longer totally free; although they might as well be free because camping charges are so low. Typically, a caretaker makes the rounds every evening and asks for a dollar or so for parking overnight. In return, the caretakers make sure things are tidy and keep an eye out for anyone who looks suspicious.

The *ejido* caretakers also keep their eyes on trailers and *palapas* left throughout the summer, when Baja sunshine makes Death Valley seem cool. From the reports we got, theft was rarely a problem. "We leave our trailer, trail bikes and boat here all summer," said one couple. "We put small things inside, and chain the bikes to the boat for safety. Yet we've never had anything stolen, not even when we've forgotten to secure things." We assume that conditions haven't changed.

Bahía de Los Angeles and South

Bahía de Los Angeles has always been a popular place with fishing enthusiasts and those who love desert solitude. Bahía has three RV parks (with boat ramps) near town and one park at the junction. The last time we were there, they charged $4 a night for electrical hookup and a cement pad. Every other day, a water truck passes through to provide fresh drinking water and will fill your tanks for about $2. The sea provides a bountiful harvest of clams and scallops, not to mention fish for those willing to toss a line in the water. Kids knock on the door every evening to see if you want to buy their freshly caught fish or pin scallops, live and still in the shell. Can't get fresher than that! A nearby restaurant serves excellent meals of fish, lobster and tough but tasty Mexican steaks.

Two little markets in the village supply rudimentary foods such as chicken, coffee and sterilized milk. Folks on tight budgets depend on the sea for much of their food, with clam chowder, sauteed scallops and rockfish fillets *a la Veracruzana* providing wonderful gourmet dinners. "We load up our cabinets with canned goods and such before we leave San Diego," said one lady in Bahía de Los Angeles. "We seldom have to buy any groceries here, other than fresh eggs and tortillas from the *tienda* and veggies from local gardens."

Farther south, in Loreto, you'll find three parks with a total of about 150 spaces. One features purified drinking water piped to your rig. Talking about the newest park in Puerto Escondido (just south of Loreto), a friend says: "One of the nicest in Mexico. You can pay a yearly rental and build your own *palapa* (a rustic, thatched roof cover that keeps the RV continually in the shade). We also have a restaurant and a market, so we don't have to run into town for groceries every day."

La Paz has six parks with a total of 411 spaces. Most of them have good water. Respondents have raved over a couple of the parks here. Not only are they topnotch, but the personnel are extremely helpful. "We came in with a blown tire," one couple reported. "The owner of the park said, *¡No hay problema!'* And before we knew what was happening, we had two men replacing the hard-to-find radial tire, which they had to run into town to locate. 'No charge for the labor, just for the tire!' said the owner. We tipped the workers, and they were delighted."

Then, farther south are two interesting places, Los Barriles and Buena Vista. These towns contain four parks, three of them (Vardugos, Playa de Oro and La Capilla) on the beach. There are 110 RV spaces in Los Barriles and 43 in Buena Vista.

The Tropics

Baja California is for winter retirees, but the tropics draw a share of summer RV visitors as well as those fleeing the rigors of northern winters. In places like Mazatlán, Puerto Vallarta and Acapulco, you'll find trailer parks with both part-time and full-time retirees living in motorhomes and trailers. Summer in the Mexican tropics is a time of high temperatures and humidity (after all this is the rainy season), not quite as humid or hot as Miami in the summer and clearly not as beastly as summer in St. Louis. It's always seemed odd to us that more RVs don't take advantage of the tropics in the summer.

For some reason, RVing further down in the mainland seems to have lost some of its popularity. At one time, almost anywhere we went in Mexico, we'd see RVs. But during our last drive through the country, in the spring of 1997, we noticed several trailer parks had closed, and there were fewer rigs in the ones that were open. Part of the problem may be the high cost of toll roads today. Since the toll is calculated on the number of axles of your vehicle (or vehicles), costs can mount if you're traveling to the Caribbean coast or deep into Chiapas.

Is RV Travel in Mexico Safe?

We've interviewed many RV owners, and most maintain that driving a rig in Mexico is no more hazardous than it is in the United States–providing you exercise common sense. Several people told of the extreme helpfulness of local people when they did have some problems. "If we have an emergency on the road, all we have to do is wait a little while and some other RV will come rolling along," said one couple. I believe them, for there have been days in Baja when I've seen RVs accounting for 30 percent of the traffic on the main highways. As far as whether or not RV travel is safe in Mexico, it apparently is, or else the insurance companies would charge higher premiums to insure RVs. On the contrary, because of the good driving records of RV people, insurance companies actually give them discounts (through travel clubs). This is understandable, because generally RV owners have a higher sense of safety in the first place.

Where North Americans Live

Our discussion of specific Mexican communities that you might want to make your retirement home is divided into two groupings. The first deals with the most popular locations, those with a substantial North American presence and a long history of welcoming retirees. Without doubt, these places will be the choices of most of our readers. However, because the most popular places are not the most economical places and because we know that some of you crave adventure, we discuss a number of other locations in a second grouping. These places have few year-round foreign residents, and are, in general, harder to get to than the communities in the first. Lacking organizations of North American residents, these communities are likely to offer a lonely life for those who do not speak enough Spanish for meaningful communication with their Mexican neighbors. At the same time, any town that has electricity is within range of satellite televison, and any house with a telephone can be hooked into the Internet. So maybe isolation is a thing of the past.

Rather than weigh down our discussion of Mexico's off-the-beaten-track retirement possibilities, we will repeat what we feel is the most important caveat for anyone considering retiring abroad: if you feel a place might be right for you, before you make any important decisions, go there and spend some time seeing what *living* there would be like.

The Guadalajara/Lake Chapala Area

No part of Mexico attracts more North American retirees than Guadalajara and neighboring towns around Lake Chapala. Estimates of the U.S. and Canadian expatriate population hereabouts range between 25,000 and 30,000–with about 8,000 living by the lake. An unusually large percentage of the expatriates here are Canadians. Long-time residents say the ratio of newcomers from Canada to U.S. citizens has changed from a ratio of one to four to about one to one. We assume these figures are correct, although we cannot explain the shift in the immigration pattern.

When you ask why so many choose to live in the Guadalajara area, the list of reasons typically starts off with "climate." The weather here, North American residents brag, is the finest in the world, and statistics consistently confirm this opinion. The Guadalajara area experiences an average of only one day completely without sunshine per month. The average daily temperatures are in the high 60s in the winter and in the high 70s to mid-80s in the summer. Most rain falls on summer evenings, (actually May through September), after a day of basking sunshine. Guadalajara's claim to being the site of "perpetual spring" obviously has some basis in fact. Should you crave the heat of a tropical sun and the crashing of waves on a sandy beach, a three-hour drive takes you to Pacific beach resorts where you can escape those "frigid" spells of 60-degree weather that occur during January.

One reason we would recommend Guadalajara or Lake Chapala as excellent places to start your quest for a retirement home is the large number of expatriates already there. By acting as a support group, they can ease the tension of your transition into a new lifestyle. Helping each other is an unwritten expatriate rule. This can make for an easy introduction to living in a foreign country. That's not to say that you will be living in an exclusively gringo compound, isolated from your Mexican neighbors. On the contrary, the vast majority of U.S. and Canadian citizens here live in homes and apartments interspersed throughout several attractive Guadalajara neighborhoods or in villages along the shores of Lake Chapala. If your next door neighbors turn out to be fellow *norteamericanos*, it's usually a coincidence. Almost all of the retired residents with whom we talked reported wonderful relations with their Mexican neighbors.

In Guadalajara, a wide variety of neighborhoods in and around the city are popular with expatriates. These neighborhoods come in all degrees of prices and elegance. According to residents, some of the nicer locations are Lomas del Valle, Colonias de San Javier, Rancho Contento, Club de Golf Santa Anita, Providencia, Ciudad Buganbilias and Barrancas de Oblatos. Housing prices in general, although fairly typical for Mexico as a whole, are somewhat lower here than in Mexico City and in some popular resort areas.

Understand, these are not simply gringo enclaves; these are the neighborhoods where most middle-class and wealthy Mexicans live. In fact, the general affluence of Guadalajara is one of its hallmarks; the city is one that has truly benefited from NAFTA. With large companies like IBM and Motorola operating factories here, large payrolls stimulate the economy. For example, IBM, the world's largest computer maker, pays workers on the disk-drive assembly line $72 a week, or about $1.40 an hour. This may not sound like much, but compare $72 a week with the $30-a-week salaries many workers earn.

Medical care in Guadalajara is tops, with two medical schools, excellent hospitals, 24-hour emergency pharmacies, and other medical care services. A new hospital affiliated with a high-tech facility in California recently opened, bringing the latest in medical treatment to the area. Through efforts of the American and Canadian expatriate associations, many U.S. health insurance companies, such as Blue Cross and Blue Shield, are accepted here, and the American Legion has a health plan that ties in with veterans' benefits from the U.S. Veterans Administration. A Guadalajara clinic, Sanatorio Americas, advertises that it not only accepts Blue Cross and Blue Shield, but also charges no deductible.

Guadalajara is one of Mexico's major transportation hubs, with an international airport and high-speed tollways connecting the city to both the U.S. and Guatemalan borders as well as to other parts of the country. These facilities make it easy for your friends and family to visit you and for you to return home occasionally, whenever you need a cultural "fix."

There's Always Something Doing

One of the reasons for Guadalajara's appeal is the plethora of recreational and cultural activities available there. Only Mexico City and Cabo San Lucas offer more golf courses than Guadalajara's five. Tennis courts, swimming pools and health clubs are plentiful. Guadalajara offers a number of movie theaters showing films in English, frequent concerts, operas and, with the great number of social organizations serving the retiree population, no end of parties, trips and other organized activities. There are at least two libraries with books in English and many bookstores and newsstands that sell U.S. publications. Cable and satellite television have revolutionized home entertainment, and videotapes of American films circulate freely in the retiree community. More than 80 religious, civic, philanthropic, social and special-interest organizations serve this huge and diverse collection of individuals.

Most American cities the same size or even larger might envy Guadalajara for its cultural richness and diversity. There is hardly a day in the week when there isn't a concert, a new art exhibition or some other event at the Institute Cultural Cabanas, the Degollado Theater or one of the city's many other museums and concert halls. A typical weekly issue of the *Colony Reporter* lists twenty or more such activities. The fare is thoroughly international, and like everything else in Guadalajara, the price is right.

A striking part of Guadalajara's cultural life is the city's numerous museums. Perhaps the best known of these was made from the studio of Clemente Orozco after the artist's death. Guadalajara residents are proud of this famous native son, whose murals embellish many public places. In addition, many other museums display the work of great artists of Mexico and the world. It is not without reason that Guadalajara has been described as "Mexico's Florence."

Shopping isn't the authors' favorite leisure activity, but we can't deny that it seems to be a popular one in Guadalajara. Every time we turn around, there seems to be a new and fancier shopping mall somewhere in the city or its environs. The North American Free Trade Agreement (NAFTA) opened the flood gates for North American merchandise, and Guadalajara has taken full advantage. The huge WalMart store here, for example, is open 24 hours a day and has over 50 checkout counters to accommodate customers. You'll also find such familiar stores as Price-Costco, Sam's Club, Sears, Radio Shack, Baskin Robbins, and Ace Hardware. The most recent addition is Office Depot! These stores are joined by Mexican shopping jumbos such as Gigante, Sanborn's and others equally modern but with less recognizable names. All of this commercialization is a far cry from the way it was when we published the first edition of *Choose Mexico;* in those days, you had difficulty finding toothpaste and diet soda. Many retirees bemoan this modernization, but they shop anyway!

We doubt that anyone has ever counted the restaurants in Guadalajara, but we have no doubt that you could go to a different one every night for several years. Before you reached the last restaurant on your list, you'd have to start over so that you could try all the new ones that had opened while you were sampling the others.

If all of that shopping and restaurant-hopping sounds exhausting, there's no reason why you can't do as we do and spend a lot of time sitting in one of the many beautiful parks and plazas scattered around the city, enjoying the sunshine, the sights, the sounds and, yes, the smells of Mexico. One of our favorite little parks is decorated with the busts of Mexicans whose heroic stature was earned in such unmilitary pursuits as poetry, philanthropy, education and music.

The center of much retiree life in Guadalajara is the American Society of Jalisco and the American-Canadian Club. The American Society, known to its several thousand members as "AmSoc," is headquartered in the pleasant Chapalita section of Guadalajara. The society's facility is a hive of activity, with bridge games, meetings (to plan the members' frequent and very economical outings) community service projects and just plain companionship that spills out of the meeting rooms and library into the lobby and dining area. The society offers low-cost medical insurance to its members, and in other ways too numerous to count, helps them to feel secure and at home in their adopted community. The AmSoc and American-Canadian Club are wonderful sources of information on just about everything you might want to know about getting comfortably settled in the Guadalajara section of Mexico. Their addresses and telephone numbers are in the "Resources" section of the appendix.

Lake Chapala and Ajijic

The 50-minute drive from Guadalajara brings you to the shores of Lake Chapala, where thousands of *norteamericanos* make their homes. These are folks who prefer small-town or village living to big-city Guadalajara, with its five million inhabitants. When we speak of Lake Chapala as a place to live, we actually refer to a half-dozen or so communities lining the northern shore of the lake, with the towns of Chapala and Ajijic as the focal points. Driving along the lakeshore, you'll encounter the villages in the following order: Vista del Lago, Chapala, Chula Vista, San Antonio, La Floresta, Ajijic, Rancho del Oro, Villa Nova, San Juan Cosal, Las Fuentes and Jocotepec. North American residents are dispersed throughout these towns and villages. They live in all manner of homes, condos and apartments as well as in several exclusive, gated communities and on small farms in outlying areas. Two golf-country club developments with upscale housing are in place, and a third was under construction at the time of this writing.

You'll find an interesting dichotomy between those who adore the intimacy of village life and those who prefer the luxurious gated villas on the hillsides. Each group can't quite understand why the other chooses the opposite lifestyle. To be perfectly honest, we can't quite figure out which side we're on. On the one hand, during a gorgeous sunset, we love having cocktails while sitting on the elegant terrace of a tasteful hillside estate (our friends, not ours). Yet there's something to be said for the quiet exhilaration of village life: the sound of church bells in the morning, the sight of burros bearing firewood, the interaction with your Mexican neighbors, and the quaint restaurant around the corner. Each lifestyle has compensating pleasures.

The mountains that loom high above the lakeside villages not only create a panoramic backdrop, but they also protect the lakeshore and the villages from prevailing northerly winds. This effect contributes to the delightful climate here and explains why the southern shore is comparatively undeveloped; the mountain ridge deflects blustery winds in that direction.

The lake does something else for the climate; the large body of water acts as a climate control. Winter days in Ajijic, for example, tend to be five degrees warmer than in nearby Guadalajara, and summer days can be five to ten degrees cooler in Ajijic. People who live around the lake are quick to point this out. This fact is ammunition in the on-going feud over which place, Guadalajara or Lake Chapala, is the best place to live. It's entertaining to listen to each camp ridicule the other's choice of living arrangements. The feud extends to the individual lakeside villages, with residents of each community maintaining they live in the best place of all! Personally, we think they're all correct.

The lake itself serves as more of a scenic treasure than as a source of recreation. Few people swim there, and fishing isn't great–it never has been. And from time to time, the water level drops drastically. In *Village in the Sun*, the charming 1945 book that popularized Lake Chapala and started the immigration of North Americans to the area, Dan Chandos described the lake:

"It is an unusual lake. Its waters, heavy with silt, are never transparent and reflect colors in curious half-tones that can turn a vulgar Wagnerian sunset into the blue-and-red fuchsia shot silk that Victorian parasols were made of."

Our observation is that sunrises too, are just as spectacular as Lake Chapala sunsets. The lake does contain fish–several kinds of small whitefish, carp and similar species–but not the kind sportsmen go after. Local fishermen harvest them with nets.

The center of the town of Chapala looks more like a small city than a village. In fact, it boasts the only traffic signal (on the corner of Hildago and Madero streets), on the lake. A wide boulevard is Chapala's main street, a kind of open mall with a tasteful center island of flowers, shrubs and tropical trees. All the way to the lakeshore, which is paved with tile, businesses, restaurants and hotels line both sides of the street. The town's centerpiece is a charming plaza, complete with a graceful bandstand, where townspeople like to congregate in the evenings.

At the other end of the spectrum is the fascinating village of San Antonio Tlayacapan. With cobblestone streets and weathered adobe buildings centered around an ancient church, San Antonio is the epitome of a Mexican village. This is the place Dan Chandos described in *Village in the Sun.* Curiously though, the gringo population isn't very dense. This makes San Antonio Tlayacapan a place for total immersion in Mexican village living. Prices are affordable here as well, with some homes being offered, when we were last here, at what seemed like bargain prices to us.

Yet another lifestyle on Lake Chapala is the Chula Vista Country Club, five minutes west of Chapala. Chula Vista's delight is its nine-hole golf course and two lighted tennis courts for the use of residents. About 200 beautifully landscaped homes, many with lake views, surround the golf course. Chula Vista is known as "the Beverly Hills" of Lake Chapala, with home prices varying from inexpensive to expensive, from $65,000 to more than $400,000.

Chula Vista maintains an active neighborhood association, which continually strives to maintain the quality of services in this area. As a result, Chula Vista is one of only two communities on the lake that enjoys pure drinking water (Villa Nova is the other). Everywhere else you must use either bottled or boiled water.

The town of Ajijic probably has the largest number of North Americans in residence, with the town of Chapala close behind. Distant Jocotepec attracts a growing number of new residents nowadays, partly because homes and land are less expensive. Most lakeside expatriates live either in the villages or on isolated acreages away from town, but several commercial subdivisions cater to North Americans and wealthy Mexicans. These residential communities vary from ordinary, low-cost places to luxurious, gated communities. Most newer developments are carefully designed to preserve the mood of a Mexican village atmosphere, featuring cobblestone streets and houses constructed to look like genuine colonial antiques.

For many residents, the *only* place to live is in the village proper, where housing is typically old Mexico. They live in apartments or houses hidden behind high walls, or in buildings with plain exteriors yielding no hint of what lies inside. Streets are typically cobblestone and many buildings are of adobe construction, occasionally of stone or antique brick. Real estate in the villages varies from cheap to expensive, and the interiors vary from rustic to fantastic. Again, the exteriors give few clues as to what lies inside.

An English-language monthly newspaper, *Ojo del Lago*, keeps lakeside residents aware of the latest news and area gossip. It opens its columns to residents who relish writing articles, editorials, book reviews–anything they care to share with the community. The content ranges from excellent reading to amateurish drivel, but it's always fun to read.

Ajijic serves as Lake Chapala's cultural and social center. It is where the Chapala Society (an expatriate association with 2,000 members) is headquartered. Even if you have no intention of choosing Lake Chapala as your retirement paradise, you owe it to yourself to take a look at the Chapala Association's library complex. Located in the center of the village, on a large estate that is full of landscaped gardens and surrounded by a wall, the facility is the heartbeat of the expatriate society. This was the estate of Neill James. A fascinating woman who lived in Ajijic for several decades, she was well liked by expatriates and adored by natives of the area. She donated everything except her living quarters to the Society, and on her recent death, at the age of 99, bequeathed these to the people of Ajijic. (By the way, it's pronounced *Aah-hee-HEEK*, with the accent on the last syllable.)

The Chapala Association's centerpiece is an extensive lending library which includes 20,000 volumes as well as 5,000 videotapes, but that's only a part of it. The association sponsors numerous social events, fund-raising activities, and special cultural offerings such as lectures, concerts and other top-notch entertainment. The library hosts a computer club and a ham-radio club with regular broadcasts and far too many activities to be listed here. The grounds have separate rooms for lectures, classes and meetings; a snack area with tables; and quiet garden areas for reading and relaxing. Even though North Americans (you needn't be a member to participate) thoroughly enjoy the library complex as a meeting place and learning facility, one of its most important functions is public relations for the expatriate community. While local people take English lessons, their children take art classes. Over the years, many successful artists received their start here, and today they donate their time to teach a new generation of artists. At the time of our last visit, club members were feverishly working on a "toys for tots" program, raising money to bring Christmas joy to over 6,000 local children. These activities go a long way toward creating a favorable image of local gringos. You sense a genuine feeling that North Americans are accepted as valued members of the community.

Another tradition here is the American Legion Post. Its large membership reflects the presence of retired military personnel near Lake Chapala. Its tree-shaded clubhouse is set behind brick walls on a quiet side street. Its members take an active part in community affairs.

The large number of active civic and social groups in Ajijic make it easy to meet people and become a part of the community. Take a look at the following list of activities and social groups in the area: Humane Society, Computer Club, Chess Club, several garden clubs, Culinary Arts Society, The Writer's Group, Genealogy Club, Duplicate and Progressive Bridge Clubs, Needle Pushers, Texas Line Dancing, Daughters of the American Revolution, Lakeside Little Theater, and two yacht clubs. This is only part of the list. All in all, more than 40 English-language clubs and charitable organizations keep people busy by the lakeside.

If the foregoing activities aren't enough, you can also take classes in art, handicrafts, music, computers and Spanish (both conversational and structured). Or you can participate in tennis, golf, walking, jogging, horseback riding, boating, fishing, mountain biking, Tai Chi and various exercise groups. A variety of passive pleasures are available too, such as taking in concerts, art galleries and museums.

Good Starting Point

In summary, we feel that unless you are familiar with Mexico or have already picked out another community in which to live, the Guadalajara-Lake Chapala area is probably the place to start your search for the ideal retirement site. It may or may not end up as the place you decide to live. Nevertheless, given its convenient location and good transportation to most parts of Mexico and given the unequalled support expatriates offer newcomers, going there first can make the choice easier and less intimidating.

San Miguel de Allende

Every time we return to San Miguel de Allende we are afraid we will find it so crowded, so Americanized and so filled with traffic as to destroy its legendary charm. The bad news is that it *is* more crowded, some parts of it are Americanized and a few of its major streets, at least at certain times of the day and week, have more traffic than we would like. The good news is that it is still a charming and delightful place for vacationers and retirees. A few blocks from the town's center, in a prosperous commercial and residential area, we could easily believe that we were the only gringos around. True, San Miguel has a high proportion of foreign residents, perhaps five percent, but that fact seems irrelevant to most of its Mexican residents.

We were also worried that the relentless march of "modernization" might have destroyed San Miguel's colonial flavor. That fear, too, proved to be unfounded. The laws that require all new building to conform to the town's architectural character continue to be enforced.

On each of our visits, we find a number of new restaurants and shops to choose from (we thought there were enough already). The existence, on the outskirts of San Miguel de Allende, of a huge, modern shopping mall, (including a well-stocked American-style supermarket, Gigante), may be an affront to those who would like time to stand still, but it is a huge convenience for anyone who would like to accomplish the purchase of such essentials as laundry detergent, vodka and lawn chairs quickly and painlessly.

Other important additions to the town include a well–equipped, modern hospital operated by a private nonprofit association. Its staff includes six specialists and one general practitioner. Less vital, perhaps, but still a big plus is the new bus terminal. We heard of one couple who looked out the bus window at the old depot and decided to travel on. If they had stayed, they might have enjoyed the chamber music festival, which has become an annual event.

Home of the Arts

There are few places in Mexico where North Americans have been as happy as in San Miguel de Allende. A colonial city just under four hours drive or bus ride from Mexico City, it draws both visitors and residents from all over the world. What many of them share is an interest in the arts. These people are attracted both by the handsomeness of the town and its natural setting and by its several excellent art schools.

The 6,300 foot altitude produces a climate that is comfortable year round, if you don't mind winter evenings that are chilly enough for a wood fire and summer afternoons that are warm enough to make swimming pool owners especially popular. San Miguel owes much of its attractiveness to three events in its history. The first, the depletion of the silver mines in Guanajuato, rendered San Miguel obsolete as a way station en route to Mexico City and left it a backwater. Consequently, its fine colonial architecture was not demolished to make way for the progress that afflicted many other Mexican towns.

The second event was the arrival in 1938 of an American, Sterling Dickinson, who founded the art school that became the world-renowned Instituto Allende, which continues to draw outstanding artists and craftspeople from all over Mexico, the United States, Europe and Asia. A second school, affiliated with Bellas Artes, Mexico City's Palace of Fine Arts, also welcomes foreign students, but it places more emphasis on the education of younger local artists. In addition to these larger institutions, there are several smaller schools and artist's studios that offer training in everything from painting and photography to weaving, stained-glass, music and dance.

The third event contributing to San Miguel's unique flavor was the Mexican government's promulgation of a law designating the entire town as a national monument. Hence, any development or construction that would change San Miguel's character or appearance must now have express permission.

Some grumble about San Miguel's narrow streets, paved with what must be the world's sharpest and most irregular cobblestones. These same people lament the government's stubborn refusal to allow the erection of gleaming aluminum and glass facades on the homes and shops facing onto the streets. But Los Angeles, Houston and parts of Mexico City are always there to welcome anyone who cannot do without these symbols of progress.

About one out of every 20 residents of San Miguel is a foreigner. That ratio is sufficient to support an active English–speaking social and cultural life, but it's not large enough to make San Miguel a little bit of the U.S. in Mexico. There is no American enclave where foreigners are concentrated and when North Americans there say that what they like best about Mexico is the people, they mean their Mexican neighbors (not just servants and shopkeepers) as well as their compatriots.

Recreation

Particularly for a town of its size, San Miguel has remarkably diverse opportunities for recreation, which ranges from golf, tennis and riding to classes in yoga and dance. You can attend lectures, play in an amateur string quartet and go bird watching with the Audubon Society. Organizations you can join include a duplicate bridge club, an amateur theatre group, an American Legion post and a garden club.

Spanish is taught at the Instituto Allende, the Academia Hispano Americana and several smaller and more informal schools. Depending on the school, these programs range from a couple of hours a day to more than forty hours a week. There are students of all ages, and among other benefits, classes, whether in language or the arts, provide excellent opportunities for meeting people.

If the concerts, dance and theater in San Miguel and nearby Guanajuato do not satisfy your cravings for culture, Mexico City is three and a half hours away by auto or bus. Some residents wish that it were a little closer, forgetting that the distance is just about right to save San Miguel from being overrun by day trippers and other tourists (especially because there is no airport in the town or nearby).

Within a short drive there are several hot-spring resorts that are open to the public where you can swim or just soak contentedly in the naturally heated water. We are not aware of any claims of curative powers, but we can testify to their calming effect on the spirit.

Restaurants

Because San Miguel is a magnet for North Americans and other foreigners, it is amply endowed with good restaurants. These range in ambiance and cuisine and from spartan vegetarian to elegant continental. Italian, French, Argentinean and Spanish food are all represented. So is the hamburger, but we are happy to report that the golden arches have not yet appeared. Specialty food stores feature items as exotic as Danish cheese, German sausage, Arab pita bread and the international bagel. Although these delicacies may not be as economical as tortillas and frijoles, they are quite reasonable by U.S. standards.

San Miguel has so many groceries, drugstores, meat markets and vegetable stands (as well as a large indoor municipal market with surrounding outdoor stalls), that each North American resident you consult is likely to give different advice about which are the most reliable and most economical. Actually, quality, selection and price tend to be similar in all stores. When you have been in San Miguel awhile and acquire Mexican friends, they can tell you the best places to buy such national specialties as *carnitas, chicharones* and *mole.*

A Most Unusual Library

San Miguel's unique public library (La Biblioteca) serves a wide variety of functions. Its outstanding collection of English-language books, including many current best sellers, is supplemented by an ample selection of classical and popular music on tape. After payment of a nominal membership fee, cassettes and books can be borrowed free of charge. (Most small or middle-sized towns in the United States do not have these literary or musical resources.)

The library is in a restored colonial mansion, whose handsome inner court serves not only as a pleasant spot to sit and read but also as a place to meet friends. Concerts and lectures are often given there in the evening. Once a week, *Conversaciones con Amigos* gathers there to provide English-speaking students of Spanish and Spanish-speaking students of English a chance to practice with each other. (Another weekly meeting of this group is held in the courtyard of one of the town's several language schools.)

In addition to the solace and stimulation the library provides to North Americans, it is also the base for an ambitious program of reading instruction and academic scholarships for underprivileged local children.

The Biblioteca and its philanthropic activities are supported financially by weekly house and garden tours that allow both tourists and curious residents to see how the most affluent live. Helping with these tours is one of the many ways that retirees in San Miguel can repay the community's hospitality. Those we questioned described a number of opportunities for public service, such as helping with the school for the handicapped, working with the local humane society, contributing to *Atención* (the weekly English-language newspaper), and participating in the cooperative burial society. In recent years, the Biblioteca has expanded into an adjacent building that once was a church and has added a pleasant cafe. One room in its original space now serves as headquarters for its computer classes. In addition, it provides numerous satellite library facilities to the Spanish-speaking residents of surrounding villages and ranchos. Work on behalf of the community and the demonstration of genuine concern for the people of San Miguel are two of the reasons for the excellent relationships that most North Americans there enjoy with their Mexican neighbors.

Because San Miguel attracts the wealthy as well as the talented from all over the world, it is entirely possible to find a house that sells for $500,000 or rents for $2,000 a month. Fortunately for the rest of us, however, residents report that you can still find unfurnished two-bedroom apartments with rents beginning at about $200. Three hundred dollars a month is a good rent to figure on for a conveniently located and attractively furnished apartment. A house is likely to rent for a little more.

The monthly salary of a maid who works eight hours a day, six days a week, is reported to be about $120 a month. Gardeners (who often serve as general handymen) are paid about 85 cents an hour. Few couples report spending more than $250 a month for all their meals, including some in restaurants. It is easy to spend $20 for a meal in the town's most luxurious eating places, but $9 is more typical for a meal in a charming, moderately priced restaurant. And there are plenty of good restaurants where a full meal costs less than $4. Much entertainment and recreation is free, and a bus trip to Mexico City, more than 160 miles away, costs about $5. San Miguel, therefore, still qualifies as a town where a comfortable life is possible within the $600-a-month figure of our subtitle. It is odd that this town is considered one of Mexico's more expensive locations, outside of the seaside vacation playgrounds.

Several retirees in other Mexican communities have made the point that if you have no interest in community service or the arts, you could feel a little out of place in San Miguel. They may be right, but this town does have so much to offer that you might want to see for yourself.

Morelia

Ask a Mexican which is his country's most beautiful state and, unless pride in his birthplace triumphs over objectivity, he or she is likely to answer Michoacán. In the summer, much of Michoacán's green, rolling landscape reminds the traveler alternatively of New England's Berkshire Hills or of a painting of peaceful rural China. Michoacán stretches from the Pacific coast almost to Mexico City.

Morelia is the capital of the state of Michoacán, and the city's colonial flavor has been maintained by ordinances that strictly control the styles of new construction. Several downtown banks, which conform to these rules, are lodged in restored mansions, which preserve the elegance of forgotten centuries while providing a place to exchange your travelers checks for pesos.

At the heart of the city, Morelia's massive cathedral boasts two soaring towers that are said to be the tallest in Mexico. Although construction began in 1640, the towers and dome took an additional hundred years to complete. Flanking the impressive cathedral, the Plaza de Armas serves as the social and commercial center. Tourists and residents gather (in cafes under the Plaza's elegant arched portals) to have a coffee and chat while waiting for the *Mexico City News* to hit the newstands. Shopping, restaurants, museums and other attractions are within easy walking distance of the Plaza de Armas. The Plaza is located a block from the city's ancient university. Dating from 1580, it is the second oldest university in the Western Hemisphere.

Morelia supports an active cultural life–music, drama, and dance thrive there as do the visual arts. A recent addition to the cultural scene is the spectacular Palacio del Arte, which boasts 5,000 seats and features internationally famous artists. The city also hosts several excellent language schools, one connected with its own bed-and-breakfast and others that can arrange home-stays with Mexican families. A home-stay is an excellent way to get to know Morelia, meet other people studying Spanish and make some friends among the Mexican community.

Morelia is indeed a colonial town, but it isn't all monuments, ancient homes and narrow cobblestone streets. Once away from the city center, a startling modern facade contrasts with the colonial style. Such contrasts are more typical on the southern edge of the city, where many expatriates prefer to live. Perhaps because Morelia's population and prosperity have increased so rapidly in the past decade, some sectors are modern and elegant. The Plaza de las Americas shopping mall is among the largest and most luxurious malls that we have ever seen. It's as if Saks Fifth Avenue, Sears, Macy's and K-Mart were combined with a luxury supermarket and for good measure, packaged with marble floors and ultra modern fixtures. Another modern convenience for lovers of the outdoors is a golf course.

Despite the fact that Morelia has been slow to catch on as a retirement site, we feel it could be a viable alternative to Guadalajara. Overall, it is much cleaner, and the nicer sections of town are just as attractive and convenient as Guadalajara. Moreover, Morelia is only a fifth of the size of Guadalaraja. A major difference between Morelia and other places of similar size is that Morelia doesn't support a well-organized expatriate group. Once a week, in the Hotel Calinda, there's an informal gathering (with an unofficial chairman), but this meeting is more of an excuse to get together and exchange news than an integrated association as you would find in Guadalajara, San Miguel de Allende or Ajijic. When and if this changes, it will be much easier to find compatible social groups.

How many foreigners live in Morelia? Jennifer Rose, who spends a great deal of time there says, "How many? That's a good question–kind of like counting the number of angels who can sit on the head of a pin. About six or seven years ago, I sat down with some friends one evening and we wrote down the name of every single expatriate we could think of, just to get a count. We quit at around 600. Some people will claim there are only 150, but they're only counting those with whom they're acquainted." She further points out that while the loose network isn't extensive, it's nevertheless big enough to have among its population "some of those gringos you assiduously avoid!" In short, the foreign colony here is large enough to support an active social life, and settling in Morelia today hardly qualifies you as a pioneer.

Easy outings from Morelia include Patzcuaro and Uruapan. The latter, justly renowned for its lacquered boxes and trays, also attracts special attention for the nearby volcano, Paricutin. In 1943, it suddenly erupted in a cornfield and spilled molten lava over the surrounding villages and countryside. Patzcuaro owes its reputation to the loveliness of its colonial buildings and of Lake

Patzcuaro. The lake is dotted with islands, including one covered by the Tarascan Indian village of Janitzio. The island is topped by a gigantic statue of José Morelos, one of Mexico's greatest heroes and a native of the locality. The lake is also the home of the *pescado blanco,* a delicious white fish caught by the Indians in their delicate "butterfly" nets and featured on the menus of the neighborhood's numerous restaurants. Patzcuaro is another location that would seem ripe for retirement relocation, but so far only a handful of North Americans have taken up the invitation.

Querétero

A couple of hours from the bustle of Mexico City, Querétero and neighboring Tequisquiapan are traditional weekend retreats for the middle-class and wealthy families from Mexico City. Those who don't own places in Cuernavaca feel obligated to have their second home in Querétero or "Tequis."

With brick-paved streets and ornate fountains decorating landscaped squares and shady parks, Querétero is a textbook example of historic preservation. Mansions and public buildings dating from the 17th and 18th centuries lend an air of elegant historicism.

Exceptionally attractive, filled with authentically restored colonial buildings and graced by tree–lined streets, Querétero–away from the bustle of Mexico City, yet only a couple of hours distant via toll road–is the "in" place for weekend homes and retirement. The fact that Querétero has almost as many golf courses as Acapulco (four of them) gives you an idea of the upper class coloring of this area.

Given the cosmopolitan colonial charm of Querétero and the ancient village atmosphere of Tequisquiapan, it isn't surprising that a number of expatriates choose to live here. Yet, curiously, their numbers are not as high as you might expect. As best we can tell, only 150 or so North American retirees live here. Part of the explanation may be the area's lack of promotion as a vacation spot for Americans and Canadians. Everyone reads about Guadalajara, Acapulco, San Miguel and all the other pouplar tourist places in Mexico, but we've seen little push for tourists in Querétero. The result is that fewer people are exposed to the charms of Querétero, so they choose other, more traditional places for relocation. This is the classic chicken-vs.-egg syndrome; large numbers of expatriates won't retire in a place where there aren't large numbers of expatriates already in place. On the other hand, there are those who don't want to live in a place crowded with gringo tourists and retirees. Querétero may be the place for them.

Not that there aren't plenty of North Americans living here. A number of multinational factories are on the outskirts of these towns, which add greatly to the general prosperity without disturbing the tranquility and charm. However, they differ slightly from traditional expatriate groups in that they tend to form friendships and social circles on the basis of their work and careers. The upper-class Mexicans who live in the Querétero area are highly educated. Most speak English to some degree or another, so you won't lack people to converse with when your Spanish becomes tedious.

Tequisquiapan holds a special place in John Howells' heart because his family bought and restored a 200-year-old home there and used it as residence for almost 20 years. The Howells' house had two-foot thick adobe walls and a large courtyard with arched portals, which was a great place for lounging on a sleepy day. Tequis has long been famous for its hot baths and swimming pools. Just about anywhere one sunk a well, hot water was available for hot tubs or swimming pools. So it was an easy task to install their own spa in the courtyard.

Tequisquiapan has of course changed over the years, as has every other town in Mexico. Many old cobblestone and flagstone streets have been paved over in the interest of speeding traffic flow through the narrow streets. Instead of lounging on the square, listening to birds and watching wood-laden burros trot past, tourists come here here to buy artwork and locally produced handicrafts. What hasn't changed is the fact that only a small number of North Americans choose to live here year-round.

We are reluctant to write off such towns as retirement possibilities, just because droves of other expatriates haven't discovered Querétero and Tequisquiapan. We realize that most of our readers will be more at ease in places like Guadalajara or

San Miguel, where they have large support groups. But some who have studied North American immigration patterns to Mexico agree that this area could be poised for a rapid increase in expatriate population. At the very least, they may be places to take another look at after you have been in Mexico long enough to have some command of Spanish and are ready to leave the bulk of your fellow expatriates behind.

Mexico City and Vicinity

Fifty years ago, when John Howells, then a teenager, lived in Mexico, the vast majority of North American residents lived in Mexico City. In those days, we, who were about 100,000 strong, called ourselves the "British-American colony." Mexico City was about the size of today's Milwaukee. Smog was a word applied mostly to places like Los Angeles, and the skies were as blue as those in Minnesota in the springtime. Off in the distance, you could see the twin volcanoes of "Popo" and "Ixti", snow-covered and glistening in the sunlight. That is, unless some fluffy white clouds happened to be lazing along to obstruct your view.

Servants worked six and one-half days a week for $10 a month, and a gallon of Bacardi rum cost about a dollar. Mexico City was *the* place to live. The rich grew richer by the day, so it seemed, and gringos with dollars lived as well as the richest of the rich. They owned huge, luxurious homes in places like Las Lomas and El Pedregal. Twenty thousand dollars would buy a mansion. A rent of $100 a month was considered extravagant.

In those days, Acapulco was an unspoiled little town with empty beaches and a sprinkling of jet-set celebrities who strived to keep the place their special secret. But Americans living in Mexico City considered Acapulco *their* private discovery! For them, it was a place to be visited in a chauffeured limousine. Why not? Hiring a limousine and reliable driver for a round-trip to Acapulco cost little more than taking a taxi from downtown Chicago to O'Hare. Besides, the old Acapulco road was curvy and picturesque and best handled by an experienced chauffeur.

In short, Mexico City of 40 years ago was a paradise for people with dollars at their disposal. A person with an income as little as $100 a month could do quite well. Hundreds of veterans who attended Mexico City College on the GI Bill reported that they had a great time on far less than $100 a month. (Remember the "52-20" club? Returning World War II veterans were given 52 weeks pay, at $20 a week, to tide them over while in school or while they looked for jobs.) Needless to say, things have changed over the years! But, do you know of *anyplace* where time hasn't marched on?

Today, with its swollen population of 15 to 20 million (no one knows how many), Mexico City suffers from Los Angeles-style smog and Rome-style traffic jams. You can no longer see Popo or Ixti except on rare, unusually clear days. Servants draw at least $100 a month and expect to have all day Sunday off, instead of just Sunday afternoons as it used to be.

The biggest change in Mexico is that, today, proportionally fewer North Americans live in Mexico City than in other parts of the country. Instead of living in the city and escaping to their "weekend retreats" in places like Cuernavaca, Tequisquiapan or San Miguel de Allende, Americans have moved away from the hustle and bustle of the city and made the "weekend retreats" their permanent homes. This way, they can visit the excitement of Mexico City whenever boredom threatens.

Today's expatriates choose to live in the hinterlands of Mexico and visit the big city for special events. No matter where you live in the country, Mexico City is always available at the cost of an inexpensive bus or train ticket. Incidentally, when residents talk about visiting "Mexico," they almost always mean "Mexico City," just as we mean "New York City" when we say "New York."

In earlier editions of *Choose Mexico* we said that we couldn't recommend Mexico City as a retirement spot for everyone. After many subsequent visits here, we still can't, but we do feel that our readers should know what an exciting and cosmopolitan city it is. We wouldn't want to live there, but we certainly would want to visit it frequently. Nevertheless, many North Americans *do* live in Mexico City; they love it and wouldn't consider any other location.

Why do North Americans choose to live in Mexico City rather than less hectic, less crowded cities? For the same reason some people love New York, Paris or London. It's difficult to explain this feeling of urban euphoria to anyone who has never fallen in love with a large city. For those who enjoy city life, Mexico City has it all–great restaurants, entertainment, outstanding museums, art exhibits, night clubs and theaters–they're all there, in one convenient, easy-to-use package. Every possible shopping convenience, from native tapestries to WalMart and Price-Costco, is at your fingertips. Mexico City is so different from Mexican villages, they could belong to a different country.

Mexico City is permeated with culture; its downtown is famous for its collection of 16th-century, colonial architectural treasures, some dating from the early 1500s. The nucleus of the city is a virtual museum of history and culture. Here you'll find the Americas' oldest cathedral sharing an enormous open *zócalo* with ancient, castle-like government buildings and a spectacular museum that displays artifacts from an Aztec temple, recently unearthed nearby. One of Mexico's cultural showplaces, Bellas Artes (Palace of Fine Arts), is also located in the center of town. One of the most beautiful opera houses in the world, Bellas Artes hosts internationally celebrated opera companies and symphony orchestras. (The ticket prices are affordable for the nightly performances.) The famous Ballet Folklórico, a prime tourist attraction, also draws crowds weekly.

Along the broad, landscaped boulevards that radiate from Mexico City's center, several modern and spacious parks and plazas have been added. These structures occupy the spaces once occupied by buildings destroyed in the earthquake of 1985.

Truly a Big City

These boulevards move outward like tentacles reaching for the city's ever expanding perimeters, for Mexico City is an enormous place. Its population is estimated to be between 17 and 20 million–nobody knows for sure. It is indeed a megalopolis. Mexico City is home to a surprising number of North American residents: retirees as well as those working for multinational corporations.

Of course, not all of Mexico City is elegant and sophisticated. As the city sprawls and expands ever outward, it creates large neighborhoods where poor families live in shoddy housing, sometimes without water or electricity.

But you won't be settling in these areas, and you'll not likely have occasion to visit them. You'll be looking at middle- and upper-class homes in those neighborhoods preferred by members of the foreign colony. These are pleasant areas of apartments, condos and houses that look out over tree-lined boulevards or quiet side streets. You'll want to live in areas like Las Lomas, Chapultepec or El Pedregal. Another favorite place (where Howells lived for some years) is the *Zona Rosa,* or Pink Zone, a place of upscale apartments, boutiques and fabulous restaurants.

Accommodations in these sections of Mexico City are not inexpensive, by any means, but the quality of life involved is well worth the money. Try to locate a house or apartment with off-street parking and near public transportation if possible. This last item is important. You'll probably not want to drive in Mexico City. A few experiences with suicidal cab drivers and incredible traffic jams will quickly turn you into a confirmed pedestrian. Many Mexico City residents don't even own autos; they prefer to use taxis, buses and the excellent subway system, and they rent cars for weekend jaunts around the country.

Pleasant Weather

Another positive side to living in Mexico City is its cool, temperate climate. Residents here neither freeze nor swelter. This is the place for those who detest hot weather and avoid tropical sunshine; they'll wear sweaters or jackets the year round and sleep under blankets every night. Some folks–especially those with heart conditions–do find Mexico City's mile-high altitude a problem but most people have no difficulty adjusting. After a day of taking it easy, we jump right back into the swing of things.

Mexico City's major problem–even outranking the impossible traffic–is smog. The pollution is at its worst in the industrial areas on the northern edge of the city. That's why affluent Mexicans and relocated North Americans choose to live in the southern neighborhoods. Despite occasional heavy smog attacks, the problem is intermittent, with many glorious days alternating with a few hazy or smoggy days. Statistically, smog in Mexico City is no worse than in Athens or Tokyo, if that makes you feel any better. We were delighted during our last recent visit by vistas of snow-capped volcanoes and of fluffy white clouds cruising across azure-blue skies.

Public Transportation and Other Amenities

Mexico City's subway system (the Metro) is one of the wonders of the modern world. Authentic Aztec relics and tasteful native murals enhance its underground stations and its rubber-tired trains whisk passengers across town with silent speed. Tracks branch out in all directions, and for the cost of just a few cents per passenger, moves an astounding number of people. Based on our experience as subway riders in New York, San Francisco, Washington, London, Madrid and elsewhere, we're convinced Mexico City is way out in front. By all means, avoid using the subway during rush hours, since the trains have to move the city's millions of commuters to and from work. They pack 'em in like sardines then.

The large number of English-speakers living in Mexico City is reflected in the scope of English-language news media. Besides a daily newspaper, the *Mexico City News,* at least one all-English FM station broadcasts network news hourly from the United States as well as daily (or more frequent) English-language features. Classical music stations abound, and many music stations feature the latest popular music from the United States. Cable TV is as popular in Mexico City as in your home town; video rental stores can be found in just about any neighborhood.

Of course, you needn't live in Mexico City to enjoy its many attractions. Buses and trains are convenient and inexpensive ways to travel here from almost anywhere in the country. Fares are inexpensive, so you can make frequent visits without putting a dent in your budget. In making your exploratory visits to the country, we strongly urge you to see Mexico's great capital city, but be sure you continue on to look at some of the other communities mentioned in this book. As mentioned earlier, living here is totally different from living in one of Mexico's smaller, more intimate communities. For the average person, Mexico City isn't well suited to retirement living.

Oaxaca

At slightly over 5,000 feet, Oaxaca's climate is a bit warmer than Mexico City's and, without the latter's industrial development, it boasts much cleaner air. Oaxaca's population is passing 300,000, but its large, spread out area and the absence of steel and concrete skyscrapers and other visible hallmarks of twentieth-century life effectively conceal that fact.

Oaxaca is easy to reach from Mexico City by air, bus or rail. The west coast beaches of Puerto Angel, Puerto Escondido and Huatulco are close by and are easily accessible by plane.

The great majority of residents, both of the city and the surrounding state of which it is the capital, are Indians. They are proud of their heritage and its resistance to assimilation into the politically, culturally and economically dominant cultures of the last five centuries, first Aztec, then Spanish, and now Mexican. Oaxaca was the birthplace of both Benito Juarez, "Mexico's Abraham Lincoln," and Porfirio Diaz, an iron-fisted president for many years, and was the home of numerous accomplished artists. It is conscious of its colonial and Indian past and has preserved much of its architectural history. Oaxaca is as different in appearance and atmosphere from cities in northern Mexico as Tucson, Arizona is different from Portland, Maine.

On Saturdays, handicrafts flood in from neighboring villages and spill out of the huge Juarez market onto the surrounding streets. Black and green glazed pottery, innumerable baskets in a great variety of shapes and sizes, handloomed textiles and many skillful copies of the Monte Alban idols and jewelry beguile even the most apathetic shopper. On other days of the week, there is a market or tianguis in one or the other of the many surrounding towns. A trip to these towns can also provide the opportunity to visit the studios of the many talented artisans whose work is sold in the shops of Oaxaca.

Every Mexican town of any size has its zócalo or town square, but few are more sumptuous or lively than Oaxaca's twin plazas. Filled with tall, handsome trees and countless wrought iron benches where locals and foreigners alike while away many sunny hours, and ringed by sidewalk cafes, it is the heart of Oaxaca.

There is an unusually handsome bandstand on which a variety of instrumental groups play several evenings a week. Almost the entire town turns out for these concerts, and parents sit around the zócalo gossiping while children play on the grassy parts of the park. The stream of peddlers whose wares include carved, painted wooden animals, bird-shaped ceramic whistles, hammocks, baskets, serapes, belts, and even elaborate carpet-sùcould become annoying after a while, were it not for the fact that a polite but firm refusal is usually sufficient to send them on their way. Then one can listen to the music, chat with friends, or just enjoy the passing parade.

In the early editions of Choose Mexico we reported that the beauty and unspoiled antiquity of Oaxaca was beginning to attract more tourists, particularly those interested in exploring the Zapotec and Mixtec ruins nearby. At that time, this mountain city still had only a small colony of North American residents. Most of those who had chosen to live there seemed to indicate that they liked it that way. One reason may be that food and housing prices have remained somewhat lower in Oaxaca than in many other parts of Mexico. We were told of apartment rentals at $200 a month and our experience was that wonderful restaurants were very affordable. Another reason may be what a retired resident described as "freedom from pressures for conformity."

By the time of our most recent visit, at the end of 1996, the number of full- or part-time foreign residents, mostly from the United States and Canada, had grown in number to what some there estimate to be 2,000 or more. It is hard to be precise because Oaxaca seems to attract retirees who are more interested in experiencing Mexican life close up than in becoming part of a foreign enclave. Certainly there are opportunities to meet and socialize with fellow norteamencanos. One is the lending library on Calle Alcala just a few blocks from the town center (which is said to have one of Mexico's best collections of English language books outside of San Miguel de Allende). It is the place to go when you want to get together with fellow expatriates to get news from home, to exchange local gossip and to get current information on such practical matters as where there is a particularly attractive house or apartment for rent at a reasonable price. We also found that there tends to be a daily early-morning cluster of English-speaking residents and tourists in one of the outdoor cafes on the zócalo. Several language schools serve the many foreign residents who want to get beneath the surface of this magical city.

A glance at the English-language *Oaxaca Times* reveals a schedule of cultural activities ranging from concerts to video showings of classical Mexican films to art exhibitions. There are ads for restaurants to suit all tastes and budgets.

One morning while we were there, more than 60 expatriates gathered for brunch in the sunny patio of a local restaurant to benefit community causes.

Because Oaxaca offers reliably comfortable winter temperatures, it attracts many part-year residents from the United States and Canada. Year after year, they desert the cold and damp of their home communities for the warmth and stimulation of Oaxaca for periods ranging from one to three months.

Many foreign residents, whether living in Oaxaca full- or part-time, seem to choose rooms, suites or cottages on the grounds of the numerous small affordable hotels, scattered throughout the city. Some are able to negotiate monthly rates lower than the $10 a day that seems to be commonplace for overnight accommodations that are more than a few blocks from the center of town.

Oaxaca is certainly an increasingly viable choice in the Mexico retirement sweepstakes and a wonderful place to visit, even if you have only a few weeks to spend in Mexico.

Cuernavaca

Cuernavaca is a special place. Montezuma knew it. So did Cortez, Emperor Maximilian, Empress Carlotta, silver baron José Borda and most of Mexico's retired presidents. Numerous Mexican and foreign millionaires knew it, too. They all chose Cuernavaca for their second homes. The location, only about an hour's drive from Mexico City, and the altitude, about two thousand feet lower, explain why so many of the capital's affluent residents make it their destination on winter days when temperatures in the capital are about a dozen degrees lower than Cuernavaca's year-round mid 70s.

The wealth that has poured into this lovely valley is readily visible in its palaces, churches, mansions and gardens. Sit in the handsome town square (it sprawls up the hill to the Palace of Cortez, which is today an outstanding historical and archaeological museum), and you will know that you are in a prosperous city.

One of the implications of this affluence is that Cuernavaca is probably one of the relatively few places in Mexico (outside of some Caribbean and Pacific resorts) where our $600-a-month figure would not allow you to live comfortably. Probably, $1,000 is a more reasonable figure for this "high-rent district." Prices in the more elegant restaurants approach those in the United States. Yet we enjoyed delicious food in some more modest spots for as little as $6 for a meal that included soup, pasta, main course, dessert and coffee. A simple breakfast in an outdoor cafe, however, was almost the same price. To live truly economically in Cuernavaca, you would have to avoid the places frequented by wealthy Mexicans, tourists and most other foreigners.

Despite the higher living costs in Cuernavaca, you'll find a thriving colony of retirees who by no means are all wealthy. The *Directory of Foreign Residents of the State of Morelos,* published under the auspices of the Navy League of the United States (and modelled after a directory published in San Miguel de Allende), lists hundreds of individuals and families. There are several pages of associations and clubs, ranging from Alcoholics Anonymous and the American Legion to a home for orphaned children supported largely by U.S. contributions and volunteers. Also in the directory, together with numerous banks, beauty salons, delicatessens and so on, are a number of veterinarians, a video club and a washing machine repair service. The physicians and dentists fill several pages. A new edition is published every two years.

July Fourth brings a big bi-national celebration of the U.S. Independence Day and Mexican-American friendship. The festivities include the trooping of the colors of the two countries, the singing of their national anthems and a feast that includes both hot dogs and *cochinito pibil*. All in all, Cuernavaca is clearly a community where you can enjoy many of the comforts of home in surroundings considerably more pleasant.

The Pacific Coast

We often hear people exclaim: "I'd never want to live in someplace like Acapulco or Puerto Vallarta! Much too tourist-plagued. I want to live some place more authentic! Someplace more truly *Mexican!*"

Think about this for a moment. Why do so many tourists travel to Mexico's beach towns in the first place? They go there simply because these are wonderful places to visit! The scenery is lush and tropical, like on a movie set. Balmy breezes caress your skin on palm-fringed beaches. Winter days are typically in the 70s, and summer highs are in the mid- to high-80s; it's shirtsleeve weather year-round. Therefore, it's not surprising that the same folks who look forward to vacations here every year also think about Mexico's west coast when it comes time for retirement. And, as for being "authentic," will someone define the term? When folks think about retiring in the United States, are they more likely to consider an "authentic" town like Soapy Springs, Nebraska, or some "touristy" place like Palm Springs, California?

When you hear people talking about the great time they had on their Mexican vacation, chances are they visited Mexico's west coast. Termed the "Gold Coast" or the "Mexican Riviera" by tourist agencies and travel writers, this section of Mexico draws by far the most tourists every year. There are many good reasons.

First of all, because of the heavy influx of tourists, accommodations are plentiful, excellent restaurants are everywhere and prices tend to be competitive. But more important is the climate, especially for those who enjoy the warmth of the tropical beaches and the warm ocean waves. The climate here is great because seasonal temperatures and rainfall are moderated by the Pacific Ocean. The Pacific, with its deep, temperate body of water, maintains a steady year-round temperature in the coastal regions.

This condition shields you from excessive summer heat, and winter "northers" that blow down from Alaska are greatly moderated by the time they reach Mexico's Gold Coast. Temperatures change very little from month to month, with most rainfall coming in the summer. Winters are almost totally rain free.

Weather on the Mexican Riviera's Pacific Coast

Month:	Jan	Feb	Mar	Apr	May	Jun	Jul	Aug	Sep	Oct	Nov	Dec
High Temp.	88	88	88	88	90	91	91	90	90	90	90	88
Low Temp.	72	72	72	73	76	77	77	77	76	76	75	73
Rain(inches)	–	–	–	–	1.5	10.4	9.0	10.5	15.0	6.5	2.0	0.5

West Coast's Desert

Not *all* of Mexico's west coast is touristy and tropical. Above Mazatlán, north of the tropic of Cancer, the country is clearly a desert. Here, the Baja California peninsula to the west across the Sea of Cortez blocks the breezes, moist from the cool Pacific currents that blow on-shore to the south and nourish the vegetation there. Also, because the Sea of Cortez is relatively shallow, it soaks up the sun's heat and radiates this warmth landward. In turn, the warm air holds its moisture, rather than dropping it as rain, thus creating a desert instead of a tropical landscape.

San Carlos Bay

On Mexico's west coast, the first place south of the border that attracts a considerable number of retirees is San Carlos Bay, located near the fairly uninteresting agricultural center of Guaymas. Originally, San Carlos was a "discovery" of winter retirees–those RV addicts who wintered in nearby Kino Bay or Puerto Peñasco. But it quickly became exceedingly popular with conventional retirees as well. With a backdrop of rugged mountains, balmy winters and gentle, protected beaches, San Carlos Bay is a place retirees come back to year after year to hold reunions with friends.

Visitors from Arizona, New Mexico and Texas began staying longer and longer; then they started building homes, both modest and elaborate. The steadily increasing numbers of North Americans sparked an astounding expansion in construction. Today, the area has the appearance of a true resort town. Locals estimate that over a thousand homes in and around San Carlos belong to gringos. The RV parks are still evident, but they're dwarfed by conventional homes and condominiums.

Several gated communities of rather elaborate homes occupy strategic positions on the shore of San Carlos Bay. These developments are popular with those who want to tie up their yachts and fishing boats at a dock in their back yard. Beachfront lots are plentiful for those who wish to build, even though prices aren't always exactly cheap, particularly in the town itself. During our last visit, we were fortunate to find four "open houses" being held the same afternoon in the main part of San Carlos. All four homes backed up against the beach. The views were spectacular, the interiors were luxurious, and the prices were exhorbitant, ranging from $175,000 to $400,000. Farther north of town, beach and view homes were considerably less expensive, ranging from $50,000 upward.

Boating is part of the scene here. During the summer while you do your retirement thing in cooler climes, a marina at San Carlos' largest RV park will store your boat. Several retiree organizations are quite active here, sponsoring Spanish lessons, dancing and art lessons for their members. North American residents also support an orphanage and buy school supplies for local children.

San Carlos Bay now has a dozen restaurants, several grocery stores, a drug store, some small shopping malls, two marinas, and everything you might need for a winter's retirement. At least one Mexican bank has established a branch here. The downside here, as anywhere along the Sea of Cortez, is the scorching summer sunshine that sends most folks scurrying north for a couple of months of cooler weather. Some may protest that, since most residents do not live here year round, they shouldn't be considered "retired" in Mexico. However, those who retire in Montana and travel to Arizona for the winter are still considered Montana retirees, aren't they? Predictably, more and more are sticking it out, enjoying having San Carlos to themselves during the hot months.

Alamos, a Ghost Town Revived

South of Guaymas you'll pass through two more agricultural cities, Ciudad Obregon and Navajoa. Neither has much to propose for retirement living. However, we can highly recommend Alamos, a fascinating colonial town about 35 miles east of Navajoa. One of Mexico's oldest silver mining cities, Alamos started its boom over four centuries ago, in the early 1500s. By the late 1700s, it had grown into a large and prosperous city with a population of over 40,000. Its many substantial buildings attest to its former grandeur. But like many mining towns, Alamos's fortunes rose and fell with changes in the world economy. After surviving a series of catastrophes, the final collapse came during the Great Depression of the 30s, when the price of silver dropped to 25 cents per ounce. Alamos became a ghost town. Today, nobody seems to remember where the original mine workings were located.

Somewhere back in the 1950s the town was "discovered" by a small group of wealthy North Americans: artists, sculptors and writers. Recognizing the ghost town's inherent beauty, they bought—for less than a song—old homes and mansions and set to work restoring them. The project was so successful that the Mexican government declared the town to be a national monument, just as they did with San Miguel de Allende and Taxco. Modern buildings are forbidden, and remodeling must faithfully preserve the structure's original appearance. Today, artists' studios and apartments are hidden away in these old colonial mansions, which once housed silver barons and wealthy merchants. Typical decor of these mansions includes Moorish arches, covered walkways decorated with intricately fashioned wrought-iron work and graceful fountains amidst landscaped gardens.

The English-speaking community is very active in Alamos and engages in several worthwhile community projects that boost the retirees' image with the local people. One fund-raising project is a regularly conducted house tour that permits tourists and residents to enjoy the restoration miracles performed on these centuries-old mansions.

The expatriate population in Alamos is small compared to other gringo colonies discussed in this book, but the residents are just as loyal to their adopted home as those living in San Miguel or Ajijic. They're totally convinced they've found Mexico's ultimate retirement Mecca. We estimate the total expatriate population to be less than 3,000. How many are North Americans is difficult to pin down, probably not much more than 10 percent. Because summers are livable in this higher altitude, many live here year round, others retire here just for the winter, and many people visit on a regular basis. Yet you never get the feeling that the place is crowded.

The Casa de los Tesoros, a remarkable hotel–claimed by some to be one of Mexico's finest–is located here. Several less expensive hotels are found on or near the main plaza. Three RV parks accommodate the motorized retiree. (Almost all of the RV folks are "snowbirds" who fly home for the summer.)

Mazatlán

Mazatlán has long been popular as a place of retirement for Americans–particularly those from the western parts of the United States and Canada–because it is the closest west-coast location where year-round retirement is practical. Mazatlán is also the first place south of the border that can be genuinely called tropical. In fact, that imaginary line (the Tropic of Cancer) that defines the tropics runs just north of the city.

Mazatlán is one of Mexico's premier beach resorts, and each year more condos, apartments and homes are built there to accommodate the swelling population. No surprise, Mazatlán is a favorite with full-time and part-time retirees from the western sections of the United States and Canada. The difference between Mazatlán and other, less touristy beach towns is that you'll not find ocean-front homes for sale. The land is too valuable; Mazatlán's precious beach properties have been claimed by large hotels and deluxe resorts. But, just a few blocks from the beach, many lovely homes are available for rent or purchase. A first-rate golf course surrounded by upscale homes attracts a large number of North Americans.

According to residents, the recent downturn in the economy had a short-term effect on prices here. At first, many homes –particularly properties owned by Mexican families–were placed on the market at reduced prices However, as in many other retirement communities in Mexico, prices asked by gringos remained fairly level, without dipping any significant degree. Since the demand for upscale homes didn't fall, there was little incentive to drop prices. (In fact, there were more buyers when the peso's value fell in 1994–1995.)

In addition to miles of sunny beaches, Mazatlán also boasts superb sports fishing and a busy commercial port. It deservedly calls itself the shrimp capital of the world. Here, shrimpers from the warm waters of the Sea of Cortez routinely unload cargoes of unbelievably enormous prawns. Sometimes as large as lobsters, most of these delicious crustaceans are unfortunately destined for Japan (where price is no object), and U.S. residents seldom get a chance to sample them. However, you can often buy some if you meet the incoming boats and do some bargaining. Jumbo shrimp taste delicious sauteed with butter, minced garlic and a pinch of chili powder! *Hay, que rico!*

Because tourists tend to throw dollars around with abandon, be prepared for higher prices and wages in Mazatlán. Don't misunderstand, these prices aren't high enough to push Mazatlán out of reason, but a tight budget could be strained somewhat. Taxi fares used to be rather expensive, but lately they have become affordable; there's too much competition to justify exor-bitant fares. You'll see a fleet of open-air taxis, which are cute but much more expensive. As a resident, you would most likely have your own auto or use public transportation. By the way, Mazatlán has greatly improved its bus system, with modern equipment replacing the old, rickety buses that used to ply the streets.

Mazatlán's major drawback is its crowded tourist section of town. As it happens, this is also the favorite area for expatriates to live–in enclaves just a few blocks off the main beach drag. Fortunately, tourists keep to their beach streets and seem to be oblivious to the peaceful neighborhoods nearby. No one we interviewed in Mazatlán felt that tourists were a particular bother. As one lady put it, "They live in their little beach world, and we live in our world. The only time we meet is when we go to the tourists' restaurants." Incidentally, several excellent restaurants, with surprisingly good food at bargain prices, cater to tourists.

When we wrote our first edition of *Choose Mexico*, we reported that traffic wasn't as bad here as in places like Puerto Vallarta or Mexico City. (No place in the world is as bad as Mexico City!) Today, we have to rescind that opinion because the population of automobiles has soared along with the population of humans, yet the streets remain the same size. Despite occasionally heavy traffic, Mazatlán drivers are unusually calm and courteous. The sound of honking horns is almost nonexistent.

Since tourism is a major industry here, many people around Mazatlán speak English. You'll discover this early on in your first visit–when you're hounded by time-share salesmen, tour guides and persistent fishing-trip operators. (We get rid of them by saying that our plane leaves in an hour.) Consequently, Mazatlán is a good place to ease into Mexican culture and practice your Spanish; you can feel confident that you can always lapse back into English for a word or two and you'll be understood. In fact, if you speak Spanish well, local people may react with astonishment.

Mazatlán's sea-level altitude is easy on those with heart problems. Residents swear that medical care and hospitals are excellent here, and they report an abundance of good, English-speaking doctors and dentists. In 1995, a new hospital with all of the latest diagnostic and surgical equipment opened here; everything is state of the art. Although Medicare isn't recognized here, most U.S. medical insurance plans cover expenses that occur outside of the country.

Mazatlán's weather is typical of the rest of Mexico's tropical coast. It's exceptionally pleasant from November until May–the dry season, a time of little or no rain and balmy temperatures. The season for rain starts in late May or June, and lasts through September. Then the weather turns warm-to-hot, and the humidity climbs. This is the most beautiful time of the year in Mexico because the hills and fields are green and fresh-looking. Yet, because of the ocean, summer temperatures are quite pleasant, with highs in the mid-80s. As in Florida, in the summertime, you need to get up early and get your tennis, bicycling or hiking over with before the weather gets too warm. A leisurely lunch is followed by a long nap and a time for reading. Later in the afternoon, you can resume outdoor activities, perhaps a swim in the surf, and be ready for a late supper, which is the norm here.

Well, what about crime in Mexican Riviera resort cities? Is it any worse than in other retirement areas in Mexico? Could it *possibly* be as dangerous as in Florida resort cities? Below is a quote from Mazatlán residents Henry and Nadine Laxen on the subject of crime in their neighborhood. (Reprinted from their Web pages, with permission. Visit their Web Site at: http://www.maztravel.com)

"To give you a feel for the level of crime in Mazatlán, let me tell you about our local newspaper, the *Noroeste*. In their local crime coverage, which is printed every day, they often include pictures of the guys who stole a bicycle, and sometimes of the gun or knife that was confiscated. Finding someone with a gun is a big deal, and gets big coverage, with pictures not only of the villain, but of the firearm as well. Can you imagine the *Los Angeles Times* doing this? They would need to publish a 100 page crime section daily if they were to include pictures of guys stealing bicycles.

"I can honestly say, that Nadine and I feel much safer living here in Mazatlán than we have living almost anywhere else in the United States. We used to live in Oakland, and going down the hill to Safeway for some milk was a truly frightening experience. Here, we have walked in the heart of downtown at midnight on several occasions, and have never felt threatened in any way. In fact, even late at night you will still pass young men and girls strolling on the streets or in the parks, holding hands and making out."

Putting all these factors together, Mazatlán might be the ideal place for a three- or six-month experiment in Mexican living. With plentiful rentals, sunny beaches and a resort atmosphere, what better place to spend a winter? If you discover that you hate Mazatlán, you can be assured that you probably won't like the rest of Mexico either. If you like most things about living here, you can consider looking for a place that suits you better.

Puerto Vallarta

For years, Puerto Vallarta was a sleepy village, isolated and cut off from the rest of Mexico–and happy to be so. The only road in was unpaved; visitors had to come by four-wheel-drive, boat or a DC3 that bounced to a landing on a dirt airstrip. When the paved road from Tepic finally broke through the tropical forest, Puerto Vallarta suddenly found itself thrust into the modern world of tourism. It also began to accumulate retirees and expatriates from the north, who formed the nucleus of today's foreign community.

Puerto Vallarta never stopped growing; today it is a thriving city of 250,000 inhabitants. Located on a long, narrow strip of land between the mountains and the sea, "PV," as its North American devotees call it, is less than a dozen blocks wide in many places. For this reason, the main part of the old town center hasn't developed the usual beach resort facade, with high-rise glass and steel buildings. Instead, hotel complexes have been forced every year to expand further north and south, where high-rise condos and luxury hotels sprout like weeds. These are the places where tourists stay–in hotels where they pay top dollar and where it costs several dollars to take a taxi into town. This north-south expansion allows the original town to retain a slight suggestion of its old village atmosphere. Cobblestone streets and ancient buildings add to the charm. The secret to affordable retirement in Puerto Vallarta is to find an apartment in the older section of town where local working people live and where permanently retired couples greatly outnumber the well-heeled. You'll find plenty of apartments available, particularly in the late spring, when the flighty "snowbirds" vacate the premises and begin their annual migration north. This is another town for testing out your tolerance for Mexico; if you find you don't care for living here, the worst that can happen is you will enjoy a long vacation at a seaside resort. The plus side is that living away from the beach is not only inexpensive, but the tourist crush isn't concentrated close to your neighborhood; it's spread out over a 20-mile stretch of beach.

Some of the more affordable housing is typically found on the hills behind town–usually eight blocks or more from the beach. Construction here is older, but in addition to favorable rent, you enjoy the bonus of gorgeous ocean views and vistas of the town below. A nice two-bedroom apartment with a view can be found for $400 per month, through one of the many English-speaking real estate agencies, But you can usually find something on your own for as little as $300. If you don't mind living a bit further from the ocean, in an all-Mexican neighborhood, (residents claim) you can find an unfurnished apartment for as little as $150 a month. Of course, you can pay much, much more for some of the gorgeous homes and villas that perch on ocean-side cliffs or cling to the hillsides above the city.

For the ultimate in elegant living, visit the luxury development north of town, Nuevo Vallarta, one of the fanciest places we've encountered in Mexico. Some houses, set back on enormous landscaped plots, would cost several millions of dollars if they were in a similar posh U.S. location. And then, other homes cost no more than you'd expect to pay for a bungalow in San Marcos, Florida, or Santa Barbara, California. (Those places aren't cheap, either.) Nuevo Vallarta is a breathtaking place, but it's not something for a couple looking for a $600-a-month retirement! For an alternative location across the bay from Puerto Vallarta, look at the discussion of Yelapa (later on in the "For the More Adventurous" section).

Many full-time American residents make their homes in Puerto Vallarta, but as in most tropical resorts, the expatriate population is somewhat impromptu. Many people stay for a few months, then they either return home or move on to try some other Mexican location. We've seen estimates ranging from 2,000 to as high as 15,000 expatriates living in Puerto Vallarta. These estimates are difficult to verify. Because people come and go so frequently, it's difficult to distinguish between retirees and visitors who are on extended vacations. Suffice to say, there are many North Americans living here; you'll have no problem finding compatible neighbors.

Because of this large foreign population, two Puerto Vallarta hospitals cater to American and Canadian patients, and they maintain bilingual staffs. These are the Medassist Hospital and the CMQ Hospital. The Crita Movil Ambulance Service, with well-equipped vehicles, is on call 24 hours a day and reportedly has English-speaking drivers.

Several public service organizations are supported by the U.S.-Canadian community. One, which was brought to our attention recently, is the America-Mexico Foundation. To raise funds, this group collects donations and holds benefits and auctions of donated goods. One major goal of the foundation is to provide scholarships for Mexican children who strive for an education but are impeded because of family financial problems. A spokesman said, "As long as the children maintain B averages or better and sustain good behavior, the foundation will help them obtain their educational goals." The program now has 200 children enrolled. Address: America-Mexico Foundation, APDO 515, Puerto Vallarta, Jalisco, Mexico 48300. Tel: (322) 3-1371.

Another organization is the The International Friendship Club (IFC), which was started in 1987 by a small group of U.S. and Canadian expatriates. Their role is organizing the international community to provide services and collect and distribute funds in response to the humanitarian and educational needs of the community. Activities of the IFC include assisting local schools, hospitals, old folks, homes, day-care centers and playgrounds. The IFC also participates in the community-wide toy distribution to children on holidays. Members started the Cleft Palate Project– which is known all over Latin America–and have helped many youngsters get the necessary operation to correct this birth defect.

Following the example of San Miguel de Allende, Ajijic and Guadalajara, Puerto Vallarta expatriates are in the process of starting a library. This project will undoubtably become the social and cultural center of the foreign community as well as further improve public relations by reaching out to the Mexican community. Those of you looking for volunteer work might seriously consider becoming part of a library-project team. This is an excellent way to become a part of the community, and meet new friends as well as to contribute to a worthwhile endeavor.

South of Puerto Vallarta, about halfway between Puerto Vallarta and Boca de Tomatlán, Mismaloya is blossoming into a retirement community. A large hillside development is underway, with some homes tucked in forest settings and others with ocean views. The beach here became famous as the film set for Richard Burton's movie "The Night of the Iguana," but Mismaloya has undergone explosive development—perhaps too fast for its size. That's the downside of Mismaloya, the danger that it might become overwhelmed by large hotels and condos and become a bit too commercial.

Time-Shares/Condominiums?

When inspecting any beach city or town along Mexico's west coast, from Mazatlán to Acapulco, you'll surely be deluged by persistent time-share salesmen. They grab you by your shirtsleeve and insist that you accept a complimentary breakfast, lunch, cruise or car rental. Should you take them up on the "free" offer, you can be sure of several hours of high-pressure sales tactics. These salespeople are experts, so keep your resistance up, or better yet, do as we learned to do when in Mazatlán: just say, "Sorry, but my plane leaves in an hour."

Time-shares are sprouting on the beaches, and a few blocks back from the water, both regular and time-share condos are popping up. Our view of time-sharing is that it should *not* have a place in anybody's retirement plans! When you pay big money for the right to stay in a condo for a couple of weeks each year, all you're doing is paying rent in advance for a condo you must share with 26 other people! It no more belongs to you than does the hotel apartment you rent for a vacation. Vacations are one thing, retirement is another. On the other hand, if you buy a condominium or house and rent it out when you don't plan on using it, that's a different story. You control all 52 weeks a year, and should you desire, you can retire full time in your condo. The key word is *control.*

We investigated one condo development in Puerto Vallarta, and we know there are similar ones in Acapulco and (probably) Mazatlán and other west coast locations. Understand, we're neither vouching for these condos nor encouraging anyone to invest, but the management rental plan sounded enticing. Prices of the condos we looked at ranged from $75,000 to $150,000 for two-bedroom units which were located on a desirable stretch of beach in a high-demand tourist area. For a percentage of the rent, a management team operates the participating units as a hotel, renting by the day or week to tourists. According to the sales force, the apartments rent for $75 per day in the low season and $125 a day during the high season. Management withholds the commission and deposits the balance of the rent money to your account.

On paper, this sounds like a great idea, but developers have a way of making things sound a lot better than they are. So beware! It all hinges upon the ability of management to keep the rentals full and to fulfill all their promises. The bottom line here is, be absolutely sure you know what you're doing when you buy this kind of condo, and *stay away* from time-shares.

Manzanillo

Manzanillo is one of Mexico's oldest cities. It was settled in the year 1522, shortly after Cortez overwhelmed the Aztecs at Tenotchtitlán (now Mexico City) during the Spanish Conquest. Manzanillo became established as Mexico's major port on the west coast. From the beginning of Spain's occupation of Mexico, treasures from China and the Philippines passed through this calm bay. Located approximately 150 miles south of Puerto Vallarta (in the state of Colima), Manzanillo isn't exactly a tourist destination in the style of Mazatlán or Acapulco. Its main occupation is as a busy marine port and railway shipping terminal. Manzanillo's downtown is strictly commercial. Devoid of elegant restaurants and tourist shops, most of the city seems rather ordinary to us.

It seems unlikely that many foreign residents would choose to live in the city of Manzanillo; instead you'll find them along the coast north of Manzanillo. This is where the resorts, condos and luxury residential communities draw tourists as well as retirees.

The number of foreigners here is small compared with the more successful resort towns along the Mexican Riviera. One reason may be that the beaches aren't as safe for swimming, due to the undertow and riptides. It's no problem for experienced swimmers or surfers, but it does keep tourism down. This doesn't displease the expatriate community at all. The places where retirees make their homes are scattered along the beaches and slightly inland. The most impressive landmark hereabouts is a magnificent complex of whitewashed villas and bungalows known as Las Hadas, or "Home of the Fairies." The architecture captures the magic of a tale out of *The Arabian Nights*. One of the attractions here is the 18-hole Las Hadas Golf Course.

Manzanillo is clearly a magnet for sports fishermen, billing itself as "the sailfish capital of the world." (Seems like we've heard this claim in other Mexican resorts!) All in all, the atmosphere here is more informal and relaxed than in Acapulco or Puerto Vallarta. Like most of the west coast, average monthly temperatures here are in the upper 70s and mid-80s year-round. The rainy months from July through September bring some hot and steamy days. (Miami, in comparison, is hotter in the summer, colder in the winter, and far more difficult to escape from when the heat becomes uncomfortable.)

Ixtapa-Zihuantanejo

Driving six hours south of Manzanillo, on a fairly good highway, you'll traverse the *Costa Grande* (the Big Coast). This is where the state of Guerrero angles 200 miles southeast from the Rio Balsas toward Acapulco. You'll travel through some interesting country– places that were unavailable to motorists until a new highway pushed through here about a decade ago. The pavement passes through quaint villages and past rustic coconut plantations, farm houses and crops of copra drying along the road shoulders. If you're looking for "authentic" Mexico, this is where you might want to visit.

The first popular retirement location you'll encounter along along the *Costa Grande* is Zihuatanejo, a little more than halfway between Manzanillo and Acapulco. Local residents affectionately refer to the town as "Zihua." The *Costa Grande* and Zihuatanejo aren't exactly newcomers to the tourist scene. Their gorgeous beaches and steep cliffs circled by forested hills in the background were attracting crowds long before the Spanish arrived. Legend has it that in the 1400s, a Tarascan Indian king built a royal bathing resort on Las Gatas Beach in Zihuatanejo Bay. However, until a paved highway from Acapulco was cut through the mountains in the 1960s, Zihua languished as a sleepy fishing village in isolated splendor. But the town woke up abruptly when developers began constructing a luxury resort on the beach at Ixtapa, a few miles north of Zihuatanejo. Before long, Zihua was being "discovered" by tourists and expatriates.

In many ways, Zihuatanejo is like the Acapulco of 40 years ago. It's evolving from a sleepy little village into a town, but mercifully it hasn't yet turned the corner to become a city. Most residents hope that it never will. Zihuatanejo's town square, the Plaza de Armas, overlooks the main beach, Playa Municipal, just beyond the palm-lined pedestrian walkway, Paseo del Pescador. At least this part hasn't changed since Zihuatanejo was still a village. In the downtown area, shops and restaurants are within a few blocks, walking distance of the Plaza de Armas.

Our favorite beach here is Playa la Ropa, a crescent of white sand about one mile in length. The beach supposedly got its name, Playa la Ropa (the clothes beach), two hundred years ago when clothing floated in from an offshore Chinese wreck. The beach is reached via the Paseo Costera, which passes some of the choice residential areas and offers great views of the nearly endless line of beaches around the bay.

Fortunately for those living in Zihuatanejo, the glamorous resort of nearby Ixtapa draws the glitzy tourist trade and crowds, thus keeping Zihuatanejo's prices within reason and its traffic flow relatively calm. Retiring here gives you the best of both worlds—quiet and affordable Zihuatanejo, with the glamour of Ixtapa just a few minutes away.

When bar-hopping in Zihuatanejo, you'll often find yacht captains and crews killing time between sailings. The harbor is popular with yachts cruising between California and Acapulco; the waterside bars never lack new faces. By the way, we always thought that retirement on a sailboat would be the ultimate. Many people do this, of course, and you'll find them in Mexican ports. However, the yachting people we've met report that getting to Mexico is a snap, but getting back north is tough, due to currents and prevailing winds. The wealthy sail their boats south, then pay someone to make the slow trek back to California.

At times, rentals are reportedly in short supply in Zihua because apartment and home building hasn't kept up with the increasing demand. Most newer construction is taking place away from the town center, especially on hills overlooking the bay. Small mountains ring the town, and the best building sites, with spectacular views of the bay, sit high on the slopes.

About 15 miles away, in Zihua's sister city of Ixtapa, ten beaches invite bathers, surfers and strollers along a dozen miles of creamy, azure coastline. Ixtapa is a luxurious beach resort with the sophistication of Acapulco but on a smaller scale and with cleaner beaches. Playa de Palmar is the main beach; protective offshore shoals and rocks break some of the surf's energy, keeping the waves safe enough for swimming and body surfing.

Ixtapa's 18-hole, professionally designed Campo de Golf is open to the public. The club has full facilities including a pro shop, a swimming pool, tennis courts, and a restaurant. Several Ixtapa hotels also have tennis courts available to the public.

Many condos going up here have time-share arrangements, and you know our opinion on that subject. Regular apartment buildings are available for rent, and an upscale housing development is underway. Therefore, Ixtapa is an alternative for those who prefer the luxury of a beach resort to the small-town environment of Zihuatanejo.

Acapulco

Most people think of Acapulco as a glamorous, expensive jet-set resort, and of course it is all of that. So, how could you consider retirement in Acapulco, with its $200-a-day hotels, costly boutiques and elegant restaurants? Impossible? Not at all. In fact, Acapulco could well be one of the more affordable of your Mexico retirement choices. The reason why is an accident of history.

Until the late 1920s, Acapulco was isolated from the outside world, until the first road was constructed that allowed anything but mules to make the trip. Suddenly, the beauty of the beaches and the idyllic climate were exposed to the world. Automobiles and buses brought tourists, and early-day airplanes started regular service. The rush was on. Hotels sprouted from nowhere, and apartments and homes went up with top speed. Later, the advent of jet travel pushed development even faster. Thus the term "jet set," which describes those characters who zipped back and forth from Hollywood and New York to their hillside homes overlooking the Bay, was coined. When John Howells was a teenager, it was common to see John Wayne, Hedy Lamar, Susan Hayward and a gaggle of other famous personalities dining in restaurants, shopping in town or playing in the surf. Of course, this was before jets, when the only air transportation was lumbering DC3s and when Acapulco's population was around 25,000. Today, there's more than a million inhabitants.

From the very beginning, Acapulco has overbuilt its facilities. Competition between hotels and rental units has always been fierce, with price-cutting the rule. The result has been a bonanza for a tourist or retiree who doesn't require the very latest of hotel or apartment accommodations.

Another important factor influencing prices in Acapulco is its geographical setting. The bay is ringed with some very steep hills. Years ago, when most people drove their autos from Mexico City and when taxis and limousines were everywhere, it was stylish to build on the hillsides for the terrific views. But today, tourist preferences have changed; people fly in and insist on hotels right on the beach. As a result, multi-story hotels and condos line the beaches like elegant monuments to the gods of tourism. And finally, Acapulco has lost favor with the world's wealthy jet setters; they've found other, more isolated hideouts. Today their homes on the hillsides are occupied by the less famous.

This shift from the hills down to the beaches rendered passé those hotels, apartments and houses that used to be luxury places up on the heights. Consequently, rents were forced downward in order to attract tenants. For less money than in Guadalajara, San Miguel de Allende or Ensenada, you can rent a spacious apartment overlooking the bay with a view that is unequaled in the world! Of course, you're not on the beach, so you can expect to climb a long way uphill to go home. Anyway, beachfront property is far too valuable to invest in single family housing!

Throughout Acapulco there is a two-tiered rental system: there are $200-a-day rooms for the two-week tourist who rents through travel agents, and there are $30-a-day rooms for the conservative tourist or retiree who doesn't demand a swimming pool and is satisfied with a ceiling fan rather than an air conditioner. To repeat: $30 a day or less can secure a clean, comfortable room in Acapulco, within a short stroll to the beach. Three hundred dollars a month can move you into an acceptable apartment, although some blocks from the beach. Luxury hotels that 30 years ago were reserved for the Hollywood crowd today are within the reach of ordinary people. Several of the more luxurious places either closed down from lack of business or have been converted into condos and apartments.

Real-estate prices, at least for properties offered for sale by expatriates, appear to be about the same as they were before the devaluation of '94–'95. Some Mexican sellers are in a mood to bargain, but local expatriates are reluctant to lower their asking prices unless they are somehow pressured to sell. Buyers often end up paying the asking price, despite vigorous bargaining. However, according to Acapulo's new U.S. Consul, a lot of homes are going on the market, so economic pressures could push prices down even more. By the way, the U.S. Consul is new to the job and well liked by Acapulco's expatriates.

One example of a bargain: a condo project called Diamante (the large, white complex you pass on your way from the airport, after Las Brisas hotel). Diamante went bankrupt after the devaluation; one bedroom condos are selling for as little as $60,000– down from the $100,000 plus before the devaluation. One Acapulco resident looked at them recently and reported the condos to be very nice, although somewhat small. He added, "I guess there are bargains here if you look hard enough, but it depends on the sellers and how badly they need the money."

As mentioned earlier in this book, with the appearance of enormous buying complexes like WalMart, K-Mart and Gigante, shopping patterns have changed in Mexico. In this respect, Acapulco was already far ahead. It had large supermarkets and malls long before the rest of the country did. Our favorite was a gourmet supermarket near Hornos Beach–a place where shopping was an adventure for luxury delicatessen treats as well as a fully stocked supermarket. We always came away burdened with goodies. This trend continues–with the full spectrum of U.S.-style shops, which carry imported goods at ordinary prices. Of course, the neighborhood markets and shops, seemingly unaffected by the wave of foreign competition, continue to serve the locals.

Restaurants are also divided into two classes. You'll find the luxurious, exquisitely designed restaurant that caters to affluent tourists, and then there are the restaurants for the rest of us ordinary residents. The basic difference, aside from the decor, is that tourist places charge the maximum and don't have to worry about serving top quality meals (because tourists in a large resort like Acapulco only visit once). The family-owned and operated establishment must serve excellent food, or they'll go out of business.

Acapulco's public transportation system is excellent; it's easy to get around on the many city buses plying the streets. Taxis are also plentiful. However, Acapulco is one place in Mexico where an auto comes in handy. Even though traffic is heavy, you will find that, with a car, you have the ability to go up into the hills and find the best view homes and bargain, quality housing. (It can be a nuisance to have to hunt down a taxi every time you want to go up or down the hill.)

Servants are more expensive here than elsewhere and may not be as loyal. This is because of the competition for help among the hotels and tourist businesses. You may find a great cook, only to have him or her discovered by a hotel restaurant and recruited away. Most North Americans aren't used to having servants anyway, so this shouldn't be any barrier to living in Acapulco.

The bottom line: if you are looking for a place in the tropics, even if only for the winter months, don't overlook Acapulco, even though you may have been told by people who have been there only as tourists that the prices are high.

Baja California

Baja California–a place with a reputation for mystery and romance–is a long peninsula that, for almost a thousand miles, juts south of the state of California. Both sides of the peninsula are lined with almost unexplored beaches. Baja is a world all its own. A wonderland of desert scenery, the peninsula is famous for secluded beaches, lost Jesuit missions, rugged mountains and deep canyons. Separated from the mainland by the blue, blue waters of the Sea of Cortez (also called the Gulf of California), the peninsula has been isolated so long that it has evolved its own flora and fauna, distinct from anywhere else in the world. Zoologists and botanists pilgrimage here to enjoy themselves.

Baja's economy, similarly isolated from the mainland, has also evolved its own economic and social characteristics. With only one highway and one railroad connecting the peninsula with Mexico's mainland, all goods and merchandise must travel over these slow routes or else arrive by ship. This increases prices to the consumer. Much merchandise comes by truck from the United States—which also makes things more expensive. Therefore, it isn't surprising to find prices and wages are higher here than on the mainland. Despite this, Baja California is still Mexico, and Baja Californians are the same friendly breed you find on the mainland.

For many people living in the western United States, Baja California is the only part of Mexico they know. This is particularly true of Californians. They fondly recall Baja's diverse attractions: long stretches of beach where enormous Pismo clams are there for the taking, moonlit grunion runs, camping, fishing, soaking up sunshine while drinking Tecate beer flavored with lemon and salt.

Baja is more than simply a place for tourists to let off steam. For uncounted numbers of West Coast residents, Baja has become a retiree's playground. In recognition of this movement, and to encourage retirement, the Mexican government relaxed the rules for property ownership in Baja, which used to be the strictest in the country. Now the land ownership laws are the same as elsewhere in Mexico. At this point, nobody knows how the rules will operate under NAFTA, but they'll probably be even more lenient.

One reason so many Californians retire in Baja California is that it's so conveniently nearby. For people retiring from southern California, having a home in Ensenada means being able to drive north to visit the grandchildren any time they choose. It means neighbors and friends they used to work with are much more likely to drop in for a weekend visit than if they had a similar residence in Puerto Vallarta or Lake Chapala. Some expatriates who own homes in the Rosarito Beach area actually commute to jobs in San Diego and vicinity.

Since most northern Baja California retirement spots are within a few hours of the border, it's no problem to run on up to San Diego or Calexico for shopping. "You'd be surprised how often I find I need a special tool or some nuts and bolts that I can't find here," said one man who is building a home in Ensenada. "In two hours, I'm in San Diego. I visit the hardware store while the wife stocks up on hard-to-find grocery items. Then it's back home after a milkshake-and-hamburger fix at some fast-food place."

Because it's convenient and close, Baja offers a way to sample Mexico's graciousness and economical living without investing excessive time or money in the adventure. Baja is an excellent place for pre-retirement planning–an opportunity to see whether you actually like Mexico and its people. Baja is a place from which to move into the Mexican culture gradually–yet be close to Hollywood and Disneyland, if that somehow makes you feel more secure. If you like what you see, you might decide to investigate a different type of Mexican retirement, on the mainland.

As we pointed out earlier, because Baja is isolated from Mexico proper, you'll find prices and wages higher and Yankee influence more apparent. Yet for the novice, these differences aren't so obvious, because prices and wages are so much less than back home that they seem downright ridiculous. In Ensenada, for example, a maid will come in to clean your house and do your laundry for $10 to $12 a day. (On the mainland, the wage might be $5 a day.) Maybe your Mexican neighbors can hire help a little cheaper, but anyone who would complain about paying these wages or even more (after all, you are comparatively wealthy) shouldn't even consider living in Mexico.

Free Zone

The northern part of Baja is known as the *zona libre* (or free zone). The government deliberately keeps this area quite relaxed as far as immigration and customs are concerned. You don't need tourist papers or an automobile permit to enter–only automobile insurance. You can usually cross the border without even saying "hello" to Mexican customs and immigration officials. Don't misunderstand: this doesn't give you any rights of residency or any legal status at all. By law, your stay is limited to 72 hours, although the law is seldom enforced–unless you're a trouble-maker. Since there is no way to prove when a tourist actually crossed the border, many Californians spend days, weeks, even months at their weekend getaways.

By no means are we encouraging you to break Mexican immigration laws by staying over the 72-hour limit–we're merely reporting on the present practices. If you plan on staying for a while, we recommend that you follow the entirely reasonable rules of the Mexican government. There are several ways to do this–all covered in the chapter on legal matters. Getting a tourist card is simple; it's yours for the asking.

Gringo investment in real estate in the *zona libre* is impressive. Everywhere you turn, particularly along the beaches, you'll find single homes, condos and luxury gated developments. But please let us encourage you to check with a locally recommended lawyer before laying out money for that ocean-view Baja property. Several scandals and horror stories have muddied the water here, with people buying homes from sellers who didn't own the property.

Rosarito Beach

Here in the *zona libre*, just a few miles from the California border, Rosarito Beach is a very popular place for retirement, second homes and vacation retreats. A four-lane highway takes you back to convenient shopping on the U.S. side of the border in short order. Rosarito Beach has a population of over 80,000, with estimates of 5,000 or more North Americans, mostly Californians, living here.

The town abounds with small ranch-style homes, crowded together and landscaped like suburban neighborhoods across the border–but with a taco flavor. Although many sections of town are typical Baja-grungy, you'll also find several upscale, gated communities reminiscent of southern California developments. Folks who live here claim that the beach is one of the finest in Baja.

The retirees here have formed a club called the "United Society of Baja California," complete with a monthly newspaper filled with local news and listings of rentals and property available in the Rosarito Beach area. This place is for those who need to be within easy driving distance to San Diego. It's Mexico, of course, but less Mexico-like than the rest of Baja.

As you travel farther south, you'll encounter numerous attractive gringo communities perched along the ocean cliffs, San Antonio Shores being one of the largest. These are mostly gated or restricted access developments, and almost exclusively inhabited by gringos. Most homes are used as weekend getaways, but many are lived in full time. The architecture trends toward tasteful old-Spanish homes with red tile roofs and adobe-like walls. Along with the upscale communities between Rosarito and Ensenada, you'll find a few areas distinguished by cheap, slapjack construction, more on the order of fishing camps. In fact, that's exactly what some places are: fishing camps. The better developments have security guards and limited access to outsiders.

Ensenada

Toward the lower limit of the *zona libre,* Ensenada is the metropolis of west-coast Baja. It's grown from the sleepy little fishing and tourist village of 40 years ago–when we used to spend some winter months there–to a bustling city of 200,000 inhabitants. Fishing and tourism are still big industries, but the momentum of industry and shipping business has grown impressively. The actual number of gringos living here is difficult to ascertain–so many are continually coming and going. But there's no question that several thousand permanently make their homes in Ensenada, and thousands more are part-time residents. Ensenada, by the way, has three language schools where you can immerse yourself in Spanish (two are listed in our Internet directory). This may be the nearest place to the border where you can get total immersion in Spanish learning, small classes, a native Spanish teacher and living quarters with a non-English-speaking family.

When asked why they chose a Ensenada as a retirement location, all those interviewed listed weather as a major consideration. "It has a balmy Mediterranean kind of climate," points out one retiree. "It rarely gets over 80 degrees and almost never below 50 degrees. With low humidity, it just seems like spring all year around." Another resident said, "I live in the most expensive neighborhood in Ensenada, yet I don't have air conditioning, nor do I know anyone who does." Few houses have heating systems, either, since the ocean keeps winter weather from dropping to extremes. For all but the most luxurious homes, an electric heater or a fireplace suffices for even the coldest January days.

Ensenada has several motels with small apartment units that rent by the month. Staying in one of these is an excellent way of trying out the area and seeing whether this might be your dream retirement place. The town itself is full of rentals, at rock-bottom prices, provided you don't insist on having English-speaking neighbors. One man we interviewed, a widower from Tacoma, reports that he pays about $80-a-month rent for his place in Ensenada. He says the neighbors are very friendly and keep an eye on his house while he is away. (We didn't check the neighborhood, so we can't guarantee that his flowery descriptions are accurate.)

A few miles south of Ensenada, just before the *zona libre* ends, you'll find the ad hoc settlement of Punta Banda. This is a large collection of the most rustic and innovative homes you can imagine. Most residents here started living in travel trailers or motor homes, many of which evolved in an interesting way. Typically, a place began with something like a 20-foot travel trailer. The first year, the owners laid out a flagstone patio and put up a picket fence to spiffy things up. Since a 20-footer is somewhat cramped for living space, the next year they built on a living room, so they could spread out a little, and perhaps added a storage room. Then, as the grandkids started coming to visit, they added on a bedroom or two. By this time, the old travel trailer was beginning to fall apart, so they pulled it out and replaced it with a kitchen. In its final stage, the compound rambles all over the place and has no relationship to the original conception of an RV lot.

The total number of residents in Punta Banda is about 800 (all gringos), and they've developed a close-knit social structure. They've organized a club they call Sociedad de Amigos de Punta Banda, an organization with about 300 members. The advantage of RV living in this part of Baja is that it can be a year-round thing; you don't have to flee furnace-like summer temperatures as you do on the Sea of Cortez side.

A few miles south of Punta Banda the *zona libre* ends. From here on you need tourist papers. (Make sure you get your papers stamped here, because the next place to do it is in La Paz.) This is where the *real* Baja starts, according to four-wheel-drive enthusiasts and true desert lovers. Here, rolling hills and rugged cliff-like mountains are sparsely covered with strange, one-of-a-kind plants, like the majestic cardon cactus (similar to the saguaro cactus on the mainland), squat barrel cactus and spiked plants of all descriptions. This is the only place on earth where you'll see things like the weird-looking cirio trees–commonly called bojuum trees–which grow like upside-down carrots or thick-trunked elephant trees which bleed a blood-colored sap when punctured with a knife. Smoke trees, salt pines and cacti of all descriptions add to the inventory of desert wonders. Several small communities, with occasional North Americans in residence, string along the paved highway. Some interesting places, like the wine-growing valleys around Santo Tomas and San Vincente, might be suitable for gringos who can get by without speaking English every day.

San Felipe

On the Sea of Cortez side of the peninsula (but still in the *zona libre* part of Baja), the town of San Felipe has mushroomed into a major center for vacationers and retirees. The attraction here is miles of sandy beaches washed with warm gulf waters–a scenic setting below the towering peaks of the Sierra San Pedro

Martir. San Felipe has become a favorite with part-time retirees, those who customarily winter in Tucson or Yuma. They've discovered that by driving 120 miles south of the border on a good paved road, they can enjoy a winter retirement in Mexico. Their grandkids and old friends can visit for the weekend without a major transportation problem.

When we first started going there 30 years ago, the town consisted of two bars, a gas station, a motel, a couple of RV parks and a row of disintegrating shrimp boats, beached by some storm of yesteryear. Probably fewer than 500 people lived there year-round. The streets were littered with broken beer bottles and trash. The town has changed tremendously over the last 30 years. For one thing, when you first come into town, you are greeted by a tasteful set of arches and desert landscaping. The main streets are now clean and paved with asphalt, whereas before, they had been paved with trash-littered sand and dirt. Today, San Felipe is bustling–with a long commercial artery, loaded with restaurants and businesses paralleling the beach. The town even boasts three banks!

Well-patronized RV and camping parks line the beach north and south of the town's center. Some of them have constructed clever, two-story shelters over the RV patios, which serve as shelters for the picnic tables. The second floor presents a shaded view of the Sea of Cortez. It's a great place to wake up in the morning and look out over the sea, shimmering and blue-green, with fishing and shrimping boats crisscrossing in the early haze.

Between 14,000 and 15,000 Mexican citizens live here today, joined by an additional 3,000 Americans and Canadians who have either part- or full-time living arrangements. During the height of the winter season, at any given time, their numbers are increased by an average of 2,000 tourists. Some of the more heat-proof northerners stick it out all year, but most flee north in the summer. The problem here–unlike on Baja's Pacific side–is fierce, incredibly hot summer weather. The sun literally bakes the town, making Death Valley look like a springtime resort in comparison. We're talking 110–120 degrees. At that level, you needn't mention low humidity; it's just plain hot! However, pleasant falls, winters, and springs make up for the fierce summer weather by providing gloriously sunny days, perfect for enjoying the outdoors. You can be pretty sure it won't rain on your picnic here–sometimes a year or two can go by without a drop. But when it does rain, as anywhere in Baja, the desert suddenly bursts into a symphony of lush green and brilliant flowers. This spectacle is an emotional experience that makes waiting worthwhile. By the way, fishing is fantastic here, with huge sea bass and enormous red snappers gnashing at your bait.

San Felipe is unusual because of the high numbers of North Americans in residence or visiting. As a result, although the ambience is Mexican, most aren't exposed to Mexican culture to any extent; most all your neighbors will be from the United States or Canada. But many prefer it this way. They don't have to adjust to another culture and don't feel pressured to learn a new language. However, those who care to, find opportunities to practice Spanish and make Mexican friends.

The winter RV population accounts for a large percentage of gringos. Like RV retirees in the United States, they waste no time in forming social organizations. The minute they move into their winter quarters, they form clubs and elect officers just as they do in the States. Among the RV groups is a chapter of Alcoholics Anonymous and an organization called Las Amigas, a ladies club that holds luncheon meetings every Friday. Although not very "Mexican," for the most part, San Felipe is becoming popular in its own way as a Mexican retirement center.

Although many North Americans own property in town, most lease or build homes to the north and south of San Felipe–either in one of the many fancy developments or on individual beach or ocean-view lots. Rentals are sometimes difficult to find because homes are rented out in advance by people who return there year after year. Several rental agents in town can usually find something, we've been told.

Labor costs are higher here than in Ensenada because of the booming economy. Still, by stateside measures, wages are very low. A maid will work for as little as $9 a day, and a gardener for $60 a week. Electricity costs from $12 to $50 a month, depending on how economical you try to be. If you use an air conditioner during the summer, expect to top that $50 figure.

To sum up, living in San Felipe makes for a different kind of Mexican retirement–one that is basically part-time and an alternative to the usual Brownsville-McAllen or Lake Havasu kind of winter escape.

Baja California Sur

The peninsula is broken into two political entities, north and south, with the territory of Baja California Sur only recently elevated to statehood. The first time John Howells visited Baja California Sur was in 1963, on a four-wheel-drive camping adventure. In those days, driving the unpaved trails of Baja was a true safari, with many hard days of bouncing through clouds of dust and climbing rocky ledges from the top to bottom of the peninsula. Baja fans formed a sort of cult in those days, with adventurers who actually made it all the way to La Paz or Cabo San Lucas being awarded the highest honors. During the journey, John reports asking himself many times, "Why am I doing this?" His wife asked the same question, although in a much more intense manner. An overnight ferry from La Paz to the mainland avoided a return trip and probably saved a marriage.

Today, a fairly good asphalt highway links the northern and southern parts of Baja; driving is a snap. A long expanse of almost uninhabited country separates the population centers of the north from the south. The drive is long, but worth it; it's liberally endowed with spectacular and unforgettable scenery. Scattered along the way are some tiny settlements, an occasional town and always friendly, helpful people. Sometimes residents seem quite shy, but if you practice your Spanish with them, you'll find they warm up very quickly.

The people in the lower parts of Baja interact with Americans differently than do Mexicans who live nearer the border–and for good reason. Here, they see a different *type* of American tourist. Those "ugly Americans" in search of boisterous weekends, gaudy souvenirs, cheap thrills and hell-raising usually don't stray very far from Tijuana or Mexicali. Tourists who bother to travel this far are different; they obviously appreciate Mexico and the fascinating Baja scenery, or they wouldn't be here. The local people sense this, and they treat you accordingly. They haven't met the other kind of gringos.

As in other parts of Mexico, you'll see the Green Angels (*Angeles Verdes*) at least once or twice a day, as they patrol for motorists in trouble. They carry a truckload of spare parts and gasoline. The drivers are excellent mechanics, speak some English, and the services are free (except for parts and gasoline, all available at cost). The trucks are all equipped with two-way radios, so they can be reached either by CB or by calling their "hotline" number, 5-20-6123.

Incidentally, along this stretch of highway are some of the most innovative automobile mechanics in the world. Just because there are few or no parts for repairs doesn't stop them. They perform miracles by recycling parts from old hulks, reworking them, and fitting them into automobiles that aren't even closely related. Still, don't let this lull you into venturing into the open country of Baja without a vehicle in good repair, and don't forget to keep an eye on your gasoline gauge.

The highway is paved and, although pock-marked in places, is in fairly good shape. Signs posted along the way proclaim that the highway was not intended to be a "high-speed" highway and caution you to drive carefully. Good advice. Many stretches have no shoulders, so wide vehicles, such as RVs and travel trailers, should use special caution. At times, every other vehicle seems to be an RV. Fortunately, traffic along the highway is usually light and relatively tension-free.

It isn't until you get as far south as La Paz that you begin to encounter North Americans in any considerable number. From here to the tip of the Baja Peninsula, the weather undergoes a subtle change. At this point, the cool water of the Pacific Ocean pushes its way into the Sea of Cortez, moderating the temperature a bit. Summers are somewhat tolerable from La Paz south to Los Cabos, at land's end, and expatriates aren't forced to evacuate every May. And here, when it rains it rains in summer rather than in winter, as is the case up north. Therefore, year-round living is feasible.

Make no mistake, this is still desert country. Rainfall is scanty, with as long as two years between rain storms—then it comes in torrential downpours that turn the arroyos into raging rivers. By the way, be very careful when driving in one of the infrequent rain storms–*anywhere* in Baja. Slight dips in the road can quickly become deep, swirling currents of water. Best wait for someone else to splash through before trying to ford what looks like a shallow rush of water crossing the highway! Okay, so it only comes halfway up on the ducks; wait anyway.

La Paz, the Pearl of Baja

The Sea of Cortez received its name when the conquistador Hernando Cortez established a town here for the purpose of collecting the fantastically rich harvest of pearls in the bay. (Some oysters today still yield an occasional pearl.) La Paz is the largest city in Baja California Sur, with close to 200,000 inhabitants. And it seems to be growing larger by the day. La Paz is an unusually clean city, and it attracts a large number of North American residents, perhaps a thousand of whom choose to live here year-round. La Paz has four well-kept trailer parks, and many RV buffs regularly bring their rigs by ferry boats. Some RV and boating enthusiasts claim this is absolutely the best place in Baja for winter retirement.

La Paz gives you the true feeling of a substantial Mexican city–more like a mainland city without the helter skelter of many Baja towns. It has an attractive downtown, nice shopping centers and many excellent restaurants.poised along the road that curves about the picturesque waterfront. The city center has businesses of all kinds, from good hardware stores to fine jewelry boutiques. Unlike northern Baja California tourist centers, the gringo presence here is subdued. That's because La Paz is a prosperous, bustling city in its own right; tourism and retirement are incidental to everyday commerce.

The harbor and marina form the focal point of the city; many North American residents live here on yachts, and many like it so well, they decide to stay. A good place to meet fellow countrymen is by the marina, at the Dock Cafe, where gringos convene for informal breakfasts every morning. Throughout the winter, a sea-going oriented group, the Club Cruceros, meets the third Tuesday of each month at Los Arcos Hotel. Meetings are open to everyone–whether you own a yacht or not–and the club maintains a trading library at its clubhouse at Marina La Paz. The clubhouse hosts informal social gatherings, where friends meet and discuss current events, lie about the fish they almost caught and surmise the best places to catch lobsters.

Several agreeable neighborhoods in the town of La Paz are quite suitable for retirement. Most are in mixed Mexican-North American areas, rather than gringo enclaves. Housing costs range from very affordable to exorbitant, all in the same neighborhoods. The bulk of the expatriates seems to gravitate toward neighborhoods on the southern edge of La Paz, where well-to-do Mexican families and gringos congregate. We enjoy visiting our friends there who have a lovely home built around a swimming pool and garden. The road into La Paz is a smooth four-laner, and shopping centers along the way make for convenience.

The local expatriate community is well regarded by its neighbors because of its participation in local affairs. With the Club Cruceros leading the way, the community holds fund-raising events to raise money for children in need of medical and other help. Every December, they host a bazaar–with an auction, food stands and entertainment. The proceeds are used for Christmas gifts and school supplies for the kids.

Daily ferry boats connect with the mainland at Mazatlán and Topolobampo, and from time to time, a ferry crosses from Cabo San Lucas (farther south) to Puerto Vallarta. If you decide to make the Topolobampo or Cabo-Vallarta ferry crossing, be sure to get your automobile papers in La Paz if you didn't already get them farther north. (It's easy to miss the customs stop.) The Registro Federal de Vehículos is near the intersection of Calle Belisario Dominguez and Calle 5 de Febrero. The papers are free, but if you don't have them, you can't get on the ferry (and if you drive to Cabo San Lucas without the documents, you'll have to return to La Paz to get them). Also, if for some reason your tourist visa hasn't been stamped by this time, go to the immigration office at Paseo Alvaro Obregon and Calle Mueller. You can't cross to the mainland without it, and you aren't legally in Mexico until this is done.

Los Cabos

One of the biggest explosions of development and population increase is underway on the lower end of the peninsula, an area known as Los Cabos. Consisting of the area between Cabo San Lucas and San José del Cabo–once widely separated, now almost twin cities–the Los Cabos area is literally sprouting hotels, condos and housing developments. Some folks come because of Los Cabos' classic desert scenery and balmy climate, but most have designs on the game fish, so abundant just off the coast. Others love the area's four excellent golf courses. Sometimes dubbed the Pebble Beach of Baja, Cabo San Lucas boasts two championship courses, and San José del Cabo claims two famous courses.

An international airport sits halfway between the towns, making it convenient for friends and family to visit those ensconced in their retirement homes. Flights to the mainland depart with great frequency, and as mentioned earlier, a ferry boat sometimes operates between Cabo San Lucas and Puerto Vallarta. I can highly recommend this trip; the staterooms for the overnight trip are comfortable, the food is okay, and there's sometimes a live orchestra for dancing in the nightclub-like lounge.

Because of its popularity, housing prices in the Cabos area can be shocking. We've seen condos, which would barely fetch $100,000 in Mazatlán, selling for over $300,000. Most houses on the beach, or with good ocean views, command prices that would be expensive even in California or Florida. To be fair, though, we also have friends who bought a very nice condo–although without an ocean view–for $45,000.

Prices go up daily, but North Americans seem to be buying condos as fast as the Mexicans can build them. The recent devaluation of the peso hasn't bothered the real-estate industry here, since prices have always been quoted in dollars.

Why the boom? We really don't understand it at all. Although Baja, is wonderful, after awhile, you may get homesick for some green plants, forests and wildflowers, instead of sand and cactus. (And the parts of Baja that we like best are the rustic, undeveloped places where gringos are still novelties.) Yet when interviewed, most North American residents insist this is the best place in all of Mexico to retire. "I wouldn't even consider living on the mainland," is the typical reply. "We love Baja, and we wouldn't care if it costs *more* to live here than it does back home!" They point to the astonishingly blue ocean, the rugged cliffs with surf frothing against the rocky shore, and the crystal-clear skies. "Where else in the world could I have a view like this from my living room?" To quote a cliché, it's all in the eye of the beholder.

This economic boom has had an effect upon the cultural atmosphere of Baja. With higher prices and almost a dollar economy, wages have naturally risen for the natives, and employment is at an all-time high. Construction workers earn from $200 to $300 a month, as opposed to $100 or less on the mainland. However, even though workers earn big money for Mexico, prices are so high in tourist facilities that Mexicans seldom patronize them. Nice restaurants and bars are exclusively gringo. After all, a worker making $12 a day can't really afford to lift many $2 beers with the gringos. Here, there are *three* economic realities–one for tourists, one for gringo residents and one for Mexicans.

San José del Cabo

In our first edition, we hinted that San José del Cabo was Baja's "well-kept secret." Today, it's undergoing an even more vigorous boom than Cabo San Lucas. Some secret! About 30 miles north of Cabo San Lucas, San José del Cabo was our favorite town in all of the peninsula; at that time, it was totally unspoiled, like something out of a Hollywood movie set. In the book, we described San José del Cabo as "an old town with sparkling white houses, dressed in flowers, neat as an old maid's bedroom."

Not surprisingly, San José del Cabo was "discovered" (we hope not because of our book) and retirees began moving in. They bought empty buildings–some centuries old–converted them into plush homes and then waited breathlessly for new condo developments to become available. Restaurants opened on side streets, competing with one another to bring in gringo customers.

Although the town doubled and then tripled in size since we reported on it in the original version of *Choose Mexico*, this growth was mostly outward. The center of town has fortunately escaped "renewal" and modernization. It looks pretty much as it must have a century and a half ago, with the landscaped squares and grassy parks intact and the old-fashioned flavor of Mexico pure.

A restaurant owner and several businessmen we spoke with insist that as much as 40 percent of San José del Cabo residents now are North American. That's somewhat difficult to believe, but there's no question that there are several thousand living there.

The southern edge of town is where the most development has taken place. If the boom continues, numerous condominium complexes and individual homes threaten to spread all the way to Cabo San Lucas. The builders deserve credit for the tasteful designs, with old Spanish colonial styles prevalent. Because of a certain amount of over-building, prices aren't as high as you might imagine. We have friends who own places here, and seem to have no problem renting them when they are back in the States.

Prices anywhere in Los Cabos are much higher than on the mainland. If you're reading this book because of its "$600 a month" subtitle, you'd better figure on a tighter budget. One woman we interviewed–a widow from Tacoma–reported that she paid $350 a month for a small apartment near the main square and that her food costs were around $200; she ate at a restaurant almost every night. That would leave $50 a month for everything else included in a budget. That would be a long stretch for a $600 budget. She does okay, only because her Social Security is around $900 a month. She reported saving a little out of that every month.

The beaches are a couple of kilometers from San José del Cabo. Oddly enough, they aren't fully developed. One would expect large hotels and condos along this nice stretch of beach. At the time of our last visit, there was just a little village called La Playa. We found one store and a couple of restaurants, and that's about it. If it hasn't boomed by now, this might still be a place to find inexpensive beach property.

Cabo San Lucas

The name Cabo San Lucas seems to have a magical quality for many people, and they're convinced that "Cabo" is the ultimate place in all of Baja California. We have never understood its fascination for many North Americans. To us, Cabo San Lucas is a large, sprawling place, without a real "downtown" section—unless you count a concentration of souvenir shops and incredibly loud gringo bars.

This is a new town, with few buildings over 30 years old, so it isn't surprising that Cabo doesn't maintain the traditional Spanish-Mexican architecture found in San José del Cabo. Most construction doesn't bother pretending to be anything other than new, utilitarian and no-nonsense.

Nevertheless, countless North Americans have fallen in love with Cabo and seem to be standing in line to buy the next new house or condo. Tourists fly down from everywhere in the United States and Canada for the incredible sailfish and marlin sport-fishing and they are happy to pay $900 a week for a one-bedroom apartment that would cost $900 for *two months* on the mainland. One development offers luxury homes and condos starting at $250,000. That's for a small one—who knows how much for a "big" one? We've heard rumors that a million bucks isn't out of range! Of course, there are affordable homes and condos, with great views of the ocean. But affordable is a relative term here. What you'd pay for a modest little home would buy something breathtaking on Mexico's mainland.

Despite our puzzlement as to why people are fighting to buy property here, the fact is that many of those who love Baja wouldn't consider living anywhere else. There's something special about the desert that attracts some people but repels others. Of course, the fishing there is marvelous, and for many Baja residents, that is reason enough to love Baja.

You needn't live in Cabo San Lucas or San José del Cabo to enjoy the best of this southern-most part of Baja. Take a look at our section on retirement sites for the more adventurous to learn about small towns, villages and beach hangouts in the Los Cabos area.

At the risk of making enemies of some Baja-lovers, we have to question the inflated prices in the lower tip of the peninsula. Is it worth the extra investment to live in Baja Sur? Obviously, the answer to the question by many who live in Cabo San Lucas and its environs is a resounding "yes." Indeed, there's a sense of romance, beauty and mystery about the Baja desert that isn't to be found elsewhere. There's a certain crispness in the dry air and the breezes off the sea that makes it a special place. The way nature balances life and environment with delicate perfection reveals some deeply miraculous secrets of the universe. Again, the only answer seems to be found within yourself. You have to go and "try it before you buy it."

Driving in Baja

Driving here is no different from driving in other parts of Mexico: don't drive at night, have insurance, drive carefully. The roads are average for Mexico–which says a lot for Baja because, until a few years ago, most roads were dirt trails liberally spotted with two-foot-deep potholes filled with powder dust.

Shirley Miller, in her travel article, "Baja Alone" (from *Mexico West Newsletter*), describes her trip driving alone from California to the tip of Baja and back. She reports, "Well, all I can say is that a woman alone driving the Baja highway from Tijuana to Cabo San Lucas is safer than she would be driving into downtown Los Angeles. Nary a problem with gasoline, my trusty 1980 Chevy pickup, the roads, or anything else, for that matter." Her only caution is that one should bring plenty of cassette tapes, because reception on the car radio fades rapidly as you get further away from civilization.

For the More Adventurous

The vast majority of North Americans who choose retirement or long-term living in Mexico will join one of the well-established English-speaking colonies in places like Guadalajara, San Miguel de Allende or Cuernavaca. This makes good sense; they know they'll find a welcoming community of expatriates and friendly neighbors to help them get settled in their new surroundings. They'll find excellent medical facilities with English-speaking doctors and nurses. Transition into a new culture is infinitely easier when you are surrounded by people who speak your language and who, themselves, have had to adapt.

However, not everybody requires the nurturing ambiance of a large gringo society. Some might prefer to blend totally into the landscape of a Mexican village or a small town where English is a foreign language. These people are more interested in adventures rather than comforts. This is particularly true of some of those newly entering the age of retirement: the advance guard of the "baby boomer" generation who are already in their 50s and rapidly moving on.

With early retirement incentives and downsizing in today's business world, many younger folks are being cut loose into the world of leisure time and retirement, whether they like it or not. This new wave of retirees (voluntary and otherwise) were just becoming adults during the Vietnam War era, and they tend to view the world differently from those who matured in Korean War times or earlier. The new retirees were the "younger generation" of the 1960s. Before they settled down to becoming successful yuppies, these baby boomers (now graying at the temples) preferred roughing it when they traveled. They enjoyed backpacking and international travel on a shoestring. Rustic accommodations were just fine–part of the adventure. For many of them, the luxury of Puerto Vallarta or the picture-book glamour of San Miguel de Allende could be a bit bourgeois and "older generation" for their taste.

For these adventurous souls–as well as any others too free-spirited to march to the conventional drumbeat–we'll now take a look at some alternative living situations in Mexico. But before you start packing, you ought to think about how you will fit in to some of these lifestyles.

Some places described here are small towns or villages with just a few expatriates in residence. In the larger towns and cities mentioned, only a handful of gringos make their homes. If you don't need a wide circle of friends and acquaintances, that's not a bad situation. It's fascinating how a tremendous level of camaraderie develops among gringos who reside in places where the English-speaking population is small. It doesn't take long before you know every expatriate in town, even those who live in the boondocks and only visit the village to shop occasionally. On the other hand, in a large city with many expatriates, you're always a stranger to those outside your immediate circle of friends.

An important item that younger retirees seldom consider is medical care. Typically one doesn't begin to worry about hospital quality and doctors until one's health begins to falter. Therefore, along with descriptions of these alternative retirement possibilities, comes a recommendation to check out the health care situation. (If you're in good health and consider yourself made of iron, you'll probably ignore this advice.) Small-town clinics can be *very* rustic, and village doctors are often newly graduated medical students fulfilling their required assignment of one-year public service. (They're stationed in the village because no regular doctor is willing to work there.)

Before deciding to live in a place where *nobody* speaks English, however, you need to examine your requirements for social interaction. Yes, living life in a totally Spanish-speaking environment sounds fascinating. But unless you speak the language, you may feel uncomfortable when you can't communicate with your neighbors beyond exchanging greetings or asking a storekeeper the price of an item. As mentioned earlier in the book, you don't "pick up" a language simply by being exposed to it. Sometimes it's essential to be near other English speakers, people to turn to in emergencies. Therefore, the places mentioned in this section have at least some English speakers, but whether they will have a "critical mass" large enough to suit you is left to your personal investigation. If you really want to immerse yourself in the culture, you can do that anywhere in Mexico; no law says you have to associate with gringos just because they are there.

Don't think that the places mentioned in this section are the only choices for off-the-beaten path retirement. Mexico is full of options. The towns discussed below are either the better-known ones or those we're personally acquainted with and enjoy visiting.

Guanajuato

Many people consider Guanajuato Mexico's most beautiful and romantic town. Certainly its architectural splendor, physical setting and pervasively European look and feel place it in the running for that title. Its location, on the slopes of a canyon, makes for narrow streets and numerous stairways. Rather than having a single central plaza or *zócalo*, like most Mexican towns, it has a number of small parks, each with its own special character.

The University of Guanajuato, with a 250-year history and a modern campus, is considered one of Mexico's best. Inside and out, the Juarez Theater displays nineteenth-century opulence, but annually plays host to the Cervantes Festival which showcases the international cultural treasures of the twentieth century.

For reasons we do not fully understand, Guanajuato, unlike nearby San Miguel de Allende, does not have many foreign retirees. The number has always been difficult to pin down. Perhaps one reason is that this community is often the choice of people who do not want to be surrounded by large numbers of their compatriots and who do not publicize their presence there. However, we do know that more than 30 U.S. and Canadian residents did meet recently to discuss their common interests. We believe that it is safe to assume that there are at least 100 North Americans settled in that community and that their numbers will grow, particularly if the number of foreigners in San Miguel continues to grow and people who want a more Mexican setting begin to look elsewhere.

Close to the Southwest Border

Several readers have asked about retirement places on the west coast that are closer to the border than Mazatlán. We wish we could locate an idyllic place for you, but it isn't all that easy. From the border south to Hermosillo, we've found few places where Americans might want to live. This is desert country without the desert attractions we expect in places like Palm Springs or Phoenix. Also, many Mexican desert towns exist on a marginal economy, and can have very rustic living conditions.

The closest nice-looking place in western Mexico is Hermosillo, about a three-and-a-half hour drive south of Nogales. Modern, clean and prosperous, Hermosillo is one of our favorite stopovers on our way south. The downtown is pleasant, with traditional parks and squares, and people seem friendly. The weather here is similar to Phoenix's, although probably with even less humidity. As you may surmise, summers are hot. Hermosillo's prosperity comes from agriculture; it's the center of a rich farming region. A number of gringos live here, most of them engaged in agriculture in some way or another.

Saltillo, a town not far from the Texas border, is another example of a modern city where you could try traditional Mexican lifestyles. Because of the university and an active student population of gringos studying Spanish, there is a contingent of North Americans residing there, so you won't be totally on your own. Since the city sits at a high elevation, summers are delightful. The downtown section, with its many good restaurants, is clean and modern. You'll find any type of residential area you might care for, ranging from luxurious to moderate to modest.

Yelapa: A Tropical Paradise

Some people dream of living in a tropical village, where there are no automobiles or electricity and where pigs and chickens run loose in the streets. Those of you who've vacationed in Puerto Vallarta have probably taken the cruise boat to Yelapa, about an hour's sail from P.V. The beach is a delightful medley of tropical sand, sun and music, with a few tequila sunrises thrown in. Typically, the visitor has lunch in one of the palm-thatched *palapa* restaurants, strolls the narrow streets of Yelapa's small village, and returns to Puerto Vallarta on the boat, with the band playing and margaritas flowing.

These visitors miss the "real" Yelapa, much to the delight of the "real" Yelapa residents. Yelapa is as different from Puerto Vallarta as different can be. With dirt streets, no electricity, and until recently, no telephone, Yelapa lives 50 years in the past. Television sets (for those who need them) are run from 12-volt car batteries, and the one lonely telephone occupies a booth in the center of the village. Residents are still debating whether a phone is a good idea or not. They fear this means electricity, which will mean the end of romantic candles and kerosene lamps, is next.

Thea and Roger, who've lived there off and on since 1981, said, "There are probably a hundred of us gringos living here at any given time. Not so many-that we don't recognize almost everyone as we do our shopping in the one grocery store." They also pointed out that the kinds of retirees living here permanently are truly unusual people. "Writers, artists, musicians, philosophers, we have 'em all."

However, it isn't all sweet music and tropical breezes. Several drawbacks prevent more people from moving to Yelapa. For one thing, you can't own the land your house is built on. This land is officially part of the Indian reservation, so title belongs to either the tribe, the municipality, or to somebody other than the residents. Nobody is completely sure. So, when a gringo "buys" a house or builds one, he is always aware of his tentative position.

Another drawback is the difficulty in getting back and forth to the mainland; the only way is by water. Until recently, the only public transportation was by the tourist steamers, but today they have five "water taxis" which carry passengers for about $7 each way. Some residents resent this innovation, for that may mean even more visitors!

San Blas

For a tropical village (small town, actually), that's "unspoiled" and truly Mexican–yet not as unspoiled as Yelapa–you might consider San Blas. Reputedly a pirate hangout during the days of the Manila galleons, the town tries to maintain a "buccaneer" motif. Actually, the town was founded as a naval base to *chase* pirates and as a place to outfit expeditions for the colonization of the west coast. Ships sailing out of San Blas established colonies as far north as Alaska. Yes, Alaska. The city of Valdez, Alaska, was named for the Spanish captain Valdez, who sailed out of San Blas to plant a royal colony there. Enough history.

As a tropical village, San Blas is a jewel. It's a subdued place of a few thousand inhabitants, where often you'll see a momma pig herding her litter of piglets along the sandy streets. (Most streets are unpaved.) Many local people live in thatched-roof houses. Some buildings along the square date back to the time when the king's sailors used San Blas's main street for shore leave.

For some reason or other, this part of the coast always seems to be green and lush while the rest of the west suffers from lack of rainfall during the winter season. Even during the severe drought of 1988, this stretch of beach looked marvelously tropical and verdant.

Housing and food are as inexpensive in San Blas as anywhere in Mexico, according to the year-round, English-speaking residents we interviewed. One person, who was in the process of finding a place for the summer, told us that he had his choice of half a dozen houses for around $200 a month. (Costs vary widely depending upon the season.) Summers here are hot and exceptionally humid–the kind of weather that makes you understand the custom of an afternoon siesta. One serious drawback to year-round living in San Blas is the seasonal appearance of "no-see-ums," tiny, almost invisible gnats that delight on feeding on any victim not liberally doused with insect repellent. The town has never been able to battle the little critters successfully. For this reason, you can have San Blas almost to yourself during the summers.

Matachén and Playa los Cocos are about a ten minute drive from San Blas, and are very rustic but picturesque villages. The view of the mountains and Matachén Bay are marvelous. Then, if you follow the road that skirts the ocean, you come to a village called Santa Cruz, which is also worth investigating. We've met several people who regularly haul fishing boats there and spend several months with the surf lapping at their beach-front site.

North of San Blas are a string of picturesque beach villages. The people here are friendly, and the villages are small. Most have a few Americans residents. A particularly inviting village is San Francisco, about an hour north of Puerto Vallarta. It is growing quickly, but prices of homes are still at bargain levels.

Boca de Tomatlán

Not very far south of Puerto Vallarta is one of west-coast Mexico's prettiest rustic villages. Boca de Tomatlán is the picture of tropical paradise as it clings to the sloping canyon walls where the Tomatlán river empties into the Pacific. The mouth of the river has a shifting sandbar which turns the river into a small lake at high tide. The steep walls of the canyon's mouth tame the surf by forming a small bay where boats can anchor and children can float on inner tubes. Add tropical vegetation, and you have an idyllic scene.

Despite Boca de Tomatlán's easy access, very few gringos make their homes there. As best we can tell, there are only two or three families who own property here, and they only stay here part time. A few years ago, before the movie actor and director John Huston died, you could occasionally see him sampling the delicious freshwater lobsters and quaffing a cold beer in one of Boca's tiny restaurants. Huston had a house on the beach just around the opening of the river. It could only be reached by boat.

In an earlier edition of *Choose Mexico*, we predicted that Boca de Tomatlán would be the next boom area for retirement, but we were mistaken. It's still on the list of possibilities, however.

Puerto Escondido

With the completion of a paved highway south from Acapulco, Mexico's southwestern corner, known as the *Costa Chica,* is now accessible. The highway passes through some fascinating places, many of which could make outstanding retirement spots for those who don't need English-speaking neighbors. In one area, the inhabitants are descendants of black slaves who have lived in isolation here and have preserved some of their old customs from Africa. Another stretch of highway takes you through the only place in Mexico we know of where women still dress every day in pre-Colombian costume: beautifully woven skirts of cochineal-dyed material.

Back in the 60s, Puerto Escondido was "discovered" by the surfing and backpacking student set. Its beaches rank among the finest on Mexico's west coast. Known as one of the premier surfing spots in all of Mexico, people come here for the huge waves that come rolling in as high as a house and then curl over to form a tube in which surfers can defy death. The waves here give the term "high-rollers" a new meaning. If you're brave enough, you can body surf along the beach with the highest waves, but most people our age tend to go to the southern portion of the beach to catch gentler rollers.

We find Puerto Escondido to be one of the most beautiful and welcoming beach communities on Mexico's west coast. Thankfully, the big developers and tourist promoters haven't discovered the place. Puerto Escondido has escaped the dramatic changes that, over the past decade, have altered the faces of less pretty beach areas.

The main street that follows the beach is lined with very pleasant and affordable small hotels and restaurants. While "P.E." or "Puerto" (as residents call it) attracts its fair share of tourists, they rarely over-crowd the town. For a few months in winter, many longer-term visitors from the United States and Canada enjoy total relaxation in the sun. But for some reason, Puerto keeps few year-round expatriate residents. According to locals, only about 50 North Americans live here more or less permanently–most of them work or operate businesses. The majority of residents are semi-permanent. Some migrate back and forth between Oaxaca and Puerto Escondido, as if they can't quite make up their minds. Because of the marvelous waves here, you'll usually find a contingent of aging surfers trying to recapture those glorious days of the 1960s. When you used to say: "Don't trust anyone over 30," it must be tough to be facing age 60!

Surfers of all ages, backpackers and conservative tourists all combine to lend a special air to P.E. One woman I interviewed described Puerto Escondido as having a combination "Haight Ashbury and Gilligan's Island" ambience.

Most construction in Escondido has been focused on tourism–hotels and time-share condos–so there aren't many apartments and houses for rent. However, just north of town several elegant subdivisions are being laid out near the Posada Real. The Zicatela Beach strip has developed, and a number of houses have been built along the main highway south of town. Again, most of these are for time-share, vacation and second homes. Residents usually don't think of these areas as part of P.E.

To sum up, Puerto Escondido could be a place to investigate for relocation in Mexico, particularly if you are into tropical beaches and monster waves. There are enough fellow North Americans to supply social needs, and developers haven't quite pushed prices out of reach or squelched the quality of life.

Puerto Angel and Huatulco

Puerto Angel is another place we predicted would become a hot spot for tourism and retirement. The area beaches are so beautiful and varied and the panorama is so gorgeous, we were convinced it couldn't miss. We envisioned cruise ships docking here, and spiffy condos and view homes going up on the steep hillsides that overlook one of the most gorgeous bays we've ever seen. Well, we were wrong again. Puerto Angel remains the charming, unsophisticated village it was 15 years ago. There are still only a couple of main streets and remarkably few tourist businesses. Until recently, the town didn't have a single curio shop–not even a place that sold postcards. There are some moderately priced hotels and some excellent restaurants specializing in the fresh fish and lobster that are brought in daily by local fishermen. But Puerto Angel is still a very quiet and restful place, with most beach activity taking place away from the village.

If you follow a dirt road a few miles west of Puerto Angel, you'll find the small village of Zipolite, with its mile-long beach of warm, white sand. A strip of tiny restaurants and bars compete for the tourist business, which isn't terribly crushing because of the beach's isolation. This is a ruler-straight beach that faces the open ocean, so riptides and currents make it rather dangerous for all but experienced swimmers. But the biggest attraction here, particularly for the younger set, is that Zipolite Beach is "clothing optional." Technically, nude bathing is against the law, but local cops seldom enforce this law. Several beaches in this area enjoy the same laxness–something unusual in Mexico.

Huatulco, about 35 kilometers from Puerto Angel, is where we should have predicted a tourist boom. But at the time, Huatulco was little more than a shabby village situated on a nice, sandy bay. When the Mexican government decided to construct a spiffy resort here, they went to work with a vengeance. Before long there was an airport, a Club Med and four large hotels, including a Sheraton. All of this expansion happened rather rapidly. Then, suddenly, things slowed to a crawl. Apparently tourism wasn't keeping pace with the expansion of facilities.

The original idea was to make the resort into an "authentic Mexican village," but the large luxury hotels destroyed this possibility. Those who've visited Huatulco as tourists rave about how wonderful their stays were, but who knows how it will be for those wishing to live there for longer. There are several condos in place, presumably time-shares, but regular housing may be in short supply.

Of the nine beautiful bays around Santa Cruz Hualtulco (its official name), only two have been opened to development (although new roads are under construction in order to develop the others). It'll probably be some time before these bays are devastated by progress. For the time being, they are just as beautiful as the travel brochures claim they are.

Taxco, the Forgotten Silver Queen

This colonial gem, nestled in the mountains just three and a half hours southwest of Mexico City, has been the favorite of John Howells since he was a teenager. In those days, when the family lived in Mexico City, they spent one or two weekends a month in Taxco. Although it's grown from a small town to a city, the main part of town hasn't changed a bit; it still looks like 1948.

Taxco is another must-visit place–a scenic delight of genuine colonial architecture (few modern reproductions here), with narrow cobblestone streets rising sharply toward the main plaza. If Walt Disney had wanted to design a 16th-century mining town, it probably would have looked just like Taxco.

Like San Miguel de Allende, Taxco owes much of its current fame and popularity with foreigners to an American. In this case it was William Spratling, an Alabama-born architect and college professor. He came for a visit in 1929, fell in love with the place and decided to stay. In 1931, he started the process of resurrecting Taxco's long-dormant silver industry. Today, his efforts can be seen today in the town's highly successful silver commerce.

Back in the eighteenth century, Taxco's wealth was based on the silver mines which had been worked since the time of Cortez. Today, the economy is based on silver far more than on tourism; the town has about 200 shops, mostly family operated, where silver is hand-crafted into jewelry and flatware. Many of today's best silversmiths are the grandchildren of Spratling's apprentices.

Why hasn't Taxco become a popular retirement center? Perhaps it is a consequence of progress. At one time, the only practical way to get from Mexico City to Acapulco was by highway, and you had to pass through Taxco. The drive used to take 12 hours, so Taxco was the logical stop-over place between Mexico City and Acapulco. Many visitors were so fascinated by the ancient town that they couldn't resist joining the artists already in residence and making Taxco their homes. Before long, several hundred expatriates owned or rented homes here, and a thousand or more stayed for lesser periods of time.

Taxco was on its way to becoming as popular with retirees as San Miguel de Allende. Then progress came in the form of a high-speed toll road, which bypassed the town and drastically cut the number of tourists who are exposed to Taxco. Now, most people drive or fly directly between Acapulco and Mexico City. Consequently, those who might have considered retirement in Taxco don't get the chance to look it over. Most tourists today are Mexican, European or Japanese. Just one factor that could account for Taxco's comparatively scanty retired population: its steep streets might intimidate older, less vigorous retirees and send them toward more level colonial towns. But with people taking retirement at much earlier ages today, we might expect to see additions to the numbers of retirees, both in town and on small ranches that sit in tropical splendor toward the base of the mountains

Puebla

What the colonial city of Puebla has is beautifully preserved sixteenth– through eighteenth–century buildings, a handsome zócalo, a regional cuisine famous throughout the country, lower prices than in many other large Mexican cities and reasonable proximity to the capital. What it does not have are any signs of poverty (at least in the center of the city) or of a large expatriate population (if you exclude the Germans employed at the huge Volkswagen plant on the outskirts).

Puebla was the site of the nineteenth–century victory of Mexican troops against a much larger French force that is celebrated each year on Cinco de Mayo, the fifth of May.

We were disappointed on our most recent trip to see that there are still few North American retirees in Puebla, but that need not be an insurmountable obstacle to its future as a retirement site. There are a couple of golf courses and tennis clubs, and as everywhere in Mexico, many of the movies shown are in English.

We continue to believe that as more prospective retirees in Mexico visit this community, more will decide that it is the place for them, and its chief drawback for many people—the lack of a large enough group of fellow expatriates—will disappear.

Baja California Off-the-Beaten Path

Driving the highway south of Ensenada, below the *zona libre,* treats you to some spectacular desert landscapes. Occasionally, but not often, you'll encounter a North American or two living in one of the small villages along the highway. Two of the most striking towns, San Ignacio and Mulegé (two of the prettiest places in Baja) have a few North Americans living there, and we suspect these places will become more popular with gringos in the near future.

San Ignacio was founded in the seventeenth century by Jesuit missionaries who discovered that the high water table around San Ignacio naturally irrigated the soil. Even before the church and mission were completed, groves of oranges and lemons, grapevines and date palms were thrusting roots into the damp soil. The Jesuits were expelled from Baja over two centuries ago, but dates, citrus and grapes survived fabulously. Today they grow like weeds, sometimes like a jungle. Not only here, but farther south in Mulegé as well, the trees and vines grow lushly. You will appreciate the meaning of oasis if you ever visit these two towns.

Mulegé was one of John Howells' favorite places anywhere (before the paved highway, that is). An old, old town–with buildings that defy centuries of weathering, tall palm trees and tropical flowers in profusion–Mulegé was in itself fascinating. But the interesting thing was that, before the new highway, it was a penal colony! On a hill overlooking the town sits a large pastel-colored building, the territorial prison. Convicts who were judged to be non-violent and who could be trusted to be part of society (yet legally couldn't) were exiled to places like Mulegé to serve out their sentences. This was not only a very humane practice, but wonderfully practical. Instead of placing a prisoner into a cage with the taxpayers spending $40,000 a year to keep him there (U.S.- style), Mexico sent non-dangerous prisoners into "exile." (They may still do this, I'm not sure.) The convict's family then joined him, and together they somehow managed to earn a living. (Remember, Mexican taxpayers are very much against pampering convicts by paying board and room for them.) The family either found jobs or started a business, much the same as if they were still on the mainland. The children went to school, the parents worked and the family lived normal lives as responsible members of the community. The prison on the hill was reserved for someone who occasionally misbehaved, perhaps appearing intoxicated in public or quarreling with neighbors. If a convict misbehaved too often, he was shipped back to the mainland and tossed into a regular prison. As you can imagine, few people ever misbehaved! If you were looking for a crime-free environment, you couldn't have found any safer place than Mulegé!

However, in the interests of tourism, the government closed the "prison" (which almost never had prisoners in the first place). Today, the children and grandchildren of convicts might be the owners of the stores or restaurants in town. Today, serious crime is almost nonexistent; Mulegé is no different from almost any small town in Mexico.

A river, slow-moving and tropical, fringed with bamboo, tall trees and massive date palms, runs through town and down to the gulf. A half-dozen trailer parks face the river. These parks are very popular with winter retirees. Although we're getting farther south, where cooler currents from the Pacific Ocean temper the warm gulf water, the summers here are still not particularly livable. Even so, there are plans for a 300-unit condo and a marina on the river.

Just south of town is a development called Villas de Mulegé. Houses there can be built to your specifications. Without electricity, this development features solar energy. Since about 98 percent of Mulegé days are sunny, this doesn't seem to be such a bad idea! Our guess is that, before long, the town is in line for development.

Loreto, a New Boomer

The oldest permanent Spanish settlement in Baja—founded in 1697, Loreto is in the early stages of a potentially big tourist development, sponsored by the Mexican government. For years, the attraction here was fishing, but lately, more and more retirees are focusing their attention on the town. There is an international airport going in at Nopolo Cove, and some ambitious facilities are underway here, particularly at Puerto Escondido (not to be confused with the mainland's west-coast town), 16 kilometers to the south. With more and more North Americans coming every day, this area is growing from a sleepy fishing resort into a bustling complex.

Some believe that when all of the projected facilities in the area are completed–including a European-styled village some-what like Manzanillo's Las Hadas, with red-tiled roofs and sparkling white walls–Loreto will be as popular as anywhere on the mainland. A new Cancun, perhaps. Maybe. Again, the problem with most of Baja California Sur is the fierce summer heat. As soon as the temperatures begin climbing in May, the gringos begin packing. Another problem is the water supply; some say it isn't adequate to support a large population.

Bahía de Palmas

On your way south, about halfway between La Paz and Cabo San Lucas, is an interesting, fast-growing North American colony, spread along the Bahía de Palmas. This colony is on the Sea of Cortez side of the peninsula (although it's just about open ocean at this point), so the weather is more civilized. Some fancy homes, as well as some ordinary places and RV lots, have been built next to the beaches. Homes aren't cheap around here, with selling prices as high as $200,000. (Of course, the price depends on what you're prepared to spend.) Nothing is crowded, and if you're looking for isolated beaches, beautiful ocean water and quiet, then you've found it.

Los Barriles and Buena Vista are the larger communities along the bay. But neither is really large enough to be called even a village. From here on southward runs a dirt and gravel road that follows the coast (and some really spectacular scenery) all the way to San José del Cabo. Very, very few people live here, but you'll find RVs and gringo houses scattered along the way, taking advantage of the view.

Because of the way the wind blows across the bay, this area is reputed to have the best windsurfing anywhere. It seems that high-velocity thermal winds swoop down from the high inland mountains, sending winds of 20 to 25 knots to really speed the windsurfers along! Better know what you're doing, though. Several really nice hotels in the area cater to the windsurfers as well as tourists who want someplace different to visit.

Just south of here is a place called Santiago, one of the most interesting towns in Baja Sur. It sits in a broad canyon that is continuously watered by volcanic springs and not affected by drought and low rainfall. The result is a lush oasis of trees, greenness and flowers. Some of the streets are lined with flowering trees with brilliant red blossoms that look almost surrealistic. The Palomar Hotel there has one of the best chefs in Baja, and it's worth a detour just to taste one of his soups. But, according to local people, not one North American resident has ever chosen to live here. We don't understand this.

Todos Santos

Todos Santos (directly west from Bahía de Palmas, on the Pacific side of the peninsula) is reached by an excellent new highway from La Paz. (If you're going directly to Cabo, this is the highway to follow, even though on most maps it looks like a secondary road.) Todos Santos is an area that obviously doesn't suffer from water shortage, because there are numerous orchards and vineyards in the area. It isn't much of a tourist center, which may be a plus, but it has attracted a few American families. Some are into farming and avocado production.

The attraction here is the beaches, which some people claim are the prettiest in Baja. At this point they *are* quite isolated and unpopulated. They are away from town by a kilometer or so, but they may possibly become popular in the near future. Until a paved highway was built in 1985, few people ever visited here. This isolation is changing. The town is growing daily. With Los Cabos becoming so expensive, Todos Santos is the place to watch.

The Yucatán

The Yucatán peninsula is easily accessible from the east coast of the U.S. and Canada—in fact it is only a couple of hours' flight from Miami. The Caribbean coast from Cancun south has some of the most delightful beaches in the world. Long stretches of sand and coral are fringed with low jungle and an occasional coconut plantation or farm.

Although much of the beach-front land is tantalizing as a site for that dream home, be warned against potential legal pitfalls. Often, people who "own" this land don't realize that they are only there because possession is that well-known percentage of the law. When they try to sell, they discover that "their" land belongs to someone else. Don't let this discourage you, however: you may always rent land, and you can even build—provided you find a reliable lawyer. Away from the beaches, land ownership is more available and more reliable but, alas, less desirable. Most of the Yucatán peninsula is thinly soiled limestone, fit only for scrub jungle and heniquen plantations. Unless you are into tropical agriculture—or isolation—you may be better off with one of the population centers such as Cancún or Mérida.

Cancún

Cancún has become one of the hemisphere's most popular beach resorts. Luxury hotels and condo developments line the beach. Prices in the tourist areas bear a much closer resemblance to those elsewhere in the Caribbean than to those in most of Mexico. Condos are being marketed aggressively, but before you sign up for one—in Cancún, Acapulco, Lake Tahoe, or any resort town—figure out what your weekly and daily costs will be. A popular ploy is to sell condos on a two- or three-week time-share basis. This is for tourists, not for anyone who seriously wants to live in Mexico. There are many small houses being built in downtown Cancún that are far less expensive than housing in the beachfront hotel area and look very comfortable.

Many Americans buy or rent south of Cancún as far as Tulum. Then, when they want to mingle with compatriots, they have only to drive the excellent road north. Playa del Carmen, where condo construction is booming, and the island of Cozumel are only 35 miles from Cancún. They, to, are starting to attract Americans and Canadians for retirement living.

Mérida

Mérida is another attractive retirement site. It has managed to maintain much of its colonial charm, and if it weren't for unmuffled motorcycles and trucks, it could be described as a sleepy paradise. One problem here is the summer weather. Without a tempering ocean to keep it cool, Mérida can become an oven, as bad as St Louis or Houston in the summer. In fact, it's even hotter than they are, although it doesn't have their oppressive humidity.

But the North Americans who live there love it! After the publication of the fourth edition of *Choose Mexico*, we received an unusually nice letter from a college administrator from Texas who had just bought a new, three-bedroom, two-and-one-half-bath, two-floor townhouse in Mérida. The purchase price (complete with full-time security) was $23,000, but it cost another $6,400 to add a carport, balcony, patio, water heater, stove, refrigerator, ceiling fans, cabinets and shelving. Furnishing the house—kitchen, bedrooms, living room and dining room—with custom-made furniture and original art brought the total close to $34,000. Our correspondent can't say enough about how delighted he is to live in the Yucatán with all its human and ecological riches. He does say, however, that there are no North Americans in his neighborhood and he is not unhappy about it. If you do not need the companionship of many compatriots and want to experience one of Mexico's most attractive areas, you might consider Mérida.

The Yucatán is historically, geographically and culturally separate from the rest of Mexico. In fact the Yucatecos do not think of themselves as Mexican. Their homeland, closer to Miami or New Orleans than to Mexico City, has become familiar to great numbers of North Americans who are drawn by the peninsula's resorts and ruins. Some, particularly those who get to know the inhabitants, are bound to make it their retirement home, overcoming all the obstacles we have mentioned. Perhaps some of them will take the time to let us know how they are doing.

Business Opportunities

Until very recently, going into business in Mexico was all but out of the question for most people. The government erected so many barriers that we used to claim that the easiest way to go into business was to marry a Mexican. One of the regulations: unless you qualified as a long-term *Inmigrado* or had a spouse who was a citizen, you needed a Mexican partner who would own 51 percent of your business. Then along came the North American Free Trade Agreement (NAFTA) and things began to change.

NAFTA has neither been the magic formula for bringing Mexico into the 21st century, as many politicians predicted, nor has it been the "sucking sound" disaster that others suggested. At first, when import restrictions into Mexico were lifted, Mexican manufacturers were devastated. Hundreds of thousands of jobs were lost in the appliance, shoe, paper, toy, candy and other industries. Consumers went for popular U.S. or Canadian brand names which used to be very expensive; they ignored locally made products. Some job recovery was made as North American industries moved south to take advantage of the four-dollar-a-day labor market. But these minimum wage jobs aren't expected to do much to build the middle-class economy that Mexico wants and needs. Minimum-wage earners can't afford to buy the products they make; they barely can afford food and clothing, especially when, after the fall of the peso in 1994–1995, the minimum wage dropped to $3 a day. In Mexico, economic betterment may prove to be a long, drawn out process.

So how does NAFTA affect expatriates living in Mexico? They're affected in two ways. First of all, prices of most imported goods are dramatically lower; you can now afford to purchase the brands you've been used to back home. And second, it's much easier to go into business in Mexico. Beginning in 1994, as an implementation of NAFTA, Mexico's Foreign Investment Law (FIL) abolished most restrictions on foreign investment. Today, foreign investors are permitted to own 100 percent of any Mexican business—your own business, a corporation or a partner-ship—except for a few restricted enterprises. Some prohibited business types are: oil drilling and refining; petrochemical indus-tries; electric or nuclear utilities; radio, telegraph and postal services; land transportation; and airports. Several large-scale businesses (mostly industries that exceed $25 million in capital investment) carry ownership restrictions which are scheduled to ease over a period of years.

Aside from the obstacle course you expect when dealing with government bureaucracy, going into business in Mexico is a lot easier today. Many restrictions have been lifted, but it's still not totally wide open. Don't confuse investment in a business and working in your business. Technically, you still need FM-2 status to actually work in your own business, although many small-business people find ways around this restriction. Besides, with labor so inexpensive, why work?

Mexico no longer requires citizenship or permanent resi-dency for professionals either, (dentists, doctors, engineers, etc.). The catch here is that, at this point in time, Mexico isn't required to recognize foreign professional licenses. And to open a prac-tice, you'll probably need a license. But under NAFTA, the government is committed to providing a procedure under which foreigners may obtain validation of their credentials.

We interviewed a number of expatriates who've gone into business in Mexico, and we asked for their insights and advice about entering the Mexican world of business. The one theme all mentioned was the importance of developing a personal relation-ship with associates, clients and customers. As a businessman in Ajijic pointed out, "If you're not willing to take time to engage in some pleasantries before starting your business meetings, you can be sure it will cost you." You see, Mexicans believe in pleasure *before* business. Exchanging pleasantries, talking about their families and maybe commenting on the weather are considered polite before jumping into the reason for the meeting. Keep your meetings easy-going and relaxed and, if the meeting is at your office or home, be a gracious host.

Like most Latin Americans, Mexicans are uncomfortable with direct confrontation, so when dealing with Mexican associates or employees, it's important not to pull rank, raise your voice or use sarcastic comments. To them, dignity and the appearance of integrity are most important. In this vein, a Mexican businessman will try to avoid giving you a direct "no" and thus avoid risking your displeasure or appearing to be rude. Pinning someone down to a final agreement usually involves a number of smaller agreements. However, even when your Mexican partner or client isn't in agreement, he might avoid saying "no" by saying "maybe" or offering some other vague reply. This is called *dar largas,* "beating around the bush" and is why getting your final agreement in writing is important. You need to recognize the difference between a "polite yes" and a "genuine yes."

To successfully function in a different culture requires patience and insight into the system. You cannot assume that everything works the same way in Mexico as it does in Canada or the United States. For one thing, you must be prepared for a great deal more government interference in your business. One bit of advice given by expatriate entrepreneurs: "Before you get too deep into the business, make sure you have a good lawyer and accountant." One lady told us that she was informed that her workers needed to belong to a union. When she explained that there was no union available for the type of work her employees were doing, she was urged to "start one for them."

South of the border, the employer-employee relationship is often on a more personal level. To Mexicans, North American management can seem rude, uncaring and demeaning. Workers here hate to be considered just another payroll number, ready to be sacrificed at any moment. Latin American concepts of time also create tension in business and employee relations. In Mexico, time is something relative. It is not, as we see it, the sacred, all important mechanism. In our value system, being late for an appointment is considered insulting; being late for work is good reason for discharging an employee. In Mexico, being late for an appointment is almost anticipated, and the more important a person is, the more tardy he or she can be expected to be. (Why this is so is something that's always eluded us.) Mostly, your employees will try to be punctual, but if something interferes with getting to work on time, they don't see this as any big deal.

The time-proven key to success for those entering business in Mexico: do something that you already know something about. Martin Parker, for example, retired to Ajijic not planning on going back to work. But because of his background in insurance, he received an offer from Sanborn's Insurance company to become a local agent. Since his wife already had her FM-2 papers, they decided to take on the job and became the first North Americans in Mexico to be licensed as insurance agents. "If you're a thinking person," Martin says, "and you find your niche, you can make it in business here." He outlined several stories of fellow expatriates who achieved success in Mexican real estate and retail businesses.

Another example of doing what you know best is David McLaughlin's partnership with Camille and Rod Collins, in the creation of Mexico Connect. This is Mexico's premier Internet connection, directed toward U.S. and Canadian citizens who want information about traveling, living and retiring in Mexico. Camille and Rod, a brother and sister team, already had a successful graphic arts and desktop publishing business, so they applied their knowledge of computer graphics to building Web pages for Mexico's booming Internet presence. David, an industrial psychologist by profession, explained that, applying the principles of his field, they combine their interests in travel, education and retirement into one all-encompassing Web Site. They started out with 800 visitors to the site each day, and by early 1997, the site was registering 9,000 "hits" daily. (You can check it out at the Web address: http://www.mexconnect.com)

More than 25 years ago, as a college student backpacking the country, Stan Gotlieb fell in love with Oaxaca. When he decided he'd had enough of the rat race in California, it seemed only natural to settle in Oaxaca. As a writer, he looked for a way to earn a living with his skills, and finally hit upon the idea of an Internet monthly magazine. For a $25 annual subscription, Stan e-mails his columns and stories to Web browsers all over the world. To supplement his writing income, he gives weekly newcomer seminars to orient folks on the ins and outs of living in Oaxaca, and he also acts as a consultant for travel agencies and researchers interested in *curanderos* (practitioners of folk medicine). He says, "I don't live in Mexico to work; I work in Mexico in order to live here." (For a for a sample copy of *Letters from Mexico,* Stan's web site is http://www.dreamagic.com/stan)

A Canadian expatriate, Curt Hyman, several years ago started a newsletter, designed to spread the news about the advantages of Mexican retirement for Canadians. Called LSMFT (Live Safely in Mexico Free of Taxes), Curt's newsletter is chock full of advice, news and the latest developments in retirement conditions (mostly in the Lake Chapala and Guadalajara areas) for Canadians. Today, he not only produces the newsletter, but does consulting and statistical work for various Mexican governmental agencies.

Another success story is Dennis Setera, a computer repairman who found a niche that needed filling and employed his special skills to start a business. During a trade mission visit to Guadalajara, Dennis realized that computer technology in Mexico lagged far behind the latest developments in the United States. Businesses here use a lot of out-dated but perfectly usable equipment that is constantly in need of maintenance and repair to keep it going. He imported some inexpensive, last-generation equipment for repairing hard disks and other computer hardware, and went into business. With virtually no competition, Dennis finds business booming. He reports his biggest difficulty is negotiating with Mexican businessmen. "They act as though they hate to make a decision. And just when you think the deal is off, they suddenly stop stalling and want to close the deal immediately."

[In a previous edition of *Choose Mexico,* we reported on the business career of John Dixon in Ensenada. John is no longer living there, but his story is worth relating here.]

John Dixon and his attractive wife, Cha Cha, looked around for a business in Ensenada, Baja California. It turned out that, while numerous restaurants were raking in tourist dollars, nobody was supplying a good old-fashioned hamburger to Ensenada's tourist trade. Since Cha Cha was a Mexican citizen, getting started was no problem. Appropriately enough, John and Cha Cha called their restaurant in Ensenada "Cha Cha Burgers" and it became an instant hit, not only with tourists who were homesick for a hamburger fix, but with local Mexicans as well.

John became the president of Amigos de Ensenada, which made him a sort of unofficial mayor for Ensenada expatriates. Although this is basically an American club, several Mexican businessmen belong. For their part, many American businessmen in Ensenada are active in the local chamber of commerce. They've undertaken some rather innovative projects, which have benefited the entire community and had positive consequences for the Americans living there. For example, they sponsor Christmas pageants, Easter parades, a wine festival, children's choirs and musical ensembles, plus library and charity events to assist the poor and needy. At first, some of these activities seemed strange to the local businessmen, who usually concern themselves with purely commercial affairs. But they've discovered that these special events generate local business and spending. Now, Mexican businesspeople join in enthusiastically.

Mexico on the Internet

One of the most exciting happenings in Mexico is the country's entry into the Internet and World Wide Web (WWW). Just a short time ago, this advanced technology was almost unknown by the rank and file citizens in Mexico. Communication in Mexico was confined to telephone (when it worked), postal mail (correctly described as "snail-mail" in Mexico) or delivering the message in person. Suddenly, the world of high-speed communication is open to anyone with a computer in Mexico. Today, in addition to many private Internet servers, both CompuServe and America-On-Line have made their services readily available. If you plan on spending a great deal of time in Mexico, we urge you to bring or buy a computer so you can enter this new world of communication.

In case you are one of those who doesn't read the business and technology section of your daily newspaper, let's briefly describe the Internet and how it can assist those who move to Mexico. The Internet is an intricate web of computers, connected via phone lines throughout the world. The phone connections link universities, government agencies, private businesses and individual computer owners. How all this happens is too complicated to explain; just accept the fact that all these computers are connected by a web of phone lines.

How will you use it in Mexico? Probably your computer's most valuable chore will be keeping you in touch with family and friends back in the United States, Canada, Germany, Bulgaria or wherever you have family and friends. With the Internet's e-mail system, you will be able to keep in constant touch, by sending as many messages as you wish—anywhere in the *world*—for absolutely nothing. Of course, you will be paying for your Internet service and your local telephone charges (which are often free for local calls), but you won't be charged for individual messages, no matter how many, or how far they travel. And the beauty of all this is: the message won't take ten days to arrive, as it does by postal delivery. It will take seconds. If the other party happens to be using a computer when you send your message, you could receive a reply while you wait! Should your granddaughter's computer be turned off when you send the message, your precious words will wait until the next time she signs on to the Internet. (Don't ask where. They hang out somewhere in outer space, I suppose.)

The other valuable use you'll have for the Internet in Mexico is keeping in touch with world news and current events. By signing on to the World Wide Web, you'll have access to the latest stories from newspapers like the *New York Times, Washington Post* or the *Wall Street Journal.* There's even a CNN page with all the current news, complete with pictures. There's a good chance your hometown newspaper has a Web page, so you can download the latest news from your old neighborhood. You can also access newspapers from all over the world as well all the leading newspapers in Mexico, including the English-language daily *The News* (formerly the *Mexico City News).*

Be warned, once you start browsing the World Wide Web, you'll be in danger of becoming addicted to the Internet. You could find yourself spending so much time glued to the screen that you won't enjoy retirement. On the Web, you can zip from one site to another, visiting a museum in India, reading speeches from the House of Representatives or the House of Commons, and on and on until dawn. You might even construct your own Web Site with pages telling about your new life in Mexico. Many people have done exactly this.

If you are a complete novice, don't shrug your shoulders and say, "I'll never learn something so complicated and new-fangled as the Internet. I don't know the first thing about computers!" The biggest mistake many people make is assuming they have to know how a computer operates before they can get on the Internet. Just as you don't need to know how your car works to learn how to drive, you needn't know beans about a computer—other than how to turn it on and start driving through the World Wide Web. However, when learning to drive a car, you have an accident. You could run into a tree, go off a bridge or get run over by a beer truck. Not so with computers and the Internet. The worst accident that can happen is that your telephone connection becomes erratic and you have to sign on again.

Don't wait until you get to Mexico to start using the Internet. The Web is loaded with pages designed to help you with your visit or relocation in Mexico. Hundreds, probably thousands, of Web sites out there provide information on the towns and cities you might consider for retirement or business. Enter some of the Web addresses listed below to get started. Once you've looked at a couple, you'll find links to other pages—which send you to still other pages—all chock full of information, color photos and advice from folks who've already made the decision to choose Mexico. Soon you'll realize why they call the Internet a "web" or "network" because these links spread out like a spider web.

It would be impossible to compile a comprehensive list of World Wide Web sites that cover Mexico. Before a list could be completed, numbers of new sites would make the list obsolete. So, below are just a few URLs collected over many evenings of browsing the Web. This is just a start—you'll quickly find lots more interesting, entertaining and fascinating Web sites.

A couple of hints:

1. If you are using one of the more popular browsers, such as Netscape or Microsoft Explorer, you don't have to add **http://** in front of each address.

2. You'll note that sometimes the address ends with the letters **html** and sometimes just **htm.** If the **html** doesn't work, remove the last character, the **l**.

3. Type all the characters as you see them; capital and lower case letters must be correct or the web can't find the address.

Let's start out by calling up Mexico City's major daily English-language newspaper, *The News*.

Enter: **http://www.novedades.com/the-news.htm**

If this doesn't work, make sure you've typed correctly (caps or lowercase as indicated), and add **http://** in front of the **www**. At the bottom of the page, you'll find a "link." That's a underlined, colored line of type that says: "Return to Group Index." If you click on that link with your mouse, you'll zip over to another page, where you can browse through the pages of *Novidades,* another Mexico City newspaper, and *Mexico,* a sister paper to *The News.*

To see a list of all of Mexico's on-line newspapers, enter: **http://www.webwombat.com.au/intercom/newsprs/mexico.htm**

Or, if you'd like to read the *Washington Post,* enter: **http://www.washingtonpost.com/**

And if you would like Washington Post news about Mexico, simply add the following to the end of the above address: **wp-srv/inatl/longterm/worldref/country/mexico.htm**

For Mexico Connect, an entry into one of Mexico's best Web Sites, enter: **http://.www.mexconnect.com/mex_/living.html**

You'll find links to every kind of information you'll ever need about Mexico. Be sure to visit their forum pages to read conversations between folks considering moving to Mexico, and those living there who like to share travel tips with others.

Let's suppose you're thinking of retirement in Mazatlán. Just enter: **http://www.maztravel.com/**

You'll find loads of information, not only about Mazatlán, but useful and interesting items about Mexico in general. To browse, click on the colored, underlined items.

Another favorite of ours is:

http://www.dreamagic.com/stan/letters.html

This site comes from Oaxaca, in southern Mexico, with information about the area and about Mexico in general. Stan Gotlieb operates these pages and offers a newsletter which is sent via e-mail to subscribers. This page contains many of Stan's letters from Oaxaca. They describe the current political, economic and cultural state of Mexico as seen by a gringo commentator.

Gateway Books has a Mexican retirement Web Site at:

http://www.discoverypress.com/mex_page.html

These pages contain information on retiring or relocating in Mexico and a forum page for comments, advice and opinions.

You can visit Gateway's home page to see what other publications they have on retirement, travel and other subjects. Just enter: **http://www.discoverypress.com/gateway.html**

To find more pages and to maximize your browsing efforts, you'll need to learn to use "search engines" such as Yahoo, Alta Vista, Excite and others. One of our favorites is Lycos, found at **http://www.lycos.com**

Just enter that site and follow instructions.

Another excellent search site is found at: **http://www.beaucoup.com/1geneng.html**

This one lists just about all of the search engines available.

Below are a few more web sites we've run across during our late-night forays into the world of the Internet, which we'd like to share with you.

http://mexico-travel.com/fiestas/fiestas.html

Fiestas of Mexico—Official Mexican Government tourism page, listing the major fiestas around the country. It also contains links to various attractions and travel information

http://www.hotwired.com/rough/mexico/ Rough Guide to Mexico—a travel guide to Mexico, with links to all parts of the country.

www.hiline.net/sanborns/insurance.html Sanborn's Insurance company's page. Get insurance rates, information about services and connections to agents, should you care to buy on-line.

http://mexico-travel.com/states/s03/76zz1.htm Baja California's Concepcion Bay...

http://www.mexconnect.com/MEX/lloyds/llydeco9.html Mexican economic report, from Lloyds, a popular investment house.

http://www.mexweb.com/guana2.htm A look at Guanajuato.

http://www.mexweb.com/retire.htm#fees General retirement information.

http://www.virtualmex.com/ensenada.htm Ensenada, Baja California.

http://mexweb.mty.itesm.mx/Info2/ Welcome to Mexico! General informtion about the country

http://virtualmex.com/acapulco.htm Acapulco home page.

http://www.hypermex.com/html/lvg_rtr.htm Inside PV Living (Retirement in Puerto Vallarta). A well-done set of pages, full of information and friendly advice for moving to Puerto Vallarta.

http://www.mexweb.com/colonial.htm A page giving an overview of Mexico's colonial towns.

http://www.reidgroup.com/~dmg/mexico/Internet/mexico.html
Comprehensive list of the Internet providers in Mexico.

http://serpiente.dgsca.unam.mx/serv_hem/nacional/home.html
Complete list of newspapers in Mexico.

http://morelia.infosel.com.mx/gdm11.htm Page for Morelia, with local newspapers

http://www.trace-sc.com/news.htm A list of 56 newspapers. Probably the best listing of newspapers in Mexico and elsewhere.

http://www1.mexassist.com.mx/mexassist/mre and

http://www.ajijic.com These are examples of real estate pages on the web; there are plenty of them. Note: our mention of these Web Sites in no way endorses or recommends the businesses that sponsor them. We know nothing about these companies, and cannot vouch for them.

http://www.anaya.es/dict/Buscar?act=HAnaya.html
How about an on-line dictionary? This one comes from Spain. You type in a word to be translated, it zips back to Spain, and in seconds the answer is on your screen! That's right, Spain!

http://daisy.uwaterloo.ca:80/~alopez-o/polind.html Letters on Mexican politics. In-depth analysis of what's happening politically in Mexico. You may or may not agree with the viewpoints, but you'll be informed of the issues.

http://www.olsen.ch/cgi-bin/w3ex-form Excellent exchange rate page; convert from any rate of exchange to another.

http://webmaster@www.coacade.uv.mx/ University of Vera Cruz. Some pages in English. Information about classes in Spanish.

http://www.mexonline.com/ Mexico OnLine home page, including Baja California, business, culture, NAFTA, real estate, travel... Everything Mexico.

Questions and Answers

We've received many letters from readers asking for more information about living in Mexico. We try to answer every letter, but cannot always provide a detailed reply to every query. Many of the questions were already answered in the book; the readers simply didn't look carefully. But we discovered many areas of information that we overlooked and/or didn't stress enough in the first four editions. We've tried to cover most of those topics in this edition, but think it may also be helpful to provide this chapter of answers to the 20 most frequently asked questions.

QUESTION: What effect has the North American Free Trade Agreement (NAFTA) had on retirees living in Mexico?

ANSWER: Its most immediate effect has been to make American and Canadian goods more available and to bring about an influx of stores like Price-Costco and WalMart. Also, it has made it much easier to start a business or to purchase property. Some people have suggested that the sharp devaluation of the peso, with the corresponding escalation of the purchasing power of the dollar, was also an effect, but that is hard to prove. The jury is still out on whether NAFTA will be good or bad for Mexico, Canada and the United States, but it certainly seems to be good, at least in the short run, for North American retirees.

QUESTION: Can a couple really live well on $600 a month?

ANSWER: Yes, definitely. We have checked prices in communities all over Mexico, and in many (but not all) of them, we have found retired North American couples who are living comfortably on that income. Of course, they have to watch their budgets carefully, just as they would in the United States or Canada, but we and they are convinced that they are better off than they would be at home. Maintaining an automobile will push the minimum figure higher, but public transportation is excellent and even the frequent use of taxis will not add substantially to your expenses.

Of course, a larger income will broaden your options and will enable you to enjoy more luxuries. Although we have not confined ourselves to writing exclusively about places where one can live on $600 a month, we have tried never to lose sight of the fact that some of our readers need to know where that can be done.

Occasionally, readers ask, "I have an income of only $400 a month. Can I get by on that?"

Well, as we've said before, $400 a month is a lot more than most Mexican families have to live on, but it's a lot less than most gringos have to live on. Figure your position from there. If you were fluent in Spanish and were willing to have a lower standard of living, you might manage to live on even less.

Personally, we would recommend against trying to live there today on much less than $600 a month, but if you are into the culture and don't mind forsaking gringo luxuries, go ahead. However, by our standards, you might find it a rather dreary living experience (but an ordinary experience by Mexican standards). On the other hand, we would be hard pressed to find a place in the United States where you could live on $400 a month with any measure of dignity.

Basically, we do not recommend that anyone move to Mexico because they are indigent. In the long run, a poor person might be much better off in the United States, given the social services and welfare grants available. In Mexico, nothing of the sort exists. Furthermore, the Mexican government dislikes the idea of someone who cannot afford to live there entering the country. People who can't support themselves often find deportation to be the remedy.

And don't expect the local North American community to come to your aid. This is one area where they are definitely not very friendly–not when it comes to people they feel are freeloaders.

QUESTION:When I look at the Foreign Currency listings in the newspaper, it seems that the peso is staying just below 8 to the U.S. dollar or just above 5 1/2 to the Canadian dollar. If inflation continues in Mexico, won't it wipe out all the gains you have written about?

ANSWER: Although inflation is now occurring at a much slower rate than a couple of years ago, yes, if it were to continue unchecked, it would cancel out the gains in the purchasing power of dollars. However, many people believe that, long before that happens, the peso will again be devalued.

QUESTION: Can I get a job in Mexico?

ANSWER: It's not altogether out of the question, but probably not, at least until you have achieved *Inmigrado* status (at least five years).

Unless you are an Inmigrado, it is illegal to work in Mexico without a work permit, which is obtained from the Department of Inmigration (with its central office in Mexico City and some branch offices elsewhere around the republic). These permits aren't easy to obtain. Unless you can do some kind of work that no Mexican citizen can perform, you aren't likely to get permission. The restrictions have relaxed somewhat over the years, particularly in real-estate sales and promotion, teaching English and so forth.

If you are caught working without a permit, you take a big risk. According to the Director of Immigration in Baja California Sur (Lic. Gabriel Cuervo), "Working without papers in Mexico is a very serious crime and comes with a generous jail sentence of 18 months or deportation." Another point is that, if you do obtain papers, they are good only for the employer specified. Should you decide to change employers, you need to apply for another permit. If you don't, you face the same serious charges as if you didn't have papers in the first place.

Finally, wages are so low in Mexico that you would have to have some kind of special talent that no Mexicans possess to demand any kind of decent salary. Real-estate and condo salesmen working on commission may do well, however, depending upon their ability and their luck. Too often, employers in Mexico believe that the minimum wage and maximum wage are identical. And with minimum wages presently below $5 a day, you probably wouldn't want to work anyway.

None of these rules applies to an artist or a writer, or to anyone who "telecommutes" via computer and modem, providing the work you do is used in the United States or Canada and you are paid in that country. The key is that there is no competition with Mexican workers.

QUESTION: Can I bring my pets with me?

ANSWER: Dogs and cats can be brought into Mexico if they are healthy and have received the required immunizations and you have a veterinarian's certificate to prove it. Birds, however, cannot be brought across the border in either direction. We advise you to check with the nearest Mexican consulate on the details of how recent your immunization certificate should be and what information it must contain.

QUESTION: How about moving my furniture there?

ANSWER You can legally move your furniture and other household goods to Mexico once you have resident status. You cannot do so when you first enter Mexico as a tourist. Whether it pays to transport your property there, rather than selling and replacing it with new purchases in Mexico, is something you will have to decide for yourself when you have been there for a while. You may be surprised at the bargains on furniture that are available to you there.

QUESTION: Do American appliances work on Mexican electrical current?

ANSWER: Yes, the current is the same as in the United States. No adapters are needed, and anything that works at home will work there (although we have heard reports that electric clocks do not keep good time).

QUESTION: Can a single woman feel safe and comfortable in Mexico?

ANSWER: Although young women alone in Mexico are sometimes annoyed by the attentions of the men, harassment is not usually an issue for those who are beyond their thirties. In communities where there are large numbers of North Americans, the problem is far less likely to arise. There, you see single women all the time traveling on buses or trains, walking around town or reading books in the town square.

Since age is respected in Mexico to a greater extent than in our youth-oriented society, residents have reported that the older the woman, the nicer local people seem to be to her. We've met many elderly ladies, some in their 70s and 80s, who have lived in Mexico for years with no problems.

Of course, the opposite can be true: the younger and prettier the woman, the more attention she will attract. Most of this attention will be in the form of sly whistles or double-entendre remarks, made for the amusement of bystanders. The best thing to do is to ignore it; Mexican men seldom say anything insulting, and you probably won't understand, anyway.

It seems that young, pretty American ladies have the reputation of being "hot" or "sexy." In a sense, this is relatively true, since Mexican girls rarely engage in pre-marital sex. Living together casually with a member of the opposite sex–as is common in the United States–is slightly scandalous in Mexico, so you can see why Mexican men can have mistaken ideas about gringo girls' morals. So when a girl dresses provocatively, in brief or clinging clothes, she can have all sorts of panting men following behind her, hoping to "get lucky."

In Puerto Escondido, we once met a stunning blonde who solved the problem of beach romeos trying to date her. She simply rolled up some newspapers and wrapped the bundle in a blanket to look like a baby. Presto: no more hassle! "I'm going to get a patent on an inflatable baby doll you can carry in your purse," she said. "Then when you want some peace, you simply blow it up."

Here are some other tips that younger single women have passed along to us. First of all, try not to give strangers casual eye contact. In Mexico, this can be interpreted as a "come-on." If you see someone you would like to know better, arrange for someone to introduce you. Otherwise they think you are "loose." Next, if someone tries to come on strong, never show fear. Culturally, Mexican women often pretend to be frightened when actually they are being coy; this turns some men on. Boredom, anger, disinterest or haughty amusement are among your most devastating weapons. Finally, if someone touches you when you don't want to be touched, make your anger known. If this doesn't cure the situation, get loud about it, very loud if necessary.

QUESTION: What income taxes do retirees in Mexico have to pay?

ANSWER: If they receive income from the United States, they have to continue filing returns and paying taxes there. They do not pay any taxes to Mexico on their U.S. income. As we have stated before, they cannot be employed in Mexico, so the only taxable income they are likely to have there is interest on their deposits in Mexican banks. The tax is withheld before the interest is paid.

QUESTION: How about golf and tennis in Mexico?

ANSWER: Tennis is a very popular game among the upper classes in Mexico. It's a sort of status symbol, and you'll find many public tennis courts in larger cities. Many more courts, however, are in private clubs or homes. If you are a real tennis buff, you might look for a condo or apartment with its own courts.

Golf is another thing entirely. While golf also carries an upper-class connotation, there aren't many courses available outside the exclusive country clubs in the larger cities. Green fees tend to be higher than on public courses at home, although not as expensive as at private clubs in the United States or Canada. Puerto

Vallarta, for example, until recently had only one golf course for the entire area. On the other hand, Palm Springs (California),with about as many residents, has over 60 golf courses.

There are several reasons for this non-popularity of golf. One is that Mexico has a perpetual water shortage in the winter, when most people would be playing golf. To expend enormous amounts of water keeping a course in playable condition would be terribly wasteful; the government hates to give well permits to golf courses when farmers anxiously wait for permission to drill for water. So, Mexican fairways are often so dry and hard that they might as well be cement. In the summers, when regular rainfall keeps the grass green, the golf-playing tourists are all at home in the United States.

Another reason for the scarcity of golf courses is that golf is a middle-class game in the United States and Canada. It's a moderately expensive pastime requiring greens fees and equip-ment, plus considerable spare time to devote to the game. But Mexico has a very small middle-class population. Most people work six days a week, sometimes 12 hours a day, and can spare neither the time nor the money to take up golf.

Don't get us wrong. There is golf in Mexico. Guadalajara alone has five courses. We just don't want to give our readers the mistaken impression that the country is a golfer's paradise or that the sport fits easily into a $600-a-month lifestyle.

QUESTION: Are insects a problem?

ANSWER: There are few unpleasant bugs in most of the areas where North Americans choose to retire. The insects we see most are flies, and they are much more likely to be found in outdoor markets than in screened kitchens. There are occasional scorpi-ons, which are seen in dry climates (especially in hot weather), but we've never heard retirees refer to them as a serious problem.

QUESTION: Isn't Mexican automobile liability insurance very expensive?

ANSWER: It is, if you buy it by the day. It costs about $7 a day to cover your car for a short stay. But just as in the United States, it becomes far less costly when you insure for a longer time period. The annual liability premium for an older car is about $150. If you have an expensive, new United States car and want collision as well as liability insurance on it, you may well have to pay more than you do in the United States, unless you join a club with insurance benefits.

QUESTION: I would like to correspond with Americans who are living in Mexico. How can I get in touch them?

ANSWER: This is the question that gives us the most trouble. Are there many people in your hometown who would be willing to spend a lot of time writing to strangers? If so, there must not be many better ways to spend your time. Most people who have retired in Mexico seem to be too busy enjoying life to develop extensive correspondences with people they don't know. In our section on resources, we've listed some people who offer information services. Their newsletters and orientation packages may be your best hope of getting current and individualized answers to your questions. Some of these Web Sites also have forums through which you can conduct on-line correspondence with others who have retired in or are considering retirement in Mexico.

QUESTION: What will my legal status be?

ANSWER: This question is answered in great detail in our "Successful Retirement" section. The most important thing to understand is that becoming a legal resident of Mexico does not impair your U.S. or Canadian citizenship in any way.

QUESTION: Are there schools for English-speaking children and adolescents?

ANSWER: Every large city in Mexico (and some smaller ones, too) has at least one bilingual school to which many American (as well as some Mexican) families send their children. Since this is primarily a book for retirees, we do not list these schools, but we advise readers with young children to visit the community they are thinking of moving to and check personally.

QUESTION: What happens if I die while I am in Mexico?

ANSWER: Your spouse or friends can get a certificate from the local authorities that allows your remains to be flown back to your home country, if that is what you wish. It is not a problem.

QUESTION: Can U.S. television programs be received in Mexico?

ANSWER: Yes, with a satellite antenna. They are becoming increasingly popular in Mexico. A recent newspaper ad offers various types for between $475 and $700. There are also English-language cable stations in most of the larger cities. Video-rental stores are everywhere, and the latest Hollywood films are available for your enjoyment. A less expensive way to see United States programs traded is to trade back and forth with friends.

QUESTION: Can you recommend a real-estate broker who can help me buy or rent a house or apartment in Mexico?

ANSWER: We don't feel that dealing with a real-estate broker long-distance is a wise way to shop for a home in Mexico. Also, the ownership and personnel of real-estate firms can change during the life of a book. As we discussed at greater length in the chapter on housing, we strongly urge you to visit a community before you make any commitments. It is also a good idea to study the real estate listing in English-language newspapers of the communities you are considering (see Appendix for names and addresses). These papers will also contain the names of real-estate brokers of whom you may want to make preliminary inquiries. However, please remember not to be discouraged by high prices, since you can almost always do much better on the spot. Bargains seldom make the newspaper ads; they are snapped up immediately.

QUESTION: How are the hunting and fishing in Mexico?

ANSWER: Fishing in Baja and along the Pacific Coast varies from good to fantastic. Licenses are usually provided by the people who rent you the boat or can be purchased in town. Companies like Mexico West Travel Club or Vagabundos del Mar (see Appendix for addresses and telephone numbers) can help you get a license before you enter Mexico. Inland communities like Guadalajara often have lakes and streams nearby where freshwater species abound. Bringing your fishing tackle into Mexico is not a problem.

Hunting, however, is somewhat more complicated. The Mexican government is very cautious about people toting guns or bringing them into the country. (Don't even think about bringing a handgun! The best advice we've heard concerning handguns is, "If you feel you can't travel without one, then better visit somewhere else.") Shotguns are about the only firearms permitted across the border. The red tape involved is incredible. Besides proof of citizenship; a character reference in duplicate from your police department; and the serial numbers, calibers and makes of your guns, you will need up to 14 passport-size photos and several days of running around to various Mexican government offices. Fees, stamps and papers will cost about $120, plus *mordidas* and a doozy of a headache.

There are people whom you can pay to do all this for you. For more information, contact Mexican Hunting Association, 3302 Josie Ave., Long Beach, CA 90808. Or, you can book a package tour with guns, permits and guides included. It's our understanding that heavier caliber hunting weapons can be rented once you are in the country.

QUESTION(S): I am a divorced woman, age 54. What are my chances of meeting eligible men, either American or Mexican?

My wife died several years ago, and I'm thinking of getting married again. Are there any single women retiring in Mexico? What about marrying a Mexican lady?

ANSWER: As far as finding companionship among other retirees and residents is concerned, our observation is that the chances can be excellent. There are several good reasons for this. First of all, there are a lot of single North Americans going to Mexico to live. When people become separated, divorced or widowed, they often think of changing their lifestyles completely, and Mexico is a great place for that. Secondly, because of the accepting nature of the English-speaking society, it's much easier to become acquainted than back home. You don't need singles bars or introduction services. Simply join in the social groups and volunteer activities or take language lessons in a school, and before long, you will come in contact with just about everyone in the foreign colony. And finally, there are certain personality types that seem to gravitate toward foreign living. They tend to be adventurous, open to new ideas and to change, perhaps brighter, and certainly more alert and active than average. When you have people with similar interests together in a setting where friendship is highly prized, you can see how odds go up as to finding compatible companions. The down side of this phenomenon that there is a higher proportion of heavy drinkers per capita in Mexico. For some reason, they are attracted by the adventure of living in Mexico, just as the others are.

As for cross-national marriages, there are some factors that should be taken into consideration. Yes, *machismo* exists in Mexico, although not to the extent that cliché would have you think. But it's definitely a man's world. It's only in hi-tech societies like the United States or Canada that women can compete with men on a more or less equal level. A woman can drive a tractor or a truck as well as a man, and she can operate a computer equally well. But in Mexico, where mules and oxen are used in the fields instead of tractors and where computers are scarce, women are not so equal. Women's lib is a foreign concept here.

For this reason, before considering marriage with a local man, an American woman should make certain she knows how he stands on many issues and how he is likely to treat her after the initial euphoria of the romance fades. You should be aware that it's culturally acceptable for a married man to have mistresses, often financially supported by the husband. Will this be acceptable to you?

Men should also know what kind of marriage they are getting into when marrying a local woman instead of one from the foreign colony. There are a number of implicit cultural differences that could cause problems. Just one problem is that many Mexican women tend to view sex differently than American women do. Sex is often looked on as a necessary evil–an act performed in order just to conceive children, not something to enjoy or for recreation. Another problem is that you might be looked upon as the beneficent caretaker for the family. When cousin Alfredo needs a new transmission for his Chevy or Aunt Claudia needs a new refrigerator, guess where they go to "borrow" the money?

In any event, there is an advantage in marrying a Mexican citizens: you immediately gain the right to become a resident, to own a business, to work, or do anything a Mexican citizen can do, except vote. This can be important in some cases; others think of nothing but love, true love!

Will You Love It?

Most foreigners either love Mexico or hate it. This phenomenon is so well known that just about every guidebook to the country, after listing the numerous reasons for the author's deep affection for the land and its people, finds it necessary to warn that "Mexico is not everybody's cup of tea." (Someone should offer a prize for an alternative to that cliché–"cup of tequila" would not qualify.) No doubt the principal reason for these strong feelings is that Mexico, like many of its favorite foods, is highly spiced. Nothing is muted, neither the colors nor the sounds. Mexico does not sneak up on you. It confronts you immediately and totally.

The shock is particularly intense for the North American who has gone right next door to find himself in a country vastly different from his own. Mexico quickly shatters the illusion that foreignness is a function of distance. More than one traveler familiar with every part of Europe, including Russia, has observed that Mexico is the most foreign country he has ever visited.

Are Mexico's differences from the United States and Canada good or bad news? We know our answer to that question, but we do not know yours. Even if we knew you very well, we are not at all sure that we could predict which it would be. Yes, there are some people whose reaction to the country we could a confidently guess. Most of them are so rigid, impatient or demanding that we cannot imagine them tolerating the inefficiencies and delays of Mexican life. We're proud that, after a number of months in Mexico, we have learned to sit in a restaurant for twenty minutes before the waiter takes our orders and for another twenty until the food arrives, without any knotting of our insides. (We're doubly proud that we can even do it back in the United States) We are not, however, sufficiently unreasonable to expect or demand that everyone master this trick. Would you be outraged or amused by the fact that, each time postage for an airmail letter to the United States goes up, it is many months before stamps are available for the new amount or that often envelopes and packages have to be mailed with wall-to-wall small denomination stamps because no larger ones are available? Trivial? Of course, but if your answer is "outraged" or even if you would merely find that situation annoying, it is quite possible that Mexico is not your "c.o.t." There are just too many little things like that which, if you let them, could add up to constant annoyance.

Somewhat more serious are the seemingly arbitrary and unpredictable shortages that plague Mexico for months at a time. Unlike the United States where many brands of almost every product are available, Mexico usually has only one brand and anything that interrupts its manufacturer's operations cuts off the supply altogether. Mexicans and longtime foreign residents there learn to deal with these shortages in a variety of ways. Approached in the right spirit, obtaining the seemingly unobtainable becomes a game. But, of course, it may not be the kind you enjoy playing.

Most North Americans are deeply offended by the sight of people spitting in the street. In the days when spittoons were a ubiquitous feature of the American domestic landscape, the aesthetic aversion to that practice was probably much weaker. However, a very effective anti-spitting campaign by the Tuberculosis Association succeeded in sensitizing our grandparents, and we continue to view it with an intense distaste that Mexicans do not seem to share. To be comfortable in Mexico, you do not have to enjoy the sight, but it does help to be able to ignore it.

Drinking only bottled or boiled water is a nuisance. How much more convenient it is to place your glass under any tap and enjoy, without any trace of concern, the clear liquid that pours out. It is also pleasant to pick up a piece of fruit in the market and eat it as you find it or, if you are fastidious, after running some cold water over it. After you have returned from Mexico, it usually takes some time before you are able to resume those practices without a moment of hesitation. Water in Mexico is not safe, and while there, you must learn to avoid everything uncooked with which it may have come in contact. Are these inconveniences serious enough to spoil your enjoyment of the country, or are they somewhat like the necessity to retrain your reflexes before you can drive or even cross streets safely in England? You may not know what your reaction will be until you have been in Mexico for a little while. Part of the initial strain is fear that you will forget and inadvertently expose yourself to danger. That worry soon fades as the required new behaviors become second nature.

Many North Americans are appalled by what they see as the pervasive corruption of Mexican political life. Indeed, it is true that few Mexican presidents have left office without arranging for themselves and their friends to live in luxury for the rest of their lives. However, to see this as contrasting sharply with universal probity north of the border requires that one forget the "sleaze" factor that has figured so prominently in the history of just about every United States presidential administration in our time. Of course every scandal on the federal level has many counterparts in our statehouses. Less visible but far more widespread are the abuses of power routinely encountered in the world of commerce. It is all too easy to jump from the unquestionable fact that United States or Canadian customs inspectors are much less likely to take bribes than their Mexican counterparts, to the dubious conclusion that North Americans are honest and Mexicans are crooked. It is not even a question of degree but rather of different culturally approved manifestations of what, sadly, appears to be a universal weakness. However, most North Americans do take awhile to become comfortable with the idea of "tipping" minor public officials.

One certainly does not have to approve of the Mexican government to be happy living there. North Americans have fallen in love with the country under regimes that have covered the full spectrum from right to left, and often their affection has been very much in spite of the ideology and behavior of the party in power. Even today, Mexico is full of Americans who deplore everything about the government's foreign and domestic policies, would love to see them become carbon copies of ours, but would not think of moving back to the United States where they could enjoy the originals. Very few, by any means, are too poor to afford the higher prices in their homeland, so there must be something else about Mexico that holds them.

This brief recitation of some things North Americans find to dislike about Mexico is far from exhaustive. It does, however, include many of the most frequently heard complaints. For those who allow them to, they constitute ample reason for choosing other places in which to spend time. For many others–the authors included–they are part of the price one must pay for sharing in the riches of Mexican life.

Uppermost among those riches are the people of Mexico. If we have repeated this observation too frequently throughout this book, it is because we know that, although anyone who has spent much time in Mexico will agree, those who have never been there will be easily convinced.

Of course there are other attractions. One is the climate. At any given time, the weather may not be perfect everywhere in Mexico, but chances are that it *is* someplace, and usually not too far from where you are. The residents of Mexico City discovered at least five centuries ago that when, as occasionally happens, the winters there are a bit too nippy, it's easy to find temperatures a dozen degrees warmer in nearby Cuernavaca. In Guadalajara, they know that, in January, descending to the Pacific Coast (only a few hours away) takes you from the fifties to the balmy eighties. In San Miguel, Morelia and dozens of other cities and towns of the Central Plateau, spring is "eternal." If you live in a climate that is bearable year-round, it may be hard to understand the thirst for warmth and sunshine that historically, for Northern Europeans from England to Russia, has made Italy an earthly Paradise, and that draws flocks of sun-starved Scandinavians to Spain every winter. Unless you have gasped for air in a New York, Washington or Houston summer, the annual exodus to the mountains and the beaches may seem inexplicable. If, on the other hand, you suffer either extreme heat or cold in the course of a year, it may not be necessary for us to tell you much more about why the Mexican climate draws so many refugees from the extremes of United States winters and summers. Yes, parts of Mexico can be hot, but the bulk of the population lives in, and visitors flock to, places where altitude or sea breezes provide year-round moderation.

It is difficult to avoid sounding crass when discussing how reasonable living in Mexico can be. Compulsive bargain hunting is an illness and, many would say, one of the least attractive characteristics of North Americans abroad. Perhaps, though, retirees who are trying to make limited incomes provide the comfort they have been encouraged to expect as the reward for a lifetime of work can be viewed a little differently than tourists seeking cheap vacations. In Mexico, we observed North Americans who would be barely making it at home living comfortably. This gave us renewed optimism about our own futures and colors our perceptions of Mexico as a place to retire. Certainly, we would not advise anyone to move there for the low prices alone. Nothing is a bargain if you do not enjoy it. Nevertheless, the stretch that the low prices give to a modest income must be counted as one of the major advantages of Mexico as a place to visit or live.

In the end, although we hope that these observations may help you make some guesses about whether you will love or hate the Mexico experience, you will not know for sure until you have tried it. If you go there expecting to find a replica of life in the United States or Canada, but with palm trees and *mariachis* in the background, you will be disappointed. Some things that you value highly are not considered important there. On the other hand, you may learn to appreciate some qualities–such as patience, courtesy and simplicity–that our cuture often slights. Even if you decide, after you have seen it for yourself, that you cannot love Mexico as we do, we doubt that you will regret having tried.

Appendix

English-Language Newspapers in Mexico

The News (A daily, sold throughout Mexico)
 Balderas 87–3rd Floor 06050 Mexico, DF, Mexico.

Mexico City Times (A new daily)
Avenida Juárez 100
Mexico, D.F. 06040

The Colony Reporter (News of the Guadalajara area)
9051-C Siempre Viva Road, Suite 5-452
San Diego, CA 922173-3628

Atención San Miguel (San Miguel de Allende weekly)
Apdo 119
San Miguel de Allende, GTO, Mexico

El Ojo del Lago (Lake Chapala Area Weekly)
P.O. Box #279
Chapala, Jalisco
Mexico 45900

Oaxaca Times (Free Weekly)
307 Macedonio Alcalá
Oaxaca, Oax. Mexico 68000

Newsletters

AIM (Adventures in Mexico)
Apdo 31-70
45050 Guadalajara, JAL, Mexico

The People's Guide to Mexico Travel Letter
P.O. Box 179
Acme, WA 98220

Retiring in Guadalajara
Apdo 5-409
Guadalajara, JAL, Mexico
This newsletter covers only Guadalajara, but in great detail.

Mexico Travel - Monthly Report
P.O. Box 1498
Imperial Beach, CA 91933-1498
Phone & Fax (619) 429-6566

CLUBMEX Newsletter
660 Bay Boulevard Suite 214
Chula Vista, CA 91910

Mexican Living & Travel Update
6301 Squaw Valley Rd.
Pahrump, NV 89041

Cuernavaca Calling
Apdo 4-587
C.P. 62431
Cuernavaca, Morelos, Mexico

L.S.M.F.T. -Live Safely in Mexico Free of Taxes
P.O. Box 531
Ajijic, Jalisco, Mexico

Other Resources

American-Canadian Club
Hotel Plaza del Sol
Lopez Mateos y Mariano Otero
45050 Guadalajara, JAL, Mexico
Phone 47-87-90 (until noon)

F.G. Furton and Bonnie Pitman
Apdo 5-409
Guadalajara, JAL, Mexico
Phones (523)121-2348 & (523) 647-9924

California Commerce Bank
615 S. Flower
Los Angeles, CA 90017 Phone (213) 624-5700
Guadalajara information number: 25-32-58.

Tourism Offices

Washington
1911 Pennsylvania Ave. NW
Washington, DC 20006
Chicago
233 North Michigan, Suite 1413
Chicago, IL 60601
New York
405 Park Avenue, Suite 1203
New York, NY 10022
Houston
2707 N. Loop West, Suite 450
Houston, TX 77006
Los Angeles
10100 Santa Monica Blvd.
Los Angeles, CA 90067
Montreal
One Place Ville Marie, Suite 2409
Montreal, Quebec H3B 3M9
Toronto
181 University Avenue, Suite 1112
Toronto, Ontario M5H 3M7

Citizens Emergency Center–U.S. State Department
Situation reports on any destination around the world; locates travelers abroad to deliver emergency messages. Phone (202) 647-5225. Available: 8:15-5:00 p.m. weekdays, 9:00-3:00 p.m. Saturdays (Eastern Time).

Background Reading

Chase, Stuart. Mexico: *A Study of Two Americas.* New York: Macmillan, 1931.

Flandrau, Charles Macomb. *Viva Mexico!* Champaign, IL: University of Illinois Press, 1964.

Franz, Carl. *The People's Guide to Mexico.* John Muir Publications, Sante Fe, New Mexico, 1995.

Johnson, William Webber. *Heroic Mexico:* The Violent Emergence of a Modern Nation. New York: Doubleday, 1968.

Kennedy, Diana. *The Cuisines of Mexico.* New York: HarperCollins, 1989.

Kennedy, Diana.. *Mexican Regional Cooking.* New York: HarperCollins, 1990.

Lincoln, John. *One's Man Mexico.* New York: Hippocrene Books, 1983.

Miller, Tom. *The Baja Book III.* Huntington Beach, CA: Baja Trail Publications, 1987.

O'Reilly, James, and Larry Habegger, eds. *Travelers' Tales Mexico.* O'Reilly and Associates, 1994.

Reavis, Dick J. *Conversations with Moctezuma: Ancient Shadows Over Modern Life in Mexico.* New York William Morrow, 1990.

Riding, Alan. *Distant Neighbors*: Portrait of the Mexicans. New York Knopf, 1985.

Rodman, Seldon. *Mexico Journal: The Conquerers Conquered*. Carbondale, IL: Southern Illinois University Press, 1964.

Sierra, Justo. *The Political Evolution of the Mexican People*. Austin, TX: University of Texas Press, 1975.

Simon, *Kate. Mexico: Places & Pleasures*. New York: Harper & Row, 1984.

Simpson, Lesley Byrd. *Many Mexicos*. Berkeley, CA: Univerity of California Press, 1967.

Strode, Hudson. *Timeless Mexico*. New York: Harcourt Brace Jovanovich, 1944.

Guidebooks

There are numerous excellent guidebooks for travelers in Mexico, most of them updated annually. A few are listed below. They are your best source of information on hotels, restaurants, museums, ruins and other attractions to enjoy while you explore the country in search of the retirement site that is just right for you. It will be worth your while to look at many of these in your library and pick up some at the bookstore before you go.

Access Mexico. HarperCollins, 1996.

Birnbaum's Mexico '97. Alexandra Mayes Birnbaum. Harper-Collins, 1996.

Central Mexico Handbook. Chicki Mallan and Oz Mallan. Moon Publications, 1994.

Fielding's Mexico 1996. Lynn V. Foster. Fielding Worldwide, 1995.

Fodor's Exploring Mexico. Fiona Dunlop. Fodor's Travel Publications, 1997.

Frommer's Mexico '97. Herb Felsted et al. Frommer, 1996.

Insight Guides: Mexico. Steve Lewers and Barbara Hendricks. Apa Productions, 1995.

Let's Go: The Budget Guide to Mexico 1997. Daniela Bleichmar and Siham Nurhussein. St. Martin's Press, 1996.

Lonely Planet Mexico (Lonely Planet Travel Survival Kit). John Noble et al. Lonely Planet, 1995.

The People's Guide to Mexico. Carl Franz et al. John Muir, 1995.

The Rough Guide Mexico (1995). John Fisher et al. Rough Guides, 1995.

Index

railroads 90-91
real estate 53-57
rents 29-33, 56
Rosarito Beach 165, 166
RVs 107-113

S

Saltillo 184
San Antonio Tlayacapan 122
San Blas 186, 187
San Carlos Bay 109, 145, 146
San Felipe 108, 168-171
San Ignacio 193
San José del Cabo 176-178
San Miguel de Allende 125-130
shopping 18, 61-65, 118, 119
singles 17, 215
Spanish, speaking 69, 70
sports 216, 217, 219, 220

T

Taxco 191, 192
television 18, 219
tennis 216, 217
Tequisquiapan 134, 135
time-shares 155, 156
Todos Santos 196
tourist disease 33-35
transportation 87-104,

W-Z

weather 21, 22, 145
World Wide Web 17, 18, 205-210
Yelapa 185, 186
Yucatán 196, 197
Zihuatanejo 157-159

About the Authors

John Howells was born in New Orleans and grew up in suburban St. Louis. His teen years, however, were spent in Mexico City, and he has been returning to Mexico as often as possible ever since. Now a resident of California, he has worked on newspapers from coast to coast—40 in all. He has been a Linotype operator, English teacher, silver miner and a travel and feature writer. John earned a B.A. in Anthropology and a M.A. in Mexican-American Graduate Studies from San Jose State University. He is the author of nine travel-retirement books.

Don Merwin is a native New Yorker who now lives in the San Francisco Bay Area. He began his career in communications as a writer for Edward R. Murrow in the early 1950s and spent the next three decades as publicist, administrator and planner in health and human service organizations. Don and his wife, Judith, are the publishers of Gateway Books. They look forward to eventual retirement in Mexico. Meanwhile, they explore new south of the border locations every chance they get.

Our books are available in most bookstores. However, if you have difficulty finding them, we will be happy to ship them to you directly. Just send your check or money order. (U. S. funds for all orders, please.)

Travel

A Traveler's Guide to Living Affordably Abroad
EUROPE THE EUROPEAN WAY $13.95 _____

An Impromptu Travel Guide
FRANCE WITHOUT RESERVATIONS $12.95 _____

Hiking Guides for Active Adults
WALKING EASY IN THE SWISS AND AUSTRIAN ALPS $14.95 _____
WALKING EASY IN THE FRENCH ALPS $11.95 _____
WALKING EASY IN THE ITALIAN ALPS $11.95 _____
WALKING EASY IN THE SAN FRANCISCO BAY AREA $11.95 _____

Retirement

Retiring, Wintering or Investing
CHOOSE COSTA RICA 3RD ED. $13.95 _____

Live Well on $600 a Month
CHOOSE MEXICO 5TH ED. $12.95 _____

Retirement Discoveries for Every Budget
CHOOSE THE SOUTHWEST $12.95 _____
CHOOSE THE NORTHWEST $12.95 _____
CHOOSE THE SOUTH (OCTOBER 1997) $13.95 _____

America's Best and Most Affordable Places
WHERE TO RETIRE $14.95 _____

Strategies for Comfortable Retirement
RETIREMENT ON A SHOESTRING $8.95 _____

Postage & Handling
First book.............................$1.90
Each additional book.........1.00   _____
California residents add 8% sales tax   _____

Total $ _____

For Credit Card ORDERS ONLY - call toll-free 1-800-669-0773
For Information - call 510-530-0299

Please ship to:

Name _____

Address _____

City/State/Zip_____

Our books are shipped bookrate. Please allow 2 - 3 weeks for delivery. If you are not satisfied, the price of the book(s) will be refunded in full.

Mail to: Gateway Books 2023 Clemens Road Oakland CA 94602